Freedom vs. Equality

The Structure and Morphology of
Contemporary World Societies

Freedom vs. Equality

The Structure and Morphology of Contemporary World Societies

Il se rencontre dans le coeur humain un goût déprave pour l'égalité...qui réduit les hommes a préférer l'égalité dans la servitude a l'inégalité dans la liberté.
Toqueville, De la Démocratie en Amérique
I, 84

Christopher Lee Bowen

Copyright © 2024 By Christopher Lee Bowen

All rights reserved. No part of this publication may be reproduced, distributed, or transmitted in any form or by any means, including photocopying, recording, or other electronic or mechanical methods, without the prior written permission of the copyright owner and the publisher, except in the case of brief quotations embodied in critical reviews and certain other noncommercial uses permitted by copyright law. For permission requests, write to the publisher, addressed "Attention: Permissions Coordinator," at the address below.

ARPress
45 Dan Road Suite 5
Canton, MA 02021

Hotline: 1(888) 821-0229
Fax: 1(508) 545-7580

Ordering Information:

Quantity sales. Special discounts are available on quantity purchases by corporations, associations, and others. For details, contact the publisher at the address above.

Printed in the United States of America.

ISBN-13:	Softcover	979-8-89389-523-0
	eBook	979-8-89389-524-7

Library of Congress Control Number: 2024919871

DEAR READER

The 21st Century is turning into an Age of Dystopia: collapse of the global economic system; rise of aggressive gangster states in Russia, China, Iran, North Korea; declining livability of cities worldwide; decline in population and economic collapse in China, Russia, Europe. You can think of a lot more.

Chaos breeds confusion. Formerly objective sources of information (press, TV, radio) and the reassuring reports of Walter Cronkite and Edward Murrow are long gone. Now we have advocacy, bias, and disinformation. Dystopia like Orwell's *1984* seems imminent. Hard to be sure who or what to believe.

News sources often cover trivial subjects and ignore major ones. For example, media covered the divorce antics of a famous Hollywood couple over a dozen news cycles but said nothing about the drastic decline in health (diabetes, dyslexia, obesity, dementia) among American children caused by chemical toxins in food. *Infotainment* is more lucrative than real news.

Which comes to the purpose of this book.

This book offers a comprehensive analysis of our 'human condition', institutions, history, events, leaders, and policies. It will help you understand the 'DNA' that underlies and makes sense of the random and seemingly incoherent news and information we are bombarded with every day.

Bonne chance!

CLB

Freedom vs. Equality
The Structure and Morphology of Contemporary World Societies

TABLE OF CONTENTS

Introduction v

PART I: Human Potential And Social Organization 1
  Human Potential
  How Society is Organized and Develops
  Framework for Understanding Non-Western Societies

PART II: Formation Of Western Civilization And The World's Encounter with West 53
  Formation of Western Civilization
  World's Encounter with the West

PART III: World Population Trends 66

PART IV: Heritage Of Theocratic Empire 79
  Russia
  China
  India
  Japan

PART V: The Heritage Of Tribal Societies 115
  Black Africa
  Islam
  Latin America

PART VI: International Issues 159
    United Nations and World Order
    Global Economic Competition

PART VII: Western Intellectual History 173
    Homer and the Founding of Classical Civilization
    Plato and the Decline of Classical Civilization
    Rousseau and the Corruption of Western Thought
    The Dark Side of Western Civilization: Calvin to Hitler

PART VIII: United States: The Last Best Hope 211
    Stages of America History
    American Subcultures

PART IX: Policy Making 250
    Foreign Policy
    Domestic Policy

Conclusion 269
    Constitution vs. Declaration of independence
    Secular State vs. Religious Society
    Social Values vs. Individual Rights
    Obsolescence and the End of History

Freedom vs. Equality
The Structure and Morphology of Contemporary World Societies

La vérité ne fait pas tant de bien dans le monde que ses apparences y font de mal.
Rochefoucauld, **Maximes**, 64

INTRODUCTION

The United States is squandering its resources on misguided foreign and domestic policies that are not addressing the major and potentially catastrophic issues and changes underway at home and abroad.

Information available from the media, government and other sources is so biased, inadequate, or irrelevant to an understanding of issues foreign and domestic that no citizen can be expected to form a sound judgement about what is at stake and what policies should adopted. It is nearly impossible to get beyond the rhetorical smoke screen that envelops media coverage and public discussion of such issues as the causes of 9/11, education policy, Islamic terrorism, budget deficits, loss of jobs, African AIDS, China's 'threat' to the US, Ukraine war, Taiwan standoff, energy policy. The list goes on. Domestic issues are obscured by political correctness and hidden agendas. Foreign issues are additionally obscured by conditions and cultural influences totally alien to our Western experience and values.

Foreign and domestic policies are formulated and defended by government officials, experts, lobbyists, academics, and interest groups, and the media funnel their opinions to the general public. Historical perspective is needed to analyze information and explain the causes and pertinence of issue and events. But the public is ill served by academics who have subdivided history, political science, economic and other subjects into specialties beyond public usefulness such that they exclude information needed for understanding how things got where they are.

A noted scholar, for example, has written a stylistically elegant but practically useless history of Islam and Islamic states from the time of Muhammad. Reading the work provides no understanding of why Islam and Islamic states pose a threat to world peace. He failed to cover aspects of Islamic society needed to understand the violent, irresponsible, and chaotic history of Arabic and Islamic peoples. These include: the disastrous nature of the "Arabic outlook" which dominates all of the Islam; the organization, principles, and power arrangements of tribal Islamic society; the role of marriage and women; tribal parochialism; and the sources of Islamic fundamentalism.

Many journalists try to provide pertinent background on current issues, but they are limited to what publishers find topical and marketable, which usually does not include historical perspective. In addition, journalists tend to be anecdotal rather than analytic in their coverage and often are as uninformed as the public.

The purpose of this book is to provide historical perspective on current conditions worldwide and explain the causes and origins of major domestic and foreign issues faced by the United States. Once the origin, basic structure, and historic evolution of a given region or issue are understood, variations in the cast of characters over time will not obscure the persistent underlying structure and morphology of the events and situations themselves. What it seeks is the DNA, as it were, of the societies and events, the underlying structure and causes that account for the endless profusions of facts that otherwise seems unrelated and confusing.

The best test of a work of this kind is how it explains and even predicts events. The first step in any impartial and independent inquiry is to take any reported fact, evidence or event and trace it back to its origins. Does an explanation make sense of the facts presented? Does it complete the sequence from cause to effect? Is what you see clearly, contradicted by what you hear others say about it? Most explanations and accounts of current events and policies in no way explain underlying causes and structures. This work attempts to offer the means to reach that kind of understanding. Along the way it will provoke controversy and disagreement with received opinions and promoted explanations. But in a long run, for an objective observer, it will be a helpful tool in dealing with the plethora of verbiage and obfuscation, much of it intentional, with which he or she is bombarded every day.

PART 1

Human Potential and Social Organization

What is man that Ye art mindful of him?
Genesis

An estimated 14 billion years ago (all datings approximate, not definitive) the Universe began with the Big Bang, creating a surge of gaseous particles that congealed into billions of stars spreading at the speed of light through infinitely expanding space. Five billion years ago a gaseous cloud circling the Sun began to cool and congeal, forming the Earth. The Earth's crust consolidated over the molten core to form continents, and condensation of hydrogen and oxygen in the atmosphere formed the oceans. Carbon later combined with hydrogen, oxygen and other elements to make possible organic life.

The first cellular life forms began some 2 billion years ago. Animal forms appeared in oceans and fresh-waters lakes and land amphibians, birds, and reptiles appeared about 500 million years ago. The Jurassic Age Reptiles came and went in the period 250 to 65 million years BC. The first mammal appeared in this interval, a very small rodent-like creature that survived and diversified. Apes appeared 4 million years ago, hominids about 1 million years ago, and homo sapiens about 200,000 years ago. *Homo sapiens* originated in Africa and remained there until 50,000 BC, when, a hunter gatherer family of men, women, and children left Africa through the Sinai into the Fertile Crescent.

Descendants of that original family expanded throughout the Earth eventually siring the Euro-Altaic, Sinic, Indo-European, Semitic, and other less numerous races from which subgroups formed to occupy the Americas the Eurasian continent and Southeast Asia. (Genome testing traces all those races back to one shared female ancestor in the group that left Africa some 50,000 years ago.) Races formed when different populations were cut off for millennia from contact with other populations during the Gunz, Mindel, Riss, and Wurm ice ages of the Pleistocene Epoch that ended about 11,500 years ago. These glaciers reached a depth of about 10,000 feet and at their greatest extent so much water was frozen in them that the sea level was at least 330 feet lower than it is now.

This telescoped version gives the general proportions of time and space within which human history occurs, subject to constant revision. Humans evolved from apelike ancestors within this context. Adaptations during human evolution included upright posture, the opposing thumb, a unique palate and tongue, which made speech possible, a large brain, extremely complicated neurological, endocrine and limbic systems, a continual capacity for sex, menstruation rather than an annual rutting season, and an extended nurturing period for young.

Because men live in a vast continuum of space and time, rational understanding of any part of this continuum requires terms, categories, and distinctions by which to group phenomena for purposes of discussion and analysis. These may lead to an imperfect approximation to the truth, but no understanding whatever is possible without them. The following discussion uses such arbitrary terms and divisions to analyze and explain the extremely complicated phenomena of human potential and social organization. They are arbitrary because other terms and divisions might be used as well. But the ones used here will at least introduce the complexity and offer an approach to understanding the evolution of our personal and social experience.

Human Potential

As a result of his evolutionary endowment, man lives in five dimensions: three dimensions of space, the dimension of time, and most important, the dimension of abstraction. The first four are familiar, the last requires some explanation.

The dimension of abstraction is rooted in the human capacity for thought, speech, and action which make possible ideas, feelings, exchange of information and opinion, forms of organization and belief, and countless other products of human interrelationship. Consequently, what men think, feel, do, and believe directly affects, changes, and creates the world in which they live. The dimension of abstraction can be displayed in simplified form based on the fundamental human capacities and needs that have become apparent over thousands of years of human existence. They range from the most spiritual and unseen to the most tangible and concrete. The list could be extended or subdivided indefinitely, but the following provide general categories that cover many basic social needs.

Religious, including mythology, cosmology, and philosophy which provide psychic certainty and understanding of the World, Universe, and Man's place in it.

Political, including all forms of organizing society to settle conflict, arrange for defense, apportion costs for public services, provide for socially important tasks such as road building and public health and so on.

Social, including all forms of association and play that satisfy the gregarious needs of humans.

Economic, including means to provide food, shelter, clothing, tools, weapons, and countless other products needed, used, and consumed by the population.

Military, including organizations that use means of violence (weapons, tactics, and strategy) to defend society from foreign and domestic enemies.

The dimension of abstraction can be called *'human culture'*. Culture comes between men and nature. Man is the only animal that has culture. Culture is the sum of tools, artifacts, buildings, organization, practices, traditions, beliefs, and relationships that a society brings into being. Culture is founded on speech and the capacity for organization that speech makes possible. Culture is actualized human potential. Without culture, men are animals but not yet men.

There are four main forms of social organization: Family, Group, Society, and Civilization.

Families are the nurturing and primary educating units of a society. A family may be nuclear, extended, polygamous, monogamous, matriarchal, patriarchal, collective, or any other combination of male and female, children and elders, or much of its nurturing role may be replaced by the state as in the Communist system. Personality develops within the family, shaped by male and female roles, sibling rivalry, real and perceived slights and favoritism, personal health, individual character, intellectual capacity, physical endowment, beauty or ugliness, the presence or absence of mentors, and countless other influences. The dynamics of a family and their effect on development of children are obscure and infinitely complicated, given the confrontation of the innate potential of the child with the cultural choices already made and the personalities already developed by the adults.

Groups form for specific purposes. They include clubs, teams, fraternities, universities, and corporations. Members of a group spend only part of their time in the group. Consequently, groups command loyalty but are not the exclusive relationship of the individual members. Groups are part of a larger society.

Society is a self-sufficient organization of families, individuals, and groups in which the members have more association with members of the society than with persons outside the society. Societies are complete and exclusive and include extended families, clans, tribes, nations, and larger associations that are independent from other people, groups, and societies.

Civilization is a society that has writing and city life. Civilizations are commonly very large and may incorporate many groups and societies that unite to form a cohesive and independent association. There have been many societies but only a few civilizations.

Societies originate from the need to associate to provide for basic human needs such as food, shelter, defense, procreation, and community. Societies are driven by necessity and tend to be hierarchical and totalitarian in the sense that every member is subordinate to the needs of the society. Few if any individual goals or life objectives occur outside or in opposition to those of the society at large. Internal control in a society is exercised through rewards for conformity and expulsion for nonconformity, and the leaders of a society, because they have been successful by adhering to the choices made by the society, tend to enforce tradition and suppress innovation.

Human Capacities

Men are social beings, unable to survive, grow, develop, and fulfill their potential without association with other men. We can't know the total range of human potential, only the many forms by which it is actualized into culture. The human brain and the neurological, endocrine, and limbic systems, which function through chemical and electrochemical reactions, give men astonishing sensibility and perception in both thought and feeling and the consciousness to conceive, remember, and ponder an infinitely subtle range of ideas and feelings.

Modern neuroscience has achieved increasing understanding of the structure and function of the brain and neural system. The function of hippocampus, amygdala, hypothalamus and other structures of the brain in shaping thought and emotions are not in dispute. Their discovery and functional analysis are among the greatest achievements of Western science. The biochemical processes of the brain and nervous system will direct 'psychotherapy' for the indefinite future. Pharmaceutical treatment of classic 'personality' disorders and dysfunctions (schizophrenia, depression, phobia, autism, etc.) will be exclusive. Traditional psychotherapy and psychiatry will become obsolete. They are fundamentally behaviorist and deterministic, and neuroscience provides a much better account for determinist behaviorism than they do. Biochemical determinism offers much more opportunity for successful treatment of disorders. What is missing is a nondeterministic non-behavioral explanation for personality based on free will, by now a naive and outmoded concept in traditional psychiatry that is confirmed nonetheless in everyday experience. Although science tends to avoid or at least postpone definitive examination of the concept of tree will, free will is essential to any volitional (read responsible and accountable) interpretation of human life and conduct. We don't take animals to court for 'murder' but we do punish humans because we believe they know better. If we have no free will, we are slaves and no meaning (i.e., agent) can be attached to our words and deeds. They are products of chemical robots and human behavior is without meaning or accountability. The following offers an interpretation of human personality based on free will that in no way conflicts with the discoveries of neuroscience. It simply explains the faculties which are manifested through the systems of the body discovered by neuroscience.

While no list can ever approach a final tally of human potential, a few of the major capacities that shape human lives and cultures are:

Thought, including reason and consciousness.

Will (or Volition) to bring about desired future conditions.

Action, which is the capacity to cooperate, to set and accomplish goals, and to begin new ways of doing things. Man is the only animal capable of action.

Emotions, such as anger, joy, and desire induced by persons, objects, and ideas and directed at the World.

Passions, such as love, hate, compassion, and grief, which are aroused involuntarily and are 'suffered' internally by the soul.

Sensations, such as hot, cold, sweet, sour, pleasure, pain, noise, touch, and color.

Human Faculties

Given these and countless other capacities, there appear to be several human faculties that actualize these capacities.

Mind: basis for intelligence, thinking, memory, consciousness, and personality.

Spirit: source of aspiration, joy, imagination, and intention directed at the unseen and the future.

Will: source of action to implement the intentions of Spirit, Mind, and Soul.

Heart: instrument for expressing emotions induced by ideas, persons, and objects directed at the World.

Soul: source of passions, love, judgment, taste, intuition, spontaneity, and identity.

Body: source of feelings and sensation and the only means for manifesting all other faculties.

Mind includes consciousness, intelligence, thought, reason, and memory. Mind is the most disembodied faculty because there is no bodily feeling associated with mental activity. Feeling and bodily stimulation disrupt mental activity, for which silence and undisturbed attention are required. ***Consciousness*** is the overall awareness we have about our activities and what takes place around us. It is the starting point for forming personality. ***Intelligence*** is the capacity to hold in the mind abstract concepts, identify connections, differences, and relationships between them, and calculate, analyze, and draw conclusions based on them. ***Thought*** is the capacity to roam mentally over a range of ideas, feelings, objects, events, and concepts, to derive observations and opinions about them, and create new ideas and concepts incorporating and synthesizing the products of intelligence, reason, spirit, and soul. ***Reason*** is the capacity to compare, contrast, analyze, synthesize and perform logical, ordered and sequential operations on mental constructs such as words and numbers and to carry out logical, sequential calculations from premises to derive consequences and conclusions. ***Memory*** is the faculty that retains and recalls previously experienced ideas, events, objects, and emotions. The hippocampus, cortex and other structures in the brain make, store, and recall memories. The mind creates and stores neural images that represent the ideas, events, objects, and feelings that were originally experienced and become memory vectors. Memory revives the stored mental image or stored feeling to evoke the remembered word, idea, object, or emotion. The biochemistry of this process in the brain has been studied and partly delineated but its underlying mystery remains. *(A pleasantly retarded mind contributes to everybody's ease Jacques Barzun)*

Spirit seems to be as abstract as the Mind, but its presence is felt through emotional elation and physical exhilaration that accompany a sense of anticipation. Interestingly, laughter is the quintessential expression of the Spirit. Spirit is the source of psychic certainty, imagination, and aspiration, and is chiefly concerned with the meaning and purpose of human existence. It deals with the unseen, future desired conditions, and manifests or brings the unseen or the 'not yet' into the World. Spirit is most often directed at the future. Spirit directs the Will to incite emotions in the Heart, concepts in the Mind, and action in the Body to make manifest what is unseen or 'not yet'. (*L'esprit ne saurait jouer longtemps le personage du Coeur. Rochefoucauld, Maximes, 108*)

Will mobilizes the mind and body through a system-wide call to endeavor. It focuses on the present and is directed at the world. It is the faculty of Volition that implements the future subjunctive, 'shall be' of the Spirit. Human culture and progress are impossible where men have lost their Spirit to conceive and their Will to make present a future. Will is the faculty for bringing about a future condition, but it is a means, not an end in itself and does not generate the objectives and plans it carries out. Soul through its grasp of meaning and truth and Spirit through imagination and aspiration direct the Will to carry out objectives those faculties devise. Mind in its critical and analytical activities and the Body through sense perception and desires provide information and mental and motor constructs for achieving what the soul and spirit direct. Willfulness is a perversion of the heart and the will by the Personality, which excites false emotions directed at persons, ideas or objects. When Willfulness enters political life, it destroys society by arousing false emotions and eliminating plurality. Will destroys plurality because Will as an end in itself must be by its nature undivided. The prime example is Adolf Hitler, whose entire life was an assertion of his Will. Another example is the French Revolution, which, following Rousseau, persecuted all social classes but the proletariat in the name of the 'General Will'. On the other hand, lack of **Will power** in political life is an indication of loss of solidarity and presages the end of the society. Will is necessary to survive and to defend a society or person. (*Les personnes faibles ne peuvent être sincères. Rochefoucauld,* ***Maximes****, 316*)

Heart is the traditional physical seat of feelings, which are expressed as emotions. E-motions, as the word suggests, are feelings enacted and 'moved outward' toward the world to manifest the condition or intentions of Spirit, Mind, and Soul. Emotion is rooted in the amygdala and other structures of the limbic system. Emotional truth is possible only when the Spirit or the Soul generates feelings. Feelings themselves are never seen but they are expressed as emotions through actions, such as crying, frowning, laughing, smiling, shouting, sobbing, staring, and countless other physical actions and manifestations the Heart executes through the Body. The emotional repertoire of the Heart is extensive and conventional, such that it can be simulated by the Mind through memory and imitation. Stage acting is based on this fact. Most daily emotions are incited by the Mind (whims) and Body (desires), not by the Spirit or Soul, and remain shallow and rootless feelings induced by memory or imitation to serve some social purpose. A tendency to emotionalize characterizes people whose feelings are induced by thought. Hypocrisy is the corruption of the Heart in which the Mind induces emotions that simulate feelings in order to deceive others, ending often in deceiving oneself. (*L'esprit est toujours la dupe du coeur. Rochefoucauld,* **Maximes***, 102)*

Soul is the most profound human faculty, the seat of the deepest and most unworldly passions and the source of overall evaluation and judgment of what appears in the world. Far from being obscure, the soul is the most manifest and yet most indeterminable human faculty. Its condition is always revealed, involuntarily, but it is inaccessible to mind and impervious to will. Interestingly, crying is the quintessential expression of the Soul, whether tears of joy and happiness and love or tears of sorrow and despair. Soul is the faculty that perceives, evaluates, and responds to the subtle expressions of feeling, such as glances, smiles, tone of voice, and *body language* that reveal the soul of another. The soul also is the source of intuition, judgment, taste, and conviction and is the overall evaluator of all perceptions. Soul is source of identity, of 'who' one is. Soul is the source of spontaneity, which is the essence of 'who' a person is, his ***daemon***, which can be seen by others but not by himself. Soul reveals and often betrays a person to others through glance, gesture, body language, and tone of voice. Soul is directly connected to the involuntary and sympathetic nervous system seated in the hippocampus and hypothalamus. Soul through the involuntary neurological system reveals 'who' a person is and is the source of the expression 'give oneself away' when attempting to conceal one's true self, beliefs, intentions, or feelings. Soul is the most manifest and the least knowable human faculty. (*Ile dolet vere, qui sine teste dolet. Martial XXXIII*)

Body is an instrument, and the mind, soul, heart, and will are the players of that instrument. Body is source of all knowledge and the instrument for all expression. It is likely that body and soul are inextricably joined ('resurrection of the body' is a profound intuition of this union) in the limbic system, since passions and convictions engage both completely, and a disembodied passion or conviction is absurd. The body is not material, it is simply the most ***manifest*** human faculty---through senses of touch, taste, smell, and sight and expressions of voice, eyes, face, gesture, and motion. Body is the ***only*** means for manifesting all other human capacities and faculties. The body is also the source or locus of compelling sensations, needs, urges, and desires. No bodily urgency can be resisted, like for example pain, which blots out all reality and consciousness. Correspondingly, no pleasure is as intense as release from pain Although the biochemical process of sensation in the body is well known, the power and intensity of such sensations and their role in revealing and intensifying reality remain unfathomable.

Personality

Foris ut mores, intus ut libet.

Given these capacities and faculties, an individual shapes a ***personality*** to face the world. This process and the need for it are among the most radical foundation experiences of humankind. It is based on the existential fact that human beings appear to one another. Appearance is the only basis on which to know or claim the existence of reality. We appear whether we like it or not. The *self* is a product of being conscious of appearing. We would not have a sense of 'selfhood' if we weren't aware of being observed by others. Appearance both reveals and conceals and can be manipulated to do more or less of either, at least for a time. Because acting, speaking, and appearing are the foundation of human existence, theater is the art form most closely related to human experience. The Greeks invented theater in this radical sense, and both Greeks and Romans provided terms to describe this entire conundrum of appearing to others. The Greek word for the mask an actor wore is **hypocritos**, from which we derive our term for someone who pretends to be what he is not and conceals who he really is. In Greek theatre, actors wore masks that presented who they were supposed to represent, while the actor spoke the lines through the mask. In Latin, this mask was called the ***persona*** (from the verb *personare*, to sound through). Persona was the appearance through (*per*) which the actor sounded (*sonare*) the role of the character he was performing.

In effect, every human creates voluntarily or presents involuntarily a ***perso**nality* through which to sound his character, or what he wishes to represent as his character. So long as Personality is congruent with the Soul and Spirit, the character is perceived as true by the observer. However, the Mind often intervenes to construct personality traits and evoke emotions, actions, and words for social display. This may be based on imitation or emulation or motivated by shame, fear, or embarrassment, self-protection, ambition, desire to deceive, or any number of motives. Personality manifests what others find intelligible and can use to decide 'who' another person is.

A person's 'personality' may be assigned by others as much as created by himself. This assigned personality is known as one's *reputation*. Once observers have concluded who a person is based on his perceived personality, it becomes both a comfort and a trap for the individual, depending on what conclusions others reach. Personality has many props that contribute to the perception if not the reality of 'who' a person is: job, income, age, looks, voice, associates, residence, possessions, taste, aggressive or passive behavior, and other 'personality traits'. Every individual is taught what society and especially the nurturing family considers fit and unfit to appear, what can be made public and what should be hidden. This is the basis for **shame**, a movement of the soul that occurs when a person is seen to do or be in a condition unfit for appearance or should be concealed because it compromises reputation. **Honor** is the opposite of shame, a censor made up of internalized judgments of what society and the individual considers admirable and dis**reputable**.

All these factors bring about a **self**, the product of a conscious sense of how we think we appear to others compared with how we appear to ourselves. Self is the creation of an individual's appearance in and evaluation by society. Self-esteem is the condition in which how we appear to ourselves is congruent with how we appear to others, and both reveal personality traits admired by the society and peers. Self-esteem is especially important in being able to project oneself forcefully into society. Traits of assertiveness and sociability rely on an individual's sense that he represents desirable qualities whereas aggressiveness and passiveness oddly share a perceived sense that one is disapproved.

Shaping personality has crucial importance for individuals and society. The incidence of achievement and failure, social responsibility and crime, dependence and resourcefulness largely depends on how newborns are nurtured to develop strong and constructive personalities. Most neurosis and psychosis not founded on purely chemical anomalies in the brain are the result of severe personality disorders caused by lack of self-esteem.

Wounds, Fear, Doubt

'Who' one is, is always in question to some degree. The reason is that we do not see ourselves, our **daemon**, so we never know how we appear to others. Photography makes possible a check on how we appear and being 'photogenic' is a litmus test for favorable or unfavorable self-evaluation. But even video and sound provide only a selective view of oneself. Self-consciousness and self-doubt is most intense in teenagers who are undergoing physical and emotional changes and are constantly being judged and evaluated by adults and peers. Sex appeal or lack of it influences popularity at that time when a person is most susceptible to social pressure. **Popularity** is the socially determined personality, *which requires constant association with and affirmation by other people.*

Just as the **public** sphere requires the **private** sphere in which to nurture life and 'depth', so the *social* requires *intimacy* to protect what should be kept private from the relentless exposure of the private in society. Photo and film make possible compete intrusion into the private realm, such that privacy and intimacy are mortally threatened. A popular person must forsake privacy and intimacy to remain popular, since he or she must adopt whatever is approved by the society. This is not much to sacrifice for the sheer bliss of being universally admired and approved, since most people have little personally distinctive character that needs privacy or intimacy to preserve. The only thing that absolutely requires privacy and intimacy is love, and where they are lost, love is soon lost.

The public is 'real' because it presents objects for common view and exchange of observation and opinion about what is commonly observed. The public is based on *'inter-est'*, the **world** of objects and actions that stands **between** individuals and **separates** and **relates** them to one another. The Social consists of private concerns made public, such as private needs for housing, food, entertainment, medical care. sexual activity, and other needs of the body. (Entertainment is a bodily need since it relaxes and renews the body for further exertion.) The private made public does not constitute a 'world', since the private is made up exclusively of needs and wants insubstantial but often urgent requirements of the body. Such needs and wants, no matter how public they become, remain urges and functions of the body and within the body and can't be shared or even seen. The most widely used example is sex, where a conventional expression of orgasm fails to change the fact that nobody can share or validate the intensity or truth of anyone else's pleasure or pain.

Intimacy is a flight from the publicity of social exposure to protect privacy. Intimacy is no more or less 'real' than the social because it deals with the same private needs and wants and yearnings, but it seeks to restore them to privacy rather than make them pubic. Making a need, want, yearning or motive for behavior public does not make it real, and in fact deprives it of the authenticity it, might have if it remained private. Making public a need, want, yearning, motive or any declaration of what can only be private falsifies them and deprives them of authenticity.

Throughout childhood and adulthood identity is subject to serious disorder. A man may become a skilled professional and rise in a corporation, retire and suffer severe depression because his entire persona or self was defined by his work. Disrupting a support system that provides security and identity can lead to suicide, insanity, addiction, and crime because the facade of personality in torn away.

Children are susceptible to wounds to the Soul, which create lifelong vulnerabilities. Most wounds are inflicted by one or both parents and cause such hurt (the spiritual version of physical pain) that they must be covered or repressed. Fear and doubt seal wounds so the hurt cannot be felt. Fear is the emotional, and doubt is the mental bandage for hurt caused by a wound. The fear and doubt protect the child from recurrence of the unbearable hurt inflicted but create in turn a sense of perpetual threat. Such wounds, when severe, can warp a child for life and may lead to sociopathic behavior. A wound binds the child's

Faith, Hope and Love to a betrayal and the feeling of consequent hurt. It impairs thereafter the child's ability to have faith, believe in hope, and give and receive love. It creates distrust and a sense of worthlessness, a sense that one is unworthy of being loved.

Fear and doubt are bearable compared to the hurt wounds cause and may persist an entire lifetime. A wound is actually a deformation or distortion of a child's Love, and by extension his Faith and Hope, caused by words, actions and feelings directed at the child from someone in whom his faith, hope, or love was confided. Normally, only parents or very close and intimate caregivers can inflict wounds, although criminal assault by a stranger can also induce trauma.

Because children are taught to believe words, not what they see or feel, they experience the contradiction between the claims of a parent's words and the facts of a parent's behavior. They cannot reconcile the parental claim of love and protection with the wounding remark or action they commit against the child. Parents use children to work out their own wounds, fears, and doubts. A common example is a mother who hates her daughter because the father or grandfather directs more affection and love to the child than to her. This jealousy may occur when the daughter is quite young, say seven or eight years old, a time at which the father's interest in the mother is abating. Similarly, a father commonly hates his sons and attempts to humiliate them because his father did the same to him or because the wife is protective and possessive of the sons. Many rivalries and antagonisms occur within families and can lead to wounds that have lifelong consequences. Antisocial behavior usually is caused by childhood wounds, which destroy self-esteem.

The wound and hurt are felt in the Soul. Only when the hurt becomes unbearable does it break through the Heart in the form of emotions. This is the 'heartbreak' whose appropriate form is convulsive weeping. The emotions of this heartbreak provide relief. They are the healthy reaction to the wound. The wound may however be so unbearable that the mind superimposes a layer of fear and doubt to numb the feeling. Fear and doubt are more bearable. Fear of feeling the hurt again and doubt about one's worth are easier to bear than the direct experience of the bitter hurt and sense of worthlessness and abandonment. Doubt is the condition of not having certainty about one's worth. Doubt of self-worth and fear of feeling the hurt of a wound again can dominate a personality and severely restrict expression, feeling, confidence, and endeavor.

The hurt eventually is filtered through fear and doubt where it is transmuted and then "breaks" out through the Heart as the emotions anger, rage, and hate. These are the toxic mimics of faith, hope and love, which are the true expressions of the Spirit and the Soul that have been entangled in the wound. Because love is the underlying constituent of the wound, tears and weeping usually accompany fits of rage, anger, or hate, as in the direct expression of the hurt in heartbreak. Fear and doubt shift personality from its bases in Spirit and Soul to the Mind, where thought contrives a defensive and concealing persona. A false persona intended to conceal rather than reveal 'who' one is, is then constructed. Wounds can heal or be mitigated if the person can get behind the fear and doubt to the original hurt and its cause. The hurt binds up love, so if the cause of the hurt can be worked through, the love can be released and the personality freed.

Relationships between Human Faculties

Emotions are inspired by and are directed at external or internal images and ideas. The faculties of Mind and Will can induce emotions, but they cannot induce passion. Passion is a suffering that arises involuntarily within the soul and is directed at another soul. Emotion is a feeling induced by an object or an idea and is intended to manifest that feeling in the world. Much of individual human failure is the result of attempts to substitute emotions of the heart induced by the mind for passions of the soul. The example of love is most pertinent. Love is a passion of the soul. People desperate for the reported blessings of love regularly attempt to simulate love by emotion. The idea of love can induce an emotion that is a toxic mimic of love. Unfortunately, ideas of love cannot induce the passion of love.

Interestingly, the only sign of true **happiness** is the combination of crying and laughter: tears as the only authentic expression of the joy of the Soul followed by laughter, the only authentic expression of elation of the Spirit. That is why in moments of extreme happiness people spontaneously cry and laugh at the same time.

None of these capacities and faculties is discrete. They exist simultaneously in a continuum that is indivisible and constantly intermixed. The *nature* of man's capacities and faculties cannot be known, although science can approximate their function, and all claims to define and determine them end in dehumanization. Neurobiology, physiology, and other investigations into the biochemical and behavioral processes of emotion and thought are remarkable and therapeutic but in no way explain or define the origin and nature of mental or emotional capacity.

How Society is Organized and Develops

Given the range and complexity of human potentiality, the forms by which it is actualized in societies, called culture, are equally varied and indeterminate.

Society combines the potentialities of all its members and chooses, develops, and intensifies certain of them. In society, human potentiality is actualized through choices, which gain loyalty, acquire momentum, persist over time, and come to characterize the members of that society as a whole.

Each society makes choices from the range of human potentiality to create a culture. The existential factors that play a role in the ordering of a society and the character of its culture are countless. These factors manifest the range of human potential and condition social interaction. A few are listed below:

> *strength*
> *power*
> *force*
> *persuasion*
> *authority*
> *love/romance*
> *compassion/pity*
> *sexuality*
> *public/private*
> *social/intimate*
> *appearance/reality*
> *equality/sameness/identity*
> *freedom/liberty/slavery*
> *birth/death*
> *hope/ forgiveness/promise*

Much confusion surrounds these subjects. No analysis of their origin, character, role, and purpose is commonly available or agreed upon. Further, there are so many inherited notions about each one that objectivity much less clarity is difficult to achieve.

A good example is the traditional interpretation of **freedom** and **equality** in the West. Men are **not** born free, although this was the founding principle of the French Revolution as formulated by Jean-Jacques Rousseau, and men are **not** created equal, although this was a primary tenet of the Declaration of Independence as conceived by Thomas Jefferson. Both freedom and equality are created, enforced, and defended only by **political** association and organization and are a product of human solidarity. They do not exist in nature or society. To posit a pre-political (social) or 'natural' freedom or equality is simply absurd, yet this is exactly what happened in two of the greatest events in human history.

Further, freedom and equality are not compatible. Freedom is possible only between peers acting and speaking together, that is, in solidarity. Freedom expresses the innate plurality of individual humans able to speak and act independently among peers, just as excellence expresses individual distinction possible only among peers (***primus inter pares***). The political risk of freedom is hubris, in which an individual may so distinguish himself as to endanger plurality. Excess of excellence was controlled in the Greek ***polis*** by ostracism, removing the proud who threaten the integrity of the State and his peers. Equality is a convention that suspends plurality. It assumes that everyone is identical or interchangeable. It can be used to a limited degree to achieve other purposes such as equal ***access*** to justice and opportunity, but it is lethal if adopted as an overall goal, outcome, or condition. Communism reduced men to a species by assuming that all men are equal to the point of identity. Equality of ***condition*** among men cannot be achieved without destroying humanity, because human plurality is the very essence of human existence and plurality by definition dictates that men are not all the same. Equality corrupts wherever it becomes the surreptitious objective of social policy. Oddly, the French Revolution made equality, ***not*** freedom, its objective and failed murderously. The American Revolution made freedom, ***not*** equality, its objective and succeeded beyond the wildest hopes of its actors.

Strength
Ita singuli pugnant, universi vincuntur.
Tacitus, ***Agricola****, 12*

Strength refers to the physical endowment, energy, agility, training, weapons, money, and other personal resources an ***individual*** has that can be used to prevent coercion by other individuals or to gain the compliance of other individuals. Every individual learns the relative distribution of strength among the people with whom he associates. Only where the balance has not been determined or settled is a test of strength likely. Playground fights and face-offs are the common means of establishing who is stronger in school. In modern society, such physical tests of strength between adults are rare because physical superiority is no longer the basis of social organization. Money, personality, contacts and influential friends and mentors are much more significant. However, the kinds and cost of weapons available can increase or decrease the relative strength of individuals in society.

Power
Nec aliad adveraus validissimus gentes pro nobis utilius quam quod in commune non consultant.
Tacitus, **Agricola**. 12

Power is the most important element in society because without power a society cannot survive. Power refers to the coordinated action and influence that a group of people can bring to bear when the members of a group organize and act together to serve a common purpose. Power is based on **solidarity**, the human capacity for mutual commitment such that every individual in the group treats the goals of every other individual in the group as his own and works to realize them. The power of a group can overwhelm the strength of an individual, but no individual can overcome the power of a group. The power of a small group can overwhelm the majority of a society where the latter have lost solidarity and no longer have power. The nature of power in its least attractive form is revealed in "social pressure", which an individual finds nearly impossible to withstand. Passive resistance as practiced by Gandhi is an example of social power exercised passively without the use of force. Power exercised through the use of force occurs when an entire nation rises to defeat an enemy. Power is always potential and exists only at the time it is exercised. It can be institutionalized in constitutions, courts, legislation, armies, and political systems which embody the principle of solidarity in a society, but the institutional embodiment requires periodic renewal of the original commitment. Outsiders can easily destroy a society in which the original solidarity between the individuals of the society no longer exists so that it cannot generate the power to resist an enemy. The fall of Rome is the classic example of a society that lost its solidarity.

Force

Force refers to the means of violence organized in a gang, militia, police force, army, or similar group. Such organized force can be controlled by a very small number of people within a society and used to coerce the larger population. Force can overcome the power of a large population that lacks the weapons to resist directly, but no stability is possible where the population maintains its solidarity and continues to resist by indirect means. The Resistance in France and Russia during WWII is an example of the power of solidarity against the force of an occupier. One force cannot resist another force unless it has overwhelmingly superior weapons or generates superior power through solidarity within its ranks, known as morale. Smaller forces motivated by greater solidarity have throughout history defeated larger forces that lack **morale**, solidarity, and therefore power. Force is the ultimate test of relative strength between political entities. Once the relative balance has been established to everyone's agreement, if not satisfaction, peace is restored. Such tests of relative power through force recur as new powers emerge and old one's decline.

Persuasion

Persuasion, which reflects the ***power*** of speech, refers to argument, debate, and discussion that convince individuals to unite in serving a common purpose. Persuasion and violence are opposites. Persuasion is based on the human faculty of speech and is the **political** means of obtaining consent and cooperation, just as violence is the ***anti-political*** means of obtaining compliance. Political life and Freedom cannot exist if violence ultimately determines outcomes in the society. Political life is made possible by the capacity for speech, and persuasion is the means by which this capacity is actualized in political life. Persuasion is the foundation of rule of law wherein disputes are settled by argument, not resort to arms. Wherever speech is no longer of importance, is no longer used to reveal truth, is no longer heard or listened to, or is suppressed, the political system will collapse into tyranny. The inability of most societies to make persuasion (and its concomitant rule of law) the basis for settling disputes accounts for the ongoing worldwide record of civil war, genocide, and war.

Authority

Authority is the second most important element in society and is directly related to the first, power. Authority refers to leadership without coercion, the most ineffable and pervasive source of cohesion in human society. Authority is the opposite of force, violence, and tyranny. Force (the organized means of violence) and authority are antithetical. Force cannot replace authority, but authority can replace force. Authority gains consent, support, or agreement without coercion. The primary question for every society is 'Where is authority?'. Every functioning society has certain principles, beliefs and moral values to which its members adhere.

Authority usually is conferred on the individuals or institutions most representative of those principles, beliefs, and values. Authority is sometimes associated with wisdom, age, and experience as in the Roman Senate, or with charismatic or spiritual individuals who gather a devoted following based on personal qualities, as did Jesus and Genghis Khan. Authority is obeyed willingly and implicitly, and there is no appeal from authority. The genius of the United States Constitution was to create a branch of Government, the Supreme Court, that embodies authority within the United States government. Loss of a source of authority within a society leads to its decline because agreement on common principles and solidarity can no longer exist without it.

Love-Romance/Compassion-Pity

Love is the union of two souls in total disregard of worldly circumstances. Compassion is the union of souls through the sympathetic suffering of one person with the suffering of another. Both love and compassion blot out consciousness of the world as the souls are consumed in each other. Love and compassion are rare compared to emotions, and in many societies are virtually nonexistent. Yet because they are among the most important influences on Western Civilization, they have acquired universal significance. Christianity introduced love and compassion as a religious and social imperative, both in the words of Jesus and the sermon of Paul on faith, hope, and love (Corinthians l,13). Their public manifestation is called charity, but love and compassion are falsified when made public, and therefore they are apolitical and asocial. Two 'mimics' of love and compassion emerged in Western Civilization: romantic love and pity.

Romantic love

Invented in the 12th Century at French troubadour courts in Aquitaine and southwestern France, it was expressed in poetry and gallantry and became an important aspect of Chivalry. It originated in the platonic love of a pledged knight for the wife of a lord. It was a courtly love that became ostentatious in its rituals and behaviors and served as a feminine, civilizing influence on the crude male warrior class of the day. It evolved over the centuries to the concept of a unique soul mate loved without regard for such worldly considerations as birth, means, and even character. It later became in American popular culture a social formula for marriage, in which 'love' was induced or simulated and then endorsed and supported through socially patterned behaviors leading to marriage. Because romantic love lacks the depth of love, most of the relationships broke down or discovered other reasons to continue. Romantic love is the driving force in popular culture.

Pity

Pity is the toxic mimic of Compassion. Like love, compassion is a personal relationship and remained largely a private matter until Rousseau and the French Revolution introduced its toxic mimic, pity, with deadly effect into political discourse. The public form compassion took in Rousseau and the French Revolution was pity for ***les miserables***, the poor and downtrodden proletariat of Paris. The difficulty lies in the nature of compassion and pity. Compassion is a passion of the soul that suffers with another suffering individual. It is the expression of a soul directly relating to another soul. Love and compassion relate one individual soul to another individual soul and cannot be generalized to groups of people. Compassion, for example, cannot be the basis for solidarity of a group. Pity is a contrived emotion of the heart presumably evoked by sympathy for the general suffering of a group of people, rather than any one individual. Pity is insincere and condescending in the sense that it is indifferent to individuals and is directed only at classes and groups. All pity is egocentric pity for the self as victim of society projected against an oppressor. This was the case of Jean-Jacques Rousseau, who considered himself the poster child of social victimization. Curiously, he was consistently disloyal to wives, lovers, his children (deserted) and associates.

Pity projects over a mass. Pity is a false, simulated expression of solidarity with a suffering group. Solidarity only occurs between individuals. Pity is directed only at groups and classes not at individuals. Pity is in fact a form of 'will to power', because it always destroys the authentic pluralism manifested by solidarity, in the name of the monolithic interest of the pitied group. Ultimately pity is more an emotion of rage at the putative oppressor than one of concern for the well-being of the oppressed. The French Revolution became the murderous instrument of pity for the proletariat of Paris directed at so-called oppressors and was embodied in later revolutionary theories of Marxism and Communism. Wherever pity becomes a political influence, political life and discourse are corrupted. Pity is by its nature hypocritical because it assigns guilt and innocence to groups rather than to individuals. In such a system, individual dignity, integrity, and especially responsibility are eliminated. Pity also eliminates the objectivity required for responsible policy. Because victims are always wronged, whatever crimes they commit are attributed to the oppressors rather than their morale culpability.

The various forms of 'woke political correctness' are inspired by pity and undermine honest discourse within a society. The politics of pity is revealed by the vocabulary it uses, which includes 'disadvantaged', 'underrepresented', 'oppressed', 'economically deprived', 'discrimination' and the like. The role of pity in the destructive ideologies of the 19th and 20th Centuries is usually overlooked because few can comprehend how pity, a seemingly innocuous even benign feeling, could corrupt polities and society or play a central and destructive role in Western society.

The only public alternative to love and compassion is **respect**, which is a principle, not a passion or emotion, and treats each individual as a person not a member of a class. Solidarity is not possible without mutual respect. Principles originate in public association wherein each individual applies to every other individual the Golden Rule. Respect is a product of solidarity where every individual considers a threat to the rights and integrity of any other individual as a threat to his own. Respect is a public virtue, not a private value, and is daily manifested in simple good manners. Where the public realm is corrupted through the loss of authority and principles, both manners and respect disappear.

Sexuality

Sexuality is the most pervasive influence on society. The influence is personal, social, political, and economic and affects how half the population relates to the other half and one generation relates to the next. Because women in most societies were subordinate to men, women played little role in the early historical records. Most primitive societies had relative equality between men and women, since both played a vital role in gathering food as well as nurturing children. In early agricultural societies, where fertility rather than virility was worshipped, women were regarded as superior because of their skill at cultivation, which did not require the strength needed for hunting, and for the earth mother mysteries of birth and reproduction. With the advent of weapons, organized warfare, and warrior societies, women became chattel just as large numbers of the male population became slaves. Because women were subject to the natural burden of pregnancy, childbirth, and nurture and the mass of men were needed to provide labor power in the absence of sufficient animal or mechanical sources of energy, both laborers and women were regarded as slavish by the ruling classes. This was particularly true in Greece where the issue achieved philosophical formulation. How a society treats women is a measure of its adaptability to change and progress. For example, the Islamic world subordinates and abases women. The inflexibility and resistance to change on the part of males in Islamic society is due largely to the fear that they will lose their power over women in their society. Islamic men are willing to forego substantial economic advantages rather than modernize and secularize, because that would emancipate women from their role as chattel without personal rights or opportunities.

Public/Private-Social/Intimate

Public and private are complementary and refer to mutually supporting domains that have entirely different but compatible and complementary purposes. Public refers to the interests of the society as a whole. Private refers to the domestic economy (shelter, job, income, etc.) every individual requires to sustain his life and to the secret, dark, and private place of withdrawal required by every individual as relief from the relentless light of public exposure. In effect the private is needed to sustain life so that the individual can participate in the public activity of society. Whenever and wherever private property and private space is destroyed or abolished, an individual or society loses its fundamental human basis and becomes totalitarian in character. The Soviet regime in Russia destroyed privacy and dehumanized Russian society for seventy years.

Social and intimate are antagonistic. Intimacy originally was discovered and explored by Rousseau as an authentic entirely private realm devised to withstand and provide refuge from the vicious gossip and treachery of court society. It was a rebellion of the heart against the cynicism of society. It was not a rebellion against the political. What made society so unbearable to Rousseau was its cheapening and rendering into social commodity of the most private aspects of human potential, especially love, friendship, and community. Court society used these, or rather their simulations, strictly as means to gain social advantage or to discredit an opponent. The social makes what is a private or personal matter into a public interest, value, or concern. Rousseau and romanticism in general turned to the intimate as a refuge, a secret, hidden, mysterious and vague inner realm where two soul mates might join in rebellion against the coercive effect of society.

The overwhelming 'social pressure' that pries open the heart and exposes the most delicate feelings to view, mockery, and false imitation became a characteristic of Western society under the middle class and working-class societies of the 19th and 20th Centuries. The associated rebellion especially by youth against the dominant society is a pattern followed by generations of Europeans and Americans to recover their privacy in particular, with enormous political and social effect. The original class of social **refusés** was defined by Murger in *La Vie de Boheme* in the 1840's in Paris and finds echoes through the Beatniks in the 1950's in the United States and the Generation X dropouts of the 1990's.

Freedom/Liberty/Slavery

Freedom is a product of political organization, not a natural endowment, and freedom is possible only within a State or society that establishes freedom by law and defends it by force. Men are not born free. Freedom is a political gift, not a personal attribute.

Liberty is relief from constraint, usually gained through wealth, which allows an individual to be free from compelled work, labor, or activity. Liberty is a negative value, in that it is the absence of compulsion.

Slavery is the condition of property in a person, through which the time and labor of an individual are entirely at the disposal of another. Slavery is a socially or legally imposed condition in which an individual is compelled to labor for another. Slavery had many definitions throughout history. Classical Civilization, which was based on chattel slavery, defined it very broadly. All labor and physical effort compelled by human metabolism was considered slavish, and whoever was compelled to labor was slavish. This view even extended to the arts, where sculptors were considered inferior to painters because their work required more physical labor. Women, because they were compelled by the 'labor' of procreation, and laborers, because they were compelled to use their bodies to earn food, were considered 'slavish' and were excluded public life. Necessity (slavery) was the basis of private life in the **oikos** or household, which ministered to the life needs of its members and liberated the master for public life in the Greek ***polis*** or Roman Republic, Classical Civilization regarded mere life as slavish and subject to metabolic compulsion and held life in low regard. Only the public realm where men could be free and seek immortality through fame was considered worthy. Western Civilization has evolved a more favorable view of 'labor' and 'life' and has much less regard for the public realm and its political fame and distinction.

Equality/Inequality

Men are distinct individuals, not a species, and the founding condition of human society is plurality, not identity. As a consequence, the role and limits of equality within a society largely determines its class and social structure. Equality and inequality pertain most to questions of opportunity and justice. A society can enforce a degree of equality of opportunity and justice, and it can impose a degree of equality of outcome. The problem is that men are born unequal in physical, intellectual, and personal qualities. Any attempt to eradicate these differences is anti-political and anti-human, reducing people to sameness, which denies their individual distinctness and humanity. The further difficulty is that men are ***similar*** in many respects. Balancing similarity and difference, equality and distinctness, is the challenge any democratic society confronts.

Appearance/Reality/Truth/Deception

Nous sommes si accoutumée à nous déguiser aux autres qu'enfin nous nous déguisons à nous-mêmes. Rochefoucauld, **Maximes***, 119.*

What seems to be a subject for philosophical speculation, how to distinguish appearance from reality, truth from deception, is one of the most basic issues in human affairs and especially political affairs. The issue arises in part from the human capacity for lying, in part from the fallibility of human perceptions, and in part from the fact that the whole truth can never be known. The only remedy is truthfulness, and the only defense is publicity. Lies can only be exposed by making them public and subject to challenges. Truth cannot be perfectly known, but it is possible to tell the truth to the extent that it is known. In human affairs, appearance is reality, since only what can appear and does appear is real.

Birth/Death

Birth and death provide the parentheses of human life and are the determinants of social change and preservation. Where men come from at birth and where they go at death is unknowable, but society is their home during the interval. The orientation of birth is the future. Birth is the beginning of someone new whose potential is actualized in society through the cultural decisions already made by past generations. Death is the end of a fully actualized member of the society trained in its culture. The orientation of death is the past.

The balance of past and future in a society is expressed demographically. Younger populations tend to be less stable, more volatile, and are often aggressive. Older populations are conservative, passive, and stable. Since both the young and the old tend to be more or less dependent on the productivity of the working adults, a heavy preponderance of either will cause social stress when the productive adults simply can't meet the demands of the dependent generations. How the young are raised and educated is the most important and characteristic feature of a society. Traditionally the young were strongly supervised and indoctrinated in the culture of their seniors. The United States devised an entirely different approach, inventing the 'teenager' and advocating that the young needed to find their own culture and mores creating endemic generation gaps in the society. This approach has spread globally, the degree depending on how conservative and dominant the older and working population is.

Hope, Promise, and Forgiveness

Prometheus made the first man and woman of clay and then stole fire from Zeus in order to bring them to life. In revenge, Zeus created Pandora's box which contained all the evils that beset mankind, including disease, labor, and hope. The box was opened and the evils spread throughout the world. Hope was included among the evils of Pandora's box, which seems incongruous to people raised in Western Civilization. Given our Christian heritage of faith, hope, and charity, hope is one of the blessings of mankind. For the Greeks, hope was a pleasant and mollifying delusion.

The difference between our view and theirs is the intervening teaching of *forgiveness* by Jesus of Nazareth as a means of breaking the relentless chain of action and reaction that makes up the daily encounters of mankind, especially in the Semitic tribes dedicated to revenge with which he was familiar. 'Trespass' or offense is inevitable in human affairs, and nothing will interrupt the cycle of revenge that such offenses set loose except the act of forgiving trespasses. This is of enormous secular importance regardless of its religious origin and inspiration. The ability to forego revenge and start over is among the highest of human capacities, literally making action and association possible. The only other means for breaking the cycle of revenge or cause and inevitable effect in human affairs is reparation or punishment, where either compensation or legal retribution completes or ends the cycle.

Promise is the human ability of solidarity to bind the future to a purpose, treating the future as if it were present. The uncertainty of the future would overcome all human endeavor if it were not possible to say, "This shall be." Contracts are the mundane version of this power to bind the future. Romans were especially sensitive to this power, which was formulated in Roman law by the dictum, **pacta sunt servanda**.

Hope in human affairs derives from this power every person has to forgive, to start over, rather than allow an inevitable chain of cause and effect to rule the future, and by the power to make promises that guarantee the future. New beginning makes the future a realm of possibilities rather than an ineluctable grinding down to inevitable conclusions. Promises that create islands of certainty in an uncertain future make continuity and duration possible. The West has made these an essential part of its Civilization. Islamic and other civilizations generally reject promise and especially forgiveness as illusory, much like the Greeks.

Socal Strata
On n'est jamais si ridicule par les qualités que l'on a que par celles que l'on affecte d'avoir. Rochefoucauld, Maximes, 134.

A society is affected by the cycle of birth and death, by its distribution of age groups, and by its class structure. Although every society seeks stability and tries to maintain itself based on its cultural choices, birth and death mean that those who inherited the culture of the society can only preserve it by passing it on to those newly born into it. This tautology conceals some very profound implications for human potential and social culture. Birth is a beginning of someone new. Only through training to imbed habits, beliefs, feelings, ways of thinking, preferences, and countless other actualizations of the range of human potential chosen by the society can the parents and elders indoctrinate the new person into their way of life. Each choice eliminates countless alternatives. This process, called education, traditionally assumed that there was a body of custom and values that distinguish members of the society and that the new person must be taught to become a member of the society. The constant departure and arrival of old and new members of the society means that no society is static. It thrives, survives, or declines, but it can't stand still.

Age distribution also profoundly affects a society. In prehistoric hunter-gatherer societies, longevity was short, and birth survival was low, so the societies tended to have few old and few young, and a preponderance of able-bodied adults. Men who lived to old age were revered for their sheer survival and wisdom, but few attained that status. As survival rates improved with agriculture and a more varied diet, the population mix tended to even out a bit, although survival at birth and into youth was never remarkable. Even in Rome, the life expectancy was about 35 years. Only with modern medicine and public health has survival increased dramatically, and average life expectancy now exceeds 80 years.

Class distribution is perhaps the most obvious influence on society. Small hunter-gatherer groups had little specialization and divided mainly on sexual and age lines. Women, children and old men might mind the store while the hunters ranged. As population increased, divisions between functions and classes became pronounced. Most early civilizations divided into:

- ***peasants and laborers (95 percent or more)***

- *middle class merchants, artisans, tradesmen*
- *bookkeepers, administrators and others who maintained the state apparatus*
- *aristocrats who owned land and led armies*
- *warriors*
- *priests*
- *King, Emperor, or Caesar and his court who guided the entire system*

The class system largely determined the fate of individuals born into each class. Social mobility was limited until the 19th and 20th Centuries, when industrialism and capitalism provided enormous opportunity for ambitious members of lower classes. Even in Russia, peasants were able to purchase their freedom and become wealthy merchants and industrialists. In this period, inequities in class systems became the fuel for social and political revolution and evolution.

The class system in every society is similar. The **lower classes** include laborers, skilled trades, and others who work with their hands in practical and necessary jobs. Adequately rewarded for their work and labor, they tend to be content with their position in society. Except for some talented individuals in the class, the members are not ambitious to rise socially or envious of those who are wealthy and prominent. They tend to be relaxed, independent, indifferent to status seeking and status symbols, and their lives are lived in close relationships with family, friends, and fellow class members.

The **upper classes** are also easygoing and content, having no one above them to excite envy and usually no one below them to provoke fear. If the upper class is not corrupt, it usually takes on the leadership work of running the state (embassies, courts, organizing capital and resources, serving as counselors, generalship, etc.) and is considered useful and necessary by the classes below them. Given their advantages, they often support and lead efforts to provide public charity and improve conditions for the poor and suffering lower classes. Where the upper class is corrupt and indifferent to the rest of the population, it tends to waste capital it controls on personal consumption and aggrandizement. This is most typical of the upper class in Latin America, which is of Spanish descent. This class controls 95 percent of the wealth, yet is indifferent to the *mestizo* and Indian population. The upper classes in Latin America use the wealth they monopolize to enjoy an international lifestyle in Europe and America while the countries endure civil war and economic stagnation.

The **middle class** usually envies and emulates the aristocratic class. They are insecure in their position, having neither birthright nor land holdings to ensure their continued prosperity. They are prosperous but live in constant fear of economic loss that may drive them into the lower class. Consequently, they tend to be more circumspect, secretive, obsequious to superiors, and respectable.

The most unstable are those at the very bottom range of the middle class, what later became known as the ***petit bourgeoisie***. Oddly this group is the most tenacious in defending and imposing the 'traditional values' of a society as a means to rise socially and financially and assuage their severe social and personal insecurity. The upper class usually lives in a style so different from the other classes that such traditional values are supported but not especially emphasized within the class. The lower class maintains the traditional value system, but their commitment is based on strong beliefs, not on opportunism as with the petit bourgeoisie.

The ***haut proletariat***, to contrive a term, is similar in some respects to the *petit bourgeoisie*. These are the ambitious and talented members of the lower class of laborers or later 'blue collars'. They tend to seek carriers where entry level opportunity is available to them, especially in the army, religious institutions, or state bureaucracy, In Africa, Latin America, the Islamic world, and Asia, the army is made up of members of this class, which tends to be the source of leadership when the upper classes lose control of the society. They invariably fail to improve conditions because they are motivated by personal ambition rather than any broader social concern. Chiang Kai-shek, Mommar Khadafi, Juan Peron, and Edi Amin are examples.

The *petit bourgeoisie* is the most neurotic and potentially violent class in a society. It a pathologically afraid of descending into the working class (which in modern times often makes more money) and clings desperately to appearances. Economic turmoil usually drives them into a lower standard of living, at which time they tend to turn to aggressive political parties for comprehensive relief. Its members pursue opportunities to rise and stridently advocate traditional values to advance their position while remaining unscrupulous. This class manned the German Nazi party and countless radical 'crackpot' groups. Its most typical representatives in the United States include J. Edgar Hoover and Richand Nixon.

The *haut proletariat* is less neurotic because they have no fear of falling in status, having come from the lower class to begin with. However, they are as ambitious as the *petit bourgeoisie* and as unscrupulous. An example is Stalin, who joined the church in order to advance in society and later became the greatest tyrant in modern history. Curiously, the petit bourgeois joined fascist organizations while the haut proletariat joined communist organizations. Both provided leadership for their respective parties in Europe in the 20th Century.

Population Growth and Society

Increase in human population is the single greatest environmental event since the meteorites struck earth and created a cloud shield that blotted out sunlight and destroyed nearly all vegetation and animal life at the end of the Jurassic Era. Humans have populated and overpopulated every habitable part of the globe and have destroyed millions of acres of habitat and ecosystems and thousands of species and there is no end in sight. Only about 10 million people lived at the beginning of the

Neolithic Period (15,000 BC). The population of the world reached about 500 million by AD 1650, 1.1 billion by 1850, 5.3 billion by 1990, 6.1 billion in 2000, and may exceed 8 billion by 2050. Ancient societies were miniscule compared to modern societies. For example, in 1200 BC, Athens had about 25,000 people. Its population reached about 155,000 by 450 BC. The Roman Empire probably had from 50 to 70 million people at its height. Of that number, about 1 million people lived in Rome, and from 5 to 6 million lived in the rest of Italy. The population of modern Italy is 57 million. In 1200 AD, Lubeck, Germany, an important city of the Hanseatic League had a population of only about 10,000. In that same period, London, with about 40,000 people, Venice about 100,000, and Paris about 150,000, ranked among the most populous cities in Europe. Even Asia was sparsely populated. In 1250 AD, Hangzhou, China, had a population of about 320,000. Guangzhou (also called Canton) had about 250,000 people.

The industrial revolution began the enormous population explosion of the 19th Century. Chicago and Manchester, England, provide two examples of the tremendous growth of industrial cities. Manchester's population grew from about 6,000 in 1685 to about 303,000 in 1851. Chicago's population jumped from about 4,000 in 1840 to more than 1 million in 1890. In the United States, the first federal census in 1790 determined that about 4 million people lived in the country compared to 300 million in the year 2000.

The gradual ending of space and time as it was once experienced is due entirely to this phenomenal crowding. The nature of societies changes qualitatively with increases in population. Politically, the greater the population, the less likely democratic forms of government can survive. Violence and civil disorder become more likely and more difficult to control, and law and order can be enforced only selectively. The Athenians of 400 BC recognized that the *Polis* had to keep its free citizenry at about 500 in order to practice direct democracy. Republican forms of government may adapt to larger populations through a system of stages of government and representation. But populations in the 100's of millions inevitably tighten the social order and reduce the scope for democratic or nonconforming political action. Socially the huge increase in population can lead to chaos, as in Africa. Lack of basic resources, such as potable water, sufficient cropland, and transportation corridors as well as lack of public health and medical services, schools, and social assistance, force residents of most third world economies into poverty and worse.

Social Instruments and Institutions

Society is made up of many activities--economic, religious, social, military, cultural, and the like--with endless subdivisions possible for each. Such activities are embodied in organizations established to achieve the objectives of the activity. For example, an army is established to develop and train with the means of violence in order to defend the society against foreign and domestic enemies. A church is established to meet the spiritual and religious needs of the population. Investment banks and corporations may be established to promote economic activity and invest in new inventions to meet the vital needs of the population. The list of needs and organizations to meet them is endless.

Originally the organizations are **instruments** for meeting the purposes for which they were established. Their members devote themselves mainly to fulfilling those purposes. Over time, however, the members acquire purposes and objectives of their own, so the instrument focuses less and less on the social needs it was established to meet and more and more on the objectives and benefits of its members. In effect they become **vested interests**. For example, an army may train and reward members who excel at using a particular kind of attack, like the cavalry charge. When more effective arms become available, like the tank, machine gun, and barbed wire, the high-ranking officers who made their careers in the now obsolete cavalry resist changing to the new and more effective weapons. The society is less able to defend itself because the army has other objectives than improving defensive and offensive capability. As a result of this scenario in WWI, millions died unnecessarily. Nearly two-thirds of the space on United States supply ships was used to ship fodder for cavalry horses that were never used in combat. At this point, the instrument becomes an ***institution***. An institution no longer meets the needs of the society at an acceptable level. Social dissatisfaction increases, as the needs for which the instrument was established are no longer met. Resistance to change on the part of members of the institution also increases. The institution can either be ***reformed*** back into an instrument, ***circumvented*** by establishing a new instrument to replace the original one, or the institution can ***successfully resist*** both reform and circumvention. The decline of societies and civilizations occurs when instruments become institutions and both reform and circumvention fail. Societies overall can become institutionalized and no longer capable of innovation or flexibility in the face of challenges. The basic characteristic of an instrument is innovation, and the basic characteristic of an institution is resistance to change.

Instrument of Expansion

Every society requires an instrument of expansion to grow and develop. The instrument of expansion ***accumulates surplus capital*** and ***invests*** it in new tools and new ways of doing things. So long as the surplus is invested, new growth, greater wealth, and social progress continue. However, when the instrument of expansion, which is the class that controls surplus investment capital, diverts that capital to personal consumption and unproductive uses the social growth rate and well-being decline.

A society or civilization declines when its instrument of expansion becomes an institution and successfully resists efforts to reform or circumvent it. Resistance to reform on the part of the capital-owning class usually takes the form of fomenting foreign conflict and creating internal political agents to undermine or divert efforts of members of the population to reform. There may also be regional conflict or class warfare as competition within the society for declining supplies of incomes, goods and services increases.

Patterns of Historical Change

Societies exist in a matrix of human potential actualized in social functions that change over time. Changes in societies are usually generated within the society or borrowed or imposed from outside the society. The degree to which a society has been institutionalized determines how adaptable it is and therefore how changes are introduced, by choice or force.

The largest societies are called Civilizations. Their principal features are writing and city life. Comparatively few civilizations have developed in human history, and all of them occurred after 4000 BC. Many have simply disappeared, such as Classical Greece and Rome, or have been assimilated into other civilizations. Civilizations go through stages, beginning with Mixture and Gestation in which several cultures and peoples mingle, compare and trade beliefs, tools, skills, and organizations. From this mixture eventually emerges a new society and instrument of expansion based on which the society expands geographically, economically, culturally, and in population. This is the stage of **Expansion** in which social functions and organizations, especially the instrument of expansion, are instruments dedicated to meeting the goals and needs of society. Expansion geographically means that the "core" area of the civilization ages faster than the outlying peripheral areas. Generally, the outlying areas continue expansion after the core area begins to decline.

When instruments become self-serving institutions that resist further growth and change in order not to threaten the established rewards and advantages within the society, the society enters a stage of **Conflict**. Conflict is internal and external, and usually involves declining innovation, productivity, growth, birth rates, and satisfaction at all levels of the society. Vested interests usually create political or social diversions to turn discontent toward targets other than themselves.

Foreign wars to gain others wealth and occupy idle males in the society are a common panacea. *Panem et circenses* (bread and circuses) forms of diversion and entertainment are created to distract the population from the causes of decline. Eventually more vigorous peripheral areas conquer or take control of depleted core areas. Nevertheless, efforts to reform institutions or create new instruments that meet social goals are made and if successful can redirect the society to a new stage of Expansion. If unsuccessful, a period of **Universal Empire** follows in which conflict ceases and a brief but golden age of peace begins based mainly on ending the waste of resources and wealth lost in the preceding conflicts.

The stage of **Decay** follows the period of Universal Empire. Decay may go on for thousands of years if there is no foreign challenger. Institutions break down, city life becomes unsupportable because agricultural production declines, the economy no longer supports a military sufficient to defend the society, and morale and solidarity disappear. When an outside society that is beginning to expand confronts the society in decay, it conquers or destroys it for all practical purposes. Such confrontations may lead to new mixing and gestation and a new civilization. Throughout the stages, the society and the people in it make choices or refuse to make choices to meet challenges and make needed changes. Where an inflexible religious, tribal, or class system is imbedded in the society, the leadership has no interest in change and successfully resists internal attempts at change. Many societies are fully prepared to give up substantial material advantages rather than change their social or power structure. This is the case in the Islamic world, Africa and to some extent Latin America today.

Framework for Understanding Non-Western Societies

The underlying social and cultural patterns of foreign societies and states determine how they are managed and how they conduct themselves. These underlying patterns help to explain an otherwise bewildering array of nations and cultures. People raised in the culture of Western Civilization assume that societies in other parts of the World are much like Western society and are motivated by similar principles and values. People are people and are basically the same wherever they happen to live.

On the contrary, other societies have traditions, cultures, and social values so different from the West that their values, behavior, and expectations are usually unlike and often entirely opposite to our own. The difference between Western and other societies derives from the entirely different organization, culture, and value systems they inherited from ancient social and political systems.

Much confusion is due to the present twofold nature of foreign cultures as observed by the West. All foreign cultures have assimilated the West's material culture to greater or less degree, Automobiles, high rises, television, movies, music, clothes, the list is endless. Some, like the Islamic world, reject and attempt to limit Western cultural influences. Others, like Japan, adopt most aspects of Western culture. Because the representatives of Asian, Islamic, African and other States speak perfect English and wear business suits, we tend to believe that their world is much like our own. But none of these States has adopted the West's nonmaterial culture, such as moral and ethical standards, science, fair play, social justice, and rule of law. There is some Institutional imitation, such as national assemblies, presidents, courts, universities and the like. But the great cultural traditions and values that underlie the West's achievements are not assimilated and, in most cases, actively resisted.

Foreign societies now are embroiled in a confrontation between their underlying cultural and social inheritance and the overwhelming power and influence of the West. The States and Empires that represented these ancient societies and cultures (Islamic, Chinese, Japanese, Indian, African) were destroyed by the West in the 19th and 20th Centuries. Understanding the nature of these underlying social and cultural systems is of great importance. Today, the West confronts the broken remnants of defeated civilizations, empires, kingdoms, and tribal societies in Africa, the Near East, Asia, and Russia, all still attempting to recover from the shock of their encounter with the West.

The following section introduces in broad outline the characteristics of civil societies, tribal societies, and theocratic empires that form the constituent elements of present States worldwide. Subsequent parts of this book will review in detail the characteristics of these societies. There are three underlying forms of social organization in world societies today: ***civil*** **societies, tribal societies** and ***theocratic empires***. Despite the proliferation of States, the Babel of languages, and the variety of cultures that confront the observer, the fundamental character of States worldwide can be identified and understood as one of these categories of social organization. Variations can be explained within the overriding form of society to which they belong. Although there are local deviations from the general form described below, the differences do not alter the basic pattern. These patterns can be used to interpret events in the respective societies. The characteristics of individual States and regions will be covered in other sections of this book.

Civil Society

Western Civilization is the only society to have developed ***civil society***, a uniquely Western form of organization. All others simulate Western institutions but have developed as and remain tribal or theocratic empires. The origins and development of Western Civilization will be covered later, but a few attributes can be mentioned for purposes of comparison with tribal societies and theocratic empires. In civil society, the state is a ***part*** of the larger society, not the overriding or primary organization of members of the society. Relationships between citizens and government are contractual based on laws that embody agreed rights and obligations. Family, occupations, professions, business, freely formed associations, all are more important than government or the State in the lives of the people, and both government and state serve the larger life interests of the members of the society.

Civil society is particularly distinguished by ***rule of law*** and ***due process***, which protects all members of the society. No one is above the law and rights of minorities or of those out of power are protected from abuses by majorities or by those in power. Officials are sworn to uphold the law fairly, and no exceptions are lawful. Religion does not override law, but is protected as part of a general right of association and belief. Religion remains a private not a public matter.

Principles of democracy, fair play, social justice, brotherhood, unbiased inquiry, and progress also are attributes of Western civil society, perhaps not always evenly observed, but universally approved. The notable fact about civil society is that the public good of all citizens is accepted as the standard for public life. Where abuses occur, institutions and measures are available and public officials and private citizens are commonly committed to correct them. Because the West has enjoyed these advantages for so long, we find it difficult to understand other societies that do not share them, much less want them.

Tribal Societies

Tribal societies are dominant in Africa, the Islamic Middle East, and Southeast Asia. Tribal societies are unstable, usually violent, and war and instability in regions where tribal societies predominate are frequent subjects for international concern. Of 16 ongoing peacekeeping missions of the United Nations worldwide, six are in Africa, six are in Muslim countries of the Middle East, and the rest are in Muslim countries in the Balkans, Central Asia, and Southeast Asia. Terrorism from Islamic extremists is a chronic threat to World peace, a threat that derives directly from the tribal value systems of Bedouin society. Given their importance to World peace, some awareness of the characteristics of tribal societies is essential if we are to develop effective policies for coping with the challenges such societies present. The principal characteristics of tribal societies are the following:

Individualism, individual freedom, and individual rights are entirely alien to tribal society. Tribal society centers on the tribe, clan, or extended family group. The most significant aspect of an individual's identity is tribal membership. The individual exists only as a member of the tribe and has no separate individual identity or rights apart from the tribe. The tribe provides a place, function, and livelihood to each of its members in return for absolute loyalty.

The concept of human rights is alien, even incomprehensible, to tribal societies. A man or woman without tribal identity or who has been ejected from his or her tribe is a non-person subject to whatever abuse others can inflict, usually in the form of domestic slavery. Correspondingly, anyone outside the tribe is not considered as human, since no concept of common humanity outside the tribe exists. The only rights anyone has are whatever the tribe chooses to bestow and is able to defend.

There is no rule of law in tribal society. The tribe is patriarchal. The head of the tribe controls all wealth and property and makes all decisions, including decisions about marriage. Law is what the head of the tribe decides. Women are regarded as chattel. Tribal societies usually are polygamous, and each male has as many wives and concubines as his station requires and his means allow. Women unrelated to the tribe and ineligible for marriage are considered fair game to be exploited sexually and economically. Women members of the tribal family in Muslim societies are usually sequestered to prevent contact with males outside the family group, and their activities outside the home are severely restricted. Tribal societies are usually patrilocal in that married couples live with the husband's father. Marriage is endogamous, and marriage of first and second cousins is practiced to preserve the integrity of the tribe.

The cohesive force of tribal societies is revenge. Each member of the tribe or clan is required to avenge any dishonor inflicted on any other member of the clan. Other tribes are considered to be enemies and a threat to the well-being and survival of one's own tribe. Alliances with other tribes and clans may occur, usually as a way to gain advantage over a common adversary. Such arrangements are always temporary and dissolve when the advantage of one or the other party is no longer served. Tribal society focuses only on its own interests and has no interest in or concern for people outside the tribe. Tribal societies are incapable of solidarity. This explains the remarkable survival of Israel, a nation of slightly more than six million that has withstood and defeated surrounding Islamic tribal societies amounting to 100 million. Tribal societies based on revenge are incapable of solidarity, externally *and* internally.

Tribal societies are not motivated primarily by economic advantage. Tribes are more interested in cohesion and survival than in long-term economic gain or social progress. Commonly tribes are quite willing to sacrifice wealth and economic progress for the psychological satisfaction of being in a closed, cohesive, and secure social setting. The Boers in South Africa are an eccentric example of this attitude. This group of

Dutch settlers 'tribalized' their society, becoming like a native African tribe, in order to enjoy the parasitic superior status provided by a white skin. The Boers trekked into the hinterland, leaving their land, homes, and possessions, in order to continue to enjoy their racial superiority over blacks in the region. This superiority was threatened by British insistence on native rights. Boers were willing to give up the economic social advantages of Western Civilization and live like their African neighbors, who performed all the labor the Boers required. They preferred a reduced standard of living in order to continue a life of ease and a sense of racial superiority.

Theocratic Empires

Theocratic empires developed in the river basins of Egypt, Mesopotamia, India, and China and in the vast steppe zone of Central Asia where large land areas and their populations were sustained by extensive agriculture or pastoralism in the case of Central Asia. Remnants of the theocratic empires of China, India, Japan, and Orthodox Russia make up nearly two thirds of the World's population to this day. India is a special variation on theocratic empire. India has a tribal society to the extent that the caste system is really a form of tribalism, but it also has traditions in Hindu religion that make it equally a theocratic empire. In all these remnant areas of theocratic empire, their original characteristics persist. In Russia and China, this legacy underlies a veneer of modern industrialism that has led people in the West into thinking such cultures are enigmatic or impenetrable to Western understanding. They are in fact quite simple in form and character. The characteristics of theocratic empire are the following.

Theocratic empires are static. Theocratic empires impose an unchanging and unalterable hierarchy and belief system, which was claimed to derive from a mandate of the gods in ancient times and from the iron law of historical necessity, Marxism, in modern times.

Theocratic empires are two class systems of rulers and ruled. A 'divine' king or leader served by priests or party ideologues and administrators supported by a military elite rule a very large, enslaved mainly agricultural population. Religion or ideology rather than honor and revenge bind the members of a theocratic empire. Worship of a divine ruler who serves as mediator between heaven and earth and who requires unqualified loyalty and obedience at the risk of divine retribution provides the principle by which theocratic empires organize and compel large populations to carry out agricultural labor year after year. In modern times, orthodox Marxism provided the organizing principle in China and Russia. India departs from their model because India was occupied and ruled by Great Britain, so its parliamentary system, language, and certain social values were partly assimilated. Japan has assimilated Western institutions and practices, if not values. The unique character of Japan is described later in this book.

A reliable living standard and psychic certainty are the rewards of a theocratic empire. The subject population divests all individual responsibility in return for an unchanging reliable living standard and belief system. Generally, citizens of theocratic empires prefer the predictable poverty of a guaranteed livelihood and position in society to the uncertainty of taking individual responsibility for their own future. This is particularly true of Russia, where a return to authoritarian rule is gradually occurring. India achieves the same result through its caste system and continuing Hinduism. China is different only because the Chinese are entrepreneurial. Once freed from the tyranny of the Communist regime the Chinese people may include more capitalist elements within their empire.

The ruler is absolute and all subjects are slaves. In theocratic empire the ruler (or party) owns or can freely dispose of all land and resources and has complete control over the lives and persons of the empire. The laboring mass of the population has no rights, is given no consideration, and is subject to constant exploitation and oppression at the whim of the ruling class. Whether Emperor, Tsar, Maharajah, or Politburo, such rulers are unrestrained by law.

Theocratic empires are not motivated by goals of economic gain or social progress. Theocratic empires are motivated by orthodoxy, to which every rational economic or social advantage may be sacrificed to maintain the divinely ideologically established system of control and belief. Economic advantage is often sacrificed to maintain exclusive control. A prime example is the refusal of Stalin to accept Marshall Plan reconstruction aid following WWII.

Theocratic empires are hermetic. Theocratic empires restrict or forbid contact with outside societies and travel to and visits from other societies. They exclude external sources of information and control internal sources of information. Foreigners are highly suspect, and any foreigners allowed to reside within a theocratic empire are required to live in areas isolated from contact with the native population. A typical example is Tsar Alexis who required all foreigners in Moscow to live in a remote suburb called *Nemetskaya Sloboda*. The Chinese and Ottomans also confined foreigners to assigned districts. The Russian and Chinese Communist regimes, which inherited and reconfigured the preceding theocratic regimes in their countries, maintained a nearly paranoiac level of restrictions against any contact with the outside world. President Putin in Russia, consistent with this characteristic, has restricted access to NGOs and religious groups from the West.

Theocratic empires are politically passive. Despite appearances to the contrary, theocratic empires tend to remain within the geographic areas they can comfortably control and are not expansionist or aggressive. Most of their apparently aggressive behavior is defensive, trying to maintain distance, create buffer states, divert foreign powers from attacking them, or create foreign threats to keep their subjects in line. The Russian Orthodox theocratic empire expanded only into regions where Mongol or Turk resistance was weak, and into Siberia, a region hardly occupied. Even after WWII, the Russian Soviet regime basically wanted buffer states not permanent annexation. China not only remained within the limits of its 'celestial' empire, the Emperor ordered a withdrawal from extensive colonial outposts gained as far away as Africa during an uncharacteristic period of exploration and expansion in the 15th and 16th Centuries.

Theocratic empires are technologically weak. Because they are orthodox, static, and hermetic, theocratic empires do not encourage innovation. They resist technological and cultural innovation because it can upset the internal balance they wish to maintain. In the 19th Century, Russia and Japan relied on imitation of Western industrial and military technology to develop sufficient defensive power against the West. Both Soviet Russia and Maoist China finally were unable to match the technological innovation and cultural superiority of the United States and had to change their theocratic empires internally to survive. The Soviet Union collapsed from sheer inanition in 1991. The Chinese under Deng Xiao-ping simply opened the floodgates to native Chinese enterprise and foreign capital investment in 1977. In China and Russia today, innovation and traditional control are in constant conflict.

> **SIDE BAR**
>
> # Pork
>
> ## *Public Treasury/Private Gain*
>
> One of the founding myths of American political argument is that the private sector provided all the major contributions to our astounding economic and social progress and the best thing government can do is to get out of the way of the private sector so it can get on with the business greater prosperity. Government spending is a drag on the economy because it withdraws money from private citizens to pay for federal projects. Partly true. At least 20 percent of the Federal budget could be cut if a serious effort were made to do so by the Executive and Legislative branches.
>
> Congress did authorize the line-item veto so the President could veto inessential items within the Federal budget, eliminating pork barrel spending that has no national advantage. Nevertheless, pork appropriations increased from $10 billion in 1995 to $27 billion in 2005 and the Executive has not used this authority. The emergency bill to deal with Hurricane Katrina and the Iraq war even included $1.8 million to promote art in West Virginia. Representatives can add line items to any bill to appropriate funds for pet projects within their districts. Because they respond to local voters, not the national electorate, such items are frequent and cumulatively quite expensive. But they are perceived as adjustments that redirect taxes paid to the Federal Government back to the local taxpayers. No Congressman challenges such line items.
>
> Throughout American history the federal government has funded economic development. The original Land Office established in

1785 surveyed public lands and transferred millions of acres to private hands over the next 150 years. Canals to move grain from the Midwest to the East were federally funded. Federal land grants to railroad developers transferred alternate sections along the track lines that subsidized rail development and were sold by the railroad companies to immigrant settlers. The patchwork land ownership of railroad and public lands still exists. Hydropower development under Franklin Delano Roosevelt included the Tennessee Valley Authority and Hoover Dam, which provided power for economic growth in the depressed region of the south and water for irrigating the arid land of the southwestern states. Without the TVA, the atomic bomb project would not have been feasible, yet right wing critics of FDR complained of 'socialism' and worse. The Federal Highway System was funded by taxpayers. The NASA space program developed countless products that were transferred to private companies for commercial production, aerosol cans among them. The National Institutes of Health helped develop the Genome Project which will transform medical practice. Federally financed research, within government and at universities, provided major advances in computer engineering, including the World Wide Web. In fact, government funding has been a crucial part of economic development since 1789. The atomic and hydrogen bomb projects, defense systems development, nuclear power, metallurgy and nonmetallic products, particle accelerators, and countless other benefits are the result of public spending. Public spending is not the problem. Misappropriation of public funds is.

PART II

Formation of Western Civilization and the World's Encounter with the West

Fortuna multis dat nimis, satis nulli.
Martial

Western Civilization, which comprises Western Europe and the United States, is the most powerful social organization the World has ever known. It has conquered, destroyed, or simply overwhelmed every society and civilization it has encountered, including the Chinese and Japanese Empires, the Soviet Empire, the Indian Mogul Empire, the Ottoman Empire and the tribal societies of Africa, the Pacific Islands, and the Americas. No other society has been able to seriously challenge Western Civilization, and no society at present, least of all the suicidal terrorist groups within the fragmented Islamic world, has any prospect of doing so.

The destruction by the West of these other civilizations is no great loss to humanity. They ended as oppressive, corrupt regimes that offered no prospect of real progress for their people. After more than a century of revolutions and wars, Japan and India appear have shed the worst characteristics of their traditional societies. Russia and China, despite economic development, appear to be regressing to their traditional authoritarian regime. Other societies destroyed by Western Civilization are doing very badly. The worst examples are in the Islamic Middle East and in Africa, where tribal societies that had fully developed civilizations remain bogged down in the corrupt and destructive social, political, and personal behavior patterns that characterized their tribal past. Disorders in these failed societies will likely occupy much World attention during the 21st Century.

Formation of Western Civilization

The core area of Western Civilization is modern day England, France, Italy and the northern Rhine areas of Belgium, Netherlands, and Western Germany. In these areas, members of Celtic, Germanic, and Scandinavian tribes assimilated Roman, Greek, and Christian religious and cultural influences under the leadership of the Roman Catholic Church.

The primary elements that went into forming Western Civilization and the most important characteristics of that civilization are seldom taught in schools and universities. 'Multicultural' electives have replaced the traditional 'Euro-centric' curricula, and Women's, Black, or other ethnocentric studies are considered equivalent alternatives. The new curriculum 'responds' to the multicultural interests and heritage of contemporary students and is considered more 'relevant'. Increasingly, citizens of the West have no clear understanding of how our civilization developed, why it is unequivocally the greatest civilization that has ever existed, and how it has affected other societies. Once the foundation and morphology of Western Civilization is understood, the measures needed to sustain that civilization will become clearer.

Civil Society

Western Civilization is the **only** social unit to develop a civil society. Civil society has never existed anywhere else the world: in Black Africa, the Arabic/Muslim Middle East and its cultural cousin Latin America, Russia, India, China, or Japan. Civil society developed as a result of:

1. The disappearance of state authority during the gestation period of Western Civilization after the fall of Rome (476 AD) and

after its aborted restoration attempted by Charlemagne in 800 AD;

2. A combination of largely incompatible elements from Greek, Roman, Christian and Jewish traditions in its cultural formation;

3. The character and traditions of the Celtic, Germanic, and Scandinavian tribes that made up the core population of the West.

The disappearance of state authority in the so-called Dark Ages was the most important event in European history. Otherwise, Western Civilization might have become like the Byzantine Empire, where Roman Imperial authority continued unbroken to form a theocratic empire based on combined religious and political authority in a virtually totalitarian state. The complete breakdown of the Roman Empire in the West eliminated the state as a factor in daily life. The Church stepped in for several centuries to provide order, but its role was ecclesiastical not statist. As the manor system developed, each unit was independent and pursued its economic and social life without interference. In essence, Europe discovered that ***society existed independently of the state***! When state power was later reintroduced in Europe by the Dynastic Monarchs of the Middle Ages and Renaissance, many restrictions were placed on their authority, both by the Church, which had operated independently and place of state power for centuries, and by the aristocrats who had pledged fealty to over lords but had never been subject to sustained state control. The English *Magna Carta* imposed by English Barons on King John is the classic example. In the West, relationships to the state were always conceived in terms of contractual rights of subjects and obligations of monarchs, and never in terms of the abject submission typical of theocratic empires.

The incompatible mix of Roman, Hebrew, Christian, and Greek culture in Western Civilization was the second extraordinary event in its formation. A later section will review this heritage and its vital significance. Suffice it to say that this jumble of contradictory and incompatible cultural influences freed Western Civilization from the curse of orthodoxy and eventually freed thought in the West to pursue entirely secular standards of truth.

The third influence on the formation of Western Civilization was the racial and tribal heritage of the Indo-Europeans who made up the new society. This heritage extends back at least 10,000 years and is of great contemporary interest. Americans play football today directly because of their Indo-European heritage of ten millennia ago. This heritage will be discussed in a later chapters.

Expansion of Western Civilization

Western Civilization has had three periods of expansion, both geographic and cultural.

> 1) The first period in the 12th and 13th Centuries was distinguished by Crusades in both the Holy Land and the Eastern Marches of Germany, the formation of Universities, the creation of Gothic Cathedrals, and the development of towns.

> 2) The second period occurred during the 16th and 17th Centuries, the great period of the Renaissance, humanism, and voyages of discovery led by Portugal, Spain, the Netherlands, and England, which opened the North American continent and extended trade to Asia and the coast of Africa.

> 3) The third period extended from 1750 to the present, a period when the world was explored and colonized, the industrial revolution transformed society, and Western dominance was irrefutably established.

During the first two periods of expansion, the West encountered other civilizations notably China and the Ottoman Empire, both relatively equal to the West in power and technology. The encounter ended in standoff. For various internal reasons, Western states either withdrew or limited their activity to trading stations. They were engaged thousands of miles from their homelands, and the technology of the time simply could not overcome this disadvantage. From roughly 1750 to the present, Western Civilization led by England entered a period of world transformation that continues to the present day.

Every civilization, tribe, and society in every part of the world has been transformed or destroyed by its encounter with the West. In the world of the 21st Century, Western Civilization is surrounded by the shattered remnants of ancient societies, cultures, tribes and civilizations that were destroyed by the onslaught of Western science and technology. The most recent victim is the Soviet Union (the culmination of a thousand years of Orthodox Russian Civilization) which collapsed because it could not meet the challenge of the microchip revolution begun in the United States in the 1970's. In Africa, the Middle East, Asia, and Russia today we confront failed states, societies, and cultural patterns, some of which date back thousands of years. The economic and social breakdown in these areas is directly the result the overwhelming power of the Western intellectual, economic, technological and social revolution that began in and was led by England beginning around 1670.

England and the Transformation of Western Civilization

The great power and overwhelming superiority of the West derives from a series of 'revolutions' that occurred in England between 1670 and 1750 that were extended throughout Western Europe and America during the 19th Century. These 'revolutions' occurred in just the right sequence so that each earlier innovation provided the basis for what followed. Resources required by each innovation were readily available due to the previous innovations within the culture. Some of the major landmarks in this revolutionary transformation of Western Civilization follow:

> **1670: Royal Society and the Secularization of Science**
> **1695: Parliamentary Government (Aristocracy not Nobility)**
> **1700: Enclosures and Creation of a Proletariat**
> **1715: Modern Banking and Capital Management**
> **1730: Agricultural Revolution**
> **1750: Ground Transportation Revolution (Macadam Roads)**
> **1750: Industrial Revolution**
> **1820: Interchangeable Parts and Cheap Amateur Weapons**
> **1820: Coal Energy**
> **1825: Railroad Transportation Revolution**
> **1830: Rise of Democracy**
> **1840: Public Health, and Modern Medicine**
> **1840: Telegraph/Telecommunications Revolution**
> **1850: Natural Gas**
> **1880: Electric Lighting and Telephone**
> **1897: Gasoline and the Internal Combustion Engine**

The sequence was self-supporting, each stage contributing to and serving as the implementing prerequisite for the next.

Scientific Revolution

Isaac Newton (1642-1727) systematized the modern, secular, experimental scientific worldview. The Newtonian System assumes that the earth and the universe obey the ***same*** laws and that truth is discovered by experiment and analysis not a priori assumptions. These simple principles freed science from Biblical estimates for the creation of the world and Platonic a priori theories, and have led every year since to new and astonishing discoveries that stimulate further inquiry leading to further invention and technology. The Royal Society of London, chartered by Charles II in 1672, arguably the most important organization in Modern European story, established an ethic of truthfulness, sharing of discovery, and recognition of distinguished effort that made science independent and free of outside influence. Secular objective standards for the discovery of truth are unique to Western Civilization. Science is a collective effort, each step building on the last, and the creation of modern experimental scientific method is the foundation of the power of the West.

Parliamentary Government by Aristocrats

Aristocratic rule through Parliament with minimum meddling from the Monarchy emerged in England following the abdication of James II in 1689 and became dominant after George I of the House of Hanover was enthroned in 1718. England has an aristocracy, not nobility, as is the rule on the Continent and especially in France. The difference is profound and reflects the pragmatism of the English people. Aristocrats are made, nobles are born. Aristocratic titles and the lands to support them were granted to able commoners by the King of England as reward for service, often simply transferred from persons who failed in this service. The rise of talented commoners to high title and office was not unusual. Modest titles that required no particular service also were available. Beginning 1610, King James created the title of Baronet to be sold to anyone able to produce the money required. He took this measure to replenish his cash-starved treasury, due largely to Parliament's reluctance to fund his questionable foreign projects and domestic largesse. Hundreds of Baronets wander the British landscape to this day thanks to the pecuniary need of James I. Prominent aristocrats married the daughters of prosperous middle class entrepreneurs, who usually managed to obtain suitable titles that made such marriages more palatable. English aristocrats were never snobs, as were the French nobles, who disdained and were legally precluded from engaging in trade or marrying outside the nobility of birth. The atrophy of the French nobility was due largely to its futile reliance on eminence of birth rather than ability and service, although able nobles did serve the Kings of France. Obsession with precedence and favor at the 'absolutist' French court of Louis XIV ruined one of the most distinguished classes in European history. In contrast, the English aristocracy became the most responsible, energetic, and progressive leadership group in history, undistracted by personal vanity regarding title and birth, and dedicated to serving society and country. They invented fair play and social improvement projects and explored the world, bringing equity and fairness to areas where such notions were entirely absent.

Enclosures

The Scottish enclosures of the 1700's that drove thousands of peasants off agricultural land to provide pasture for more profitable sheep ultimately provided the manpower needed for colonial expansion and later industrial development. The romantic movement excoriated the Sutherlands of northern Scotland for driving the honest peasants from the fields to provide grazing, but the Scottish diaspora provided some of the most enterprising characters in Western history, and the general decline in farm labor required to produce much greater yields, freed rural labor for urban mills and factories that made England the richest country in the world.

Modern Banking

The banking revolution, begun by John Law in 1715 with the creation of the Bank of England, made possible capital markets, accumulation, and distribution needed to foster new enterprises. Although John Law and his bank ended in scandal and financial ruin during the South Sea bubble, a paradigm for future market speculation the basic principles and advantages of credit banking were confirmed.

Agricultural Revolution

The agricultural revolution around 1750, using legume crops and fertilizers to renew the soil, made possible larger harvests and feed for livestock, which increased the supply of mutton and beef, and reduced the labor requirement, permitting more peasants to leave the land. Increased agricultural production made it possible to support the urban population engaged in trade and industry. As a result of improved crops, much increased cattle and sheep, and adequate transportation to move goods to city markets, the diet and health of Englanders improved.

Ground Transportation Revolution

In 1750, Macadam invented the modern roadbed, designed to provide adequate drainage and a stable surface. The road transportation revolution made transportation overland reliable for the first time since the height of the Roman Empire. Improved ground transportation made it possible to ship goods to the expanding urban mass market. Not since the Roman road system fell into decay in the 4th Century, had ground transportation been practical over long distances. The roadbeds laid down by the Romans were still used but they were in such disarray that moving large volumes of traffic at reasonable speed between widely separated major commercial areas was either impractical or an endlessly lamented ordeal. River transport was the fastest and preferred method. The Macadam road transformed ground transportation, as wagons and other vehicles designed for comfortable travel could now be successfully used.

Industrial Revolution

The industrial revolution beginning around 1760 applied non-animal energy and machine tools, rather than animal and human labor and hand-guided tools, to produce goods, vastly increasing productivity. Moving from waterpower, to steam, to electricity, to petroleum, to hydropower, it transformed the entire world economy.

Interchangeable Parts

Interchangeable parts was a manufacturing revolution first applied systematically in the Connecticut River Valley for the manufacture of rifles. This method made weapons in particular cheaper in England and especially the United States, reinforcing the move toward democracy. But the principle revolutionized all manufacture and led to standardization in all aspects of production. During the Civil War, standardized clothing and shoe sizes were introduced.

Railroad Transportation Revolution

About 1800, the English inventor Richard Trevithick experimented with the first engines capable of using high-pressure steam. He mounted one of the engines on a four-wheeled undercarriage designed to roll along a track. In 1804, Trevithick used this vehicle to pull 10 tons of iron, 70 men, and 5 wagons along 9 1/2 miles of track. Trevithick's invention thus became the world's first successful railroad locomotive. Soon, other English inventors built successful locomotives. An English railway engineer named George Stephenson constructed the world's first public railroad, the Stockton and Darlington, which opened in 1825 over a distance of about 20 miles. Stephenson's second railroad opened in 1830. It ran 30 miles from Liverpool to Manchester. It was the first railroad to run steam passenger trains on a regular schedule. Stephenson also originated the idea that railroads should all have a standard gauge. The gauge he selected for the railroads he built--4 feet 8 1/2 inches--corresponded to the length of the axles on many horse-drawn wagons. This gauge was eventually adopted by most European railroads and then by railroads in other parts of the world.

Public Health and Modern Medicine

Finally, the invention of modern medicine and public health policy based on the bacterial cause of disease in the mid-19th Century increased birth and survival rates, eventually reducing the need for women to have large numbers of children and leading to the "nuclear family" idealized in the mid 1800's. The increased population of survivors could be supported in England and the United States by the ever increasingly productive agricultural technology (McCormack harvesters 1840), fertilizers and improved seed crops.

The revolution in culture, technology and management described above happened later and at different rates and to differing degrees but in approximately the same sequence in France beginning in 1830, Germany beginning in 1850, and Italy beginning in 1870. This transformation of Western Civilization into a secular, scientific, industrial society, led to overwhelming industrial and technological advances and the greatest geographic expansion in World history.

The World's Encounter with the West
On fait souvent du bien pour pouvoir impunément faire du mal.
Rochefoucauld, Maximes, 121.

The most important fact about the encounter of other Civilizations and societies with the West is that the revolutions described above ***occurred in reverse order and incompletely or not at all in other parts of the World.*** As other civilizations and tribal societies encountered Western industrial powers, they adopted the material culture of the West first, particularly weapons systems, but for the most part rejected the most important part of Western culture, the humanist, scientific outlook that made possible the invention and power of the West. Their rejection was based on the realization by the ruling class that the Western outlook was antithetical to the values and beliefs of tribal societies and theocratic empires, the two systems that prevail worldwide. The failed systems common worldwide are largely the result of the following practices when dealing with Western impacts on their societies.

Weapons Systems and Authoritarian Rule
The Muslim, African, Chinese, and Japanese cultures kept their traditional outlooks. assimilating first Western weapon systems which, unlike in the United States, were extremely expensive in terms of the local economy and were monopolized by the local elite to control their populations and engage in wars with traditional rivals. The weapons were paid for by extorting greater taxes from their backward agricultural sectors, further impoverishing the rural populations often to the point

of desperation. The role of military juntas in Latin America, Africa, the Near East and Asia is due entirely to this practice. In Africa, so-called states ruled by a given tribe regularly purchase weapons with scarce local or borrowed international capital in order to repress rival tribes within and adjacent to their borders. Arab Islamic states in the Middle East are ruled by tribes and clans that use revenue from natural resources, notably oil, to buy weapons in order to attack neighbors or repress internal opposition. Armies in most parts of the world have become a routine source of new leadership, when existing regimes degenerate beyond the point at which they can retain control. Chiang Kai-chek in 1927 and Mao Zse-dong in 1949 led military coups that seized the state apparatus from corrupt regimes. Latin America has become a byword for military juntas and takeovers.

International Loans and Corruption

Diversion of scarce resources to military rather than needed economic investment characterizes most of the third world. The pattern of World Bank, IMF, and private bank loans that eventually disappear in default with no benefit to the people of the country is due to wasteful spending on armies and weapons and to massive misappropriation of state revenues for personal use. For example, Yasser Arafat, leader of the beleaguered Palestinians, redirected millions of dollars in aid and revenue belonging to the Palestinians to recharge his personal bank holdings and support his wife, who lived luxuriously in Paris, while their people subsisted in refugee camps. The practice of diverting public revenue for private benefit is endemic in Latin America, Africa, the Near East and Asia. Only Japan and India following WWII, and China following the reforms of Deng Xiao-ping in the 1970's, have introduced agricultural, industrial and economic reforms required to modernize at the level of Western Civilization.

Public Health and Population Explosion

The rapid application of modern medicine and public health practices to backward areas simply increased population, but no agricultural revolution had occurred to provide food, so control of the food supply by the state using weapons acquired from the West became a common method of controlling the population. Famine periodically thinned out the burgeoning population and now HIV AIDS is devastating populations in Central Africa. The Green Revolution of the 1960's and 1970's transformed Asian agriculture and has made it possible in India and elsewhere to feed the overwhelming increases in population. Again, Western Civilization has provided the means for the rest of the world to survive and prosper. The genetic revolution in agriculture begun in the West will likely serve the same purpose in the next decades of population increase.

PART III

World Population Trends

The distribution of and projected growth in world population will largely determine international economic and political affairs over the next fifty years. Within an individual country, the size, distribution by age, urban vs. rural concentration, health, and education of its population will determine its economic and social future. Current demographic trends, both domestic and international, are likely to adversely affect the supply and distribution of resources worldwide and could lead to major conflicts and civil wars. The overriding trend is that Russia, China, and Europe are facing dramatic declines in population. Offsetting that decrease, the so-called third world of Africa, Middle East and Southeast Asia population is rapidly increasing.

Given these trends the overall population may increase to more than 8 billion by 2050. Demand for food and mineral resources remains high. But the war in Ukraine the world's third largest grain producer, destruction of crops by drought and flooding in Africa, China and elsewhere, shortage of phosphates and other fertilizers, and political disruptions of supply routes are decreasing the foreseeable supply of wheat, soybeans, and rice.

Only developed economies can acquire the foreign exchange needed to compete for resources worldwide. For decades, China remained insular and relatively poor, neither able economically nor inclined for ideological reasons to compete with Western States in global markets. China is in a position to bid up grain prices to provide for its population, which will lead to unprecedented prosperity in the US agricultural sector but may cause substantial inflation in food prices worldwide, prices that historically have been remarkably low. The era of inexpensive food in the United States may end.

Population Distribution Worldwide

World population increase will affect power relationships and world peace and have incalculable political, social and economic consequences. Whether current methods and rates of food production can meet the needs of two billion more people is debatable. Genetically modified crops that can insure high productivity at low cost offer the best prospect of meeting the challenge although their initial reception in Europe and elsewhere has been cool. In 2002, Zambia refused shipments of genetically modified grain from the United States even though some 2.3 million of the 10 million Zambians faced starvation due to government corruption and mismanagement of the agricultural sector (in addition, 20 percent of the population is infected with HIV AIDS). Such scruples likely will be short-lived. Like the "green revolution" which made agriculture more productive and starvation less likely in Asia in the 1970's, genetic crops will be the only likely alternative to starvation for billions of people in the underdeveloped world by the year 2050.

Although the current world reserves of many raw materials may not match the consumer needs of such an increase in population except at the most elemental level, new supplies may be found, especially on the ocean floor where abundant deposits of copper and other ores occur. Measures to meet the needs of this increase in population will depend on Western science and technology, either to grow crops or to recover raw materials. Whatever happens, population and demographics will drive political affairs worldwide. The current and projected population distribution worldwide follows:

Europe is aging and declining demographically, which may presage economic and military weakness, somewhat offset by the economic union, free trade and common currency introduced in 2000. Dramatic decline in population in every European country is projected, especially in Germany the powerhouse of the European economy. Equally striking is the projected decline in population in Russia and Ukraine where the decline is irreversible.

China controlled its population by its one-child policy such that now faces a dramatic decline in population. Accurate counting of population was discontinued and publishing inaccurate but favorable estimates is done mainly to maintain local levels of central government financial support. Instead of the 1.4 billion, the real population is about 1.1 billion and likely to decline to as low as 750 million by 2050. China also faces a number of natural disasters (flooding, hydroelectric dam failures, drought, severe decrease in potable water) that affect population growth. The ongoing economic collapse as a result of ending international trade and investment in China also suppresses family formation.

India has not controlled its population growth, now at about 1.5 billion and far exceeding China's population. Poverty, social stress, and unrest in some areas can be expected. India developed its agriculture following the 'green revolution' and now is self-sufficient, but more than 400 million more people by 2050 will present a substantial test to that achievement. India's high technology sector located mainly in Bangalore is a major force for developing a high profit technology sector to lift the Indian economy, but it rewards an infinitesimal part of the population. The rest live in extreme poverty.

Japan the world's third largest economy is declining in population in a pattern similar to that of Europe. After a decade of economic stagnation and low growth rates, Japan is becoming aware of the need to recover its economic dynamism in the face of the emerging Asian 'tiger' economies. Innovation and competitiveness may overcome the demographic drag of its aging population. Lack of growth has severely strained Japan's cradle-to-grave guarantee of education, employment and retirement with substantial changes in the social assumptions of lifelong employment and corporate paternalism. Young Japanese are for the first time trying entrepreneurial rather than safe corporate career paths.

The populations of Asian states other than China and Japan are growing substantially and will provide an inexpensive, highly skilled and motivated labor force that will make possible low-cost production of manufactured goods. Singapore, one of the most economically advanced states in Asia, is likely to make a bid to become a genetic engineering center. Other states have the intelligent and motivated populations needed to compete in high technology as well. The United States is the only major economic power expected to substantially increase in population over the period 2000 to 2050.

Population Distribution by Age

Equally dramatic are the differences in existing and projected age distribution of populations within countries worldwide. Economically speaking, population can be divided into three main sectors: ***Dependent*** people who are expected to become productively employed such as children, students, temporarily unemployed); ***Productive***: people who are employed and producing goods and providing services); ***Parasitic***: people who are not expected to be employed such as the retired, indigent, welfare recipients, chronically unemployed, and aged).

The ***dependent sector*** is in training for future productivity or only temporarily unemployed and expected to resume working in the not-too-distant future. The ***parasitic*** elderly retired sector presumably has saved from earnings during its period of productivity and draws on that account in retirement. To that extent their economic effect is neutral, except for their disproportionate use of medical services, which the ***productive*** sector must subsidize through higher insurance premiums.

The balance between the three sectors can be maintained so long as the incomes of the productive sector plus savings and invested assets from the other sectors can remain sufficiently productive to support the needs of all three sectors. Cyclic economic recessions and permanent structural changes in the economy, like outsourcing jobs abroad, reduce productive opportunities and cause economic dislocations when the productive sector can no longer pay for services provided to the other sectors. Those services have to be reduced or funded by borrowing.

Such reductions usually involve ***public services*** (public education, health care, public housing, and welfare) that the dependent and parasitic sectors rely on. Cuts in school and other budgets and increased tuition at State colleges and universities due to reduced tax revenues are familiar examples. Changes in services to the dependent and parasitic sectors involve political disruption as well as economic dislocation. Political measures are taken by beneficiaries to maintain services even when taxes and other sources of income are not adequate to fund them.

Population distribution by age correlates with distribution by dependent, productive, and parasitic sectors and has enormous effects on the economic, social and political life of a country. Where older people preponderate, countries tend to be politically conservative because older populations prefer security and stability to change. Younger populations are more enterprising, but large numbers of very young tend to create instability. They have many demands and expectations, but opportunities may not exist in sufficient abundance to accommodate them, or they may not be trained sufficiently to take advantage of them. In poor countries, large young, dependent populations are easy to exploit and especially disruptive.

Africa and the Islamic States have large, young dependent populations that are placing enormous pressure on their governments to provide housing, education, food, employment and services. Unrest in these areas can be expected to increase, especially because their societies and governments are endemically corrupt and incapable of substantial reform. These areas are discussed in later sections of this book.

The tragedy undergone by **Russia** since the collapse of the Soviet Union is evident in the demographic pattern shown above. Russia has the lowest percentage of children up to 15-years old of any major country in the World. The devastating breakdown in medical care, social services, and economic opportunity is well documented and appalling, especially for children and the retired and elderly indigent population. The reasons for Russia's problems are long standing and will be discussed later in some detail. However, at this point it is possible to point out that Russia cannot sustain any major military, economic, or political role internationally for the indefinite future. Putin's venture into Ukraine was a strategic blunder that will drain Russia's economy, force talented citizens to migrate and increase Russia's dependence on China. Their military establishment is in a shambles and male population in the age group 18 to 25 is not able to provide enough manpower to defeat and occupy Ukraine permanently. The economy depends on selling oil and gas to India and China at bargain rates to finance the war and maintain the government.

The demographic decline in **Germany** is remarkable. Germany has very negative future population gradients. Its population is expected to decline about 30 percent by 2050, when it will be only slightly larger than that of the United Kingdom. The economic consequences are substantial. With a declining and aging domestic market and labor force, German social services and workers benefits are likely to be reduced. Especially because the millions of Islamic 'refugees' admitted to Germany by Angela Merkel are almost all dependent of welfare payments, overload schools, and get free medical treatment and social services. Current levels of vacations, retirement, health care, and family subsidies for native Germans will be less and less affordable as more of the aging productive population enters the parasitic sector. Recipients used to these benefits will use the political system to maintain them through higher taxes and benefit charges to employers, placing a major strain on the profitability and competitiveness of German business. Relocating production in Eastern Europe and Asia will be strongly opposed. Similar attempts to use politics to reverse or stall inevitable economic and demographic change are likely to emerge in France and elsewhere in Europe.

Urban vs. Rural Population

For 150 years a worldwide change in population distribution from rural to urban areas has occurred. In 1850, nearly 70 percent of the population in the United States worked on farms and lived in rural areas. By the year 2000, less than 3 percent of the population worked in agriculture, and 95 percent of the population lives in urban agglomerations. In developed industrial countries, high percentages of urban population are normal and reflect the industrial and commercial growth that occurred over the same period. These countries have developed employment, housing, transportation, food supplies, schools, and medical facilities to support large urban populations.

In contrast, many countries in Africa and Asia have very large urban populations due to movement of rural populations to cities in search of employment. Unfortunately, cities in Africa, the Islamic world, and Southeast Asia have limited employment opportunities or inadequate infrastructure to support them. All have millions of people living in improvised shelters or on the street and are undernourished or starving and subject to multiple diseases and disabilities. Their governments are unable to begin providing for their needs, much less law enforcement and civic order. Crime is rampant and political violence is always a potential threat to domestic stability from those clearly unable to perform. These cities are overcrowded with peasant populations that have left the countryside but have no prospects for adequate employment or for achieving an adequate living standard. They constitute a neglected and potentially violent population that may contribute to widespread political instability over the coming decades.

Dysgenics

Intellect is not the only or most important characteristic in human personality. But further growth in intellectually demanding fields required by highly developed societies depends entirely on rearing capable and motivated youth to assume these responsibilities. Intellectual incapacity closely correlates with social costs within the society caused by criminality, welfare, and chronic unemployment. Dysgenics refers to the social deficits caused by lower intelligent levels within sectors of the population. Intellectual capacity and performance of the population significantly affects prospects for economic development and the supply of qualified candidates for demanding scientific, technical and professional fields.

It should be emphasized that capability can only be demonstrated by performance. Objections to Intelligent Quotient evaluations are understandable. Reasoning, analytical ability, mathematics, chemistry, physics and other skills require strong intellectual capacity that can be measured and is necessarily attainable by only a minority of the population so endowed. We all sense a dehumanizing determinist element in such evaluations of people. They are depressing because they suggest limited potential for many students.

In the United States, tests designed to measure intelligence have been given students at all levels of the educational system for decades. These tests come under severe criticism as being biased or skewed in favor of middle class and white values and expectations. Yet if workplace success depends on mastering those values and expectations, we have no choice but to evaluate performance on their terms. So called IQ tests, when correlated to a number of social problems, show that crime, welfare dependency, and chronic unemployment consistently occur mainly among the lowest IQ levels.

IQ levels of the population significantly affect development and investment. Foreign investment in China is directly related to the intelligence, work ethic, and adaptable skills of the population. Investment in Islamic and African countries other than for resource extraction is low by comparison, because the local populations do not have a similar work ethic or the intellectual capacity or temperament to perform regular, high-tech work required by advanced industry. This deficiency will increase existing discrepancies in rates of growth and standards of living worldwide.

IQ and Education

The most obvious effect of IQ is on educational achievement. Persistent failure in education leads to failure in life. Worldwide, educational systems differ dramatically. The most advanced are in the United States, Europe, Japan, Russia, China, parts of India and Southeast Asia where high levels of scientific education are provided.

Education in Islamic states consists mainly of indoctrination into the teachings or Islam and study of the Qur'an, rather than study of modern science and a liberal curriculum. This formation produces narrow, parochial, and often fanatical religious belief but does not prepare the students for work in the advanced technical professions or develop a tolerance and interest in foreign cultures. Consider that only one Pakistani and one Egyptian (working in the United States) received a Nobel Prize from 1901 to the present. The problem is not IQ, with which Muslim populations clearly are well endowed. The problem is the tribal organization and outlook, which prevent modernization of Islamic States.

Africa has limited educational facilities, and the general population is dominantly illiterate, although a very small, privileged minority studies abroad. The problem is not that there are no high IQ blacks. Obviously, there are many. But in Black Africa many of the most intelligent have no sense of responsibility for their fellow citizens, preferring to acquire personal wealth and power at the expense of the common good. The endemic tribal outlook throughout Africa simply reinforces this attitude.

Latin America has limited educational facilities and large numbers are illiterate. Throughout Latin America, a sharp division exists between the Indian and mestizo (mixed Indian and Spanish) population and the dominantly Spanish minority that controls 98 percent of the land and wealth. A small irresponsible wealthy class dominates and exploits the large numbers of abject, ignorant, and poor. Much of this condition is due to 700 years of Arabic influence on Spain during the Caliphate. Patterns similar to those in Arabic tribal societies filtered into Spanish culture and outlook. Exploitation of and indifference toward people beneath them is their most common trait of the upper class. Instead of solidarity at the lowest levels of society, there is a corresponding attitude of machismo, which devalues women and elevates violence and fatalism.

Politics and schools

The educational crisis in the United States largely derives from the dysgenic distribution of IQ. The United States has adopted, for practical and political reasons, the assumption that all students are created equal. Assuming that each student has equal potential ensures that no one is prejudged, and everyone gets a chance to learn and develop his or her abilities. But the differences in students' intellect, drive, motivation become apparent at some point, and sorting out the achievers and non-achievers becomes necessary. Schools are established to provide every child the minimum skills needed to function in society and develop his or her potential. School also is intended to train the skilled workers we need to sustain our society and economy, not to focus on lazy and incapable students. Low IQ correlates with crime, welfare dependence, poor work performance, and drug and health problems, regardless of race. Education is intended to develop differences in talent and ability that result in unequal outcomes. It is intended to train the talented to assume responsibility and provide the less talented with sufficient skills to perform successfully. Equality of condition or outcome is not the intention or purpose of education. Attempts to equalize can only equalize downward. Reducing able students to the level of the less able defeats the purpose of education and undermines the well-being of society. Flight from public schools to parochial and private schools is evidence that all groups want a rigorous public school system that will develop their child's potential to its fullest.

Population and Health

Health of the population is another major determinant of social progress. The world faces a split between:

- **developed countries** with aging populations subject to individual degenerative diseases and
- **underdeveloped countries** with young populations subject to public communicable diseases.

For example, cardiovascular disease is the leading cause of death in the United States and Europe, whereas HIV AIDS, malaria and diarrhea are the leading cause of death in Africa. The most common cause of disease in the United States is obesity, whereas polluted water supplies, poor public sanitation, sexually transmitted diseases, and malnutrition are primary causes of death and disease in most of the undeveloped world.

Medical treatment also differs as between the developed industrial states and the underdeveloped countries. Of the 25 worst countries in terms of medical systems, 16 are in Africa. The United States provides a striking example of this dichotomy in health care. Infant mortality averages 86 per thousand births in Africa and 6.9 per thousand in the United States. The United States has 360 persons per doctor, whereas Central and Eastern Africa have 13,000 per doctor. Life expectancy of males in East Africa is about 45 years compared with 75 in the United States. Malnutrition, lack of safe drinking water and public sanitation, poor medical facilities, and especially political corruption that diverts money provided for health care to other purposes are the main causes of this situation.

The HIV AIDS crisis in Africa is an interesting example of a medical disaster totally mismanaged. Some governments simply refused to accept that it is a behavioral disease. In the West, a litany of obligation to expend enormous resources to curtail its spread in Africa is advanced, and drug companies are blamed for not providing the expensive treatments that ostensibly could arrest its spread. As with most issues involving Blacks (in Africa, the United States and elsewhere), the history of slavery and discrimination tends to create martyr image in which they are not to blame for *anything* that happens to them and others are to blame for everything. HIV AIDS is a behavioral disease (85 percent transmitted by sexual intercourse) and has now reached a point of no return in Africa. The infection rate is now so high, and the rate of infection is increasing so rapidly, that little can realistically be done to reverse the trend.

Of roughly 36 million cases worldwide in 2003, 25.3 million were in Black Africa (70 percent) and 5.8 million (16 percent) in Southeast Asia. Each year about 5.5 million new cases develop, 3 million people die, and the rate of increase grows each year. Since its first detection in the late 1970's, HIV AIDS has infected at least 58 million people worldwide and some 22 million have died.

In the United States, HIV AIDS first occurred among homosexuals in San Francisco and other large cities. Attempting to avoid "discriminatory" practices with regard to this minority, doctors and officials were very slow to address the behavioral origins of the disease. Consequently, it spread much more rapidly than necessary because early detection did not lead to early prevention measures. Measures to close bathhouses and promote safe sex among homosexuals were finally taken, but much damage was done to accommodate a "politically correct" approach to the problem.

In Africa, the same "politically correct" reluctance to face the behavioral causes of the disease have led to disaster. In effect nothing can now be done. The political regimes in Africa are so corrupt that any aid sent to support medical intervention will be diverted to private use by the government officials responsible to distribute it. Medical infrastructure in Africa has systematically been undermined by such practices. This combined with active denial that HIV AIDS exists on the part of such African leaders as President Mugabe of Zimbabwe, where 25 percent of the population is infected, would make any effort entirely futile.

PART IV

Heritage of Theocratic Empire
Russia China India Japan

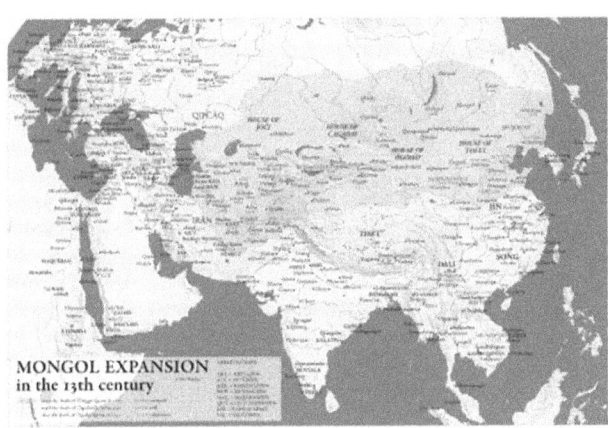

Theocratic empire refers principally to Russia, China, Japan, and India. The formative influence on each of them was the great Mongol Empire of the 13th and 14th Centuries. Its influence was enormous and continues to this day. The Mongol Empire was the largest in history. Its territory extended from the Yellow Sea in eastern Asia to the borders of Eastern Europe. At various times it included China, Korea, Mongolia, Persia (now Iran), Turkistan, and Armenia and parts of Burma, Vietnam, Thailand, and Russia. It directly controlled the Eurasian landmass and was the formative influence on Russia, China, and India and a significant influence on Japan for different reasons.

The Mongols attempted but did not succeed in conquering Japan and reducing it to servitude. Russia was entirely subdued and for 300 years was dominated by the Golden Horde. China was ruled directly by Mongol dynasty, which divided the country on class and race lines. The Mongols also established the Mogul Empire in India.

In 1218, Genghis Khan broke off his attack on China and turned west toward central Asia and Eastern Europe. His armies charged into the steppes of Russia and the Muslim lands, including Persia. They came within reach of Constantinople (now Istanbul) and destroyed much of Islamic-Arabic civilization. In 1241, about 150,000 Mongol riders laid waste a large part of Hungary and Poland, threatening the civilization of Western Europe.

Genghis Khan died in 1227. Kublai Khan, a grandson of Genghis Khan, completed the conquest of China in 1279, after attacking the Song dynasty in South China. Kublai Khan's Yuan dynasty lasted until 1368. He established the Mongol winter capital at the site of present-day Beijing. The Mongols under Kublai Khan had a reputation for greater tolerance than that shown under earlier Mongol rulers. The Khan permitted the existence of various religions. He enlisted the services of Muslims, Christians, Buddhists, and Taoists. He supported Confucianism and Chinese political ideas, though he avoided having too many Chinese in high offices. In Persia and other Islamic lands, many Mongols adopted Muslim customs and the Muslim faith.

In his travel records Marco Polo provided information about the Mongols. His reports of beautiful Chinese cities and the riches of the country he called Cathay did much to arouse the interest of Europeans in exploring the possibilities of trade with the Orient. Many Europeans, including Christopher Columbus, then sought to go to the Orient by the sea route. Kublai Khan expressed a desire to have more missionaries sent to China. Dominican and Franciscan missionaries were welcomed by the Khan and the Franciscan John of Montecorvino, built a church in the capital and converted many people to Christianity.

The Mongol Empire did not last long, because it was too big and had no unity of culture. When Kublai Khan died, his empire broke up into several parts. These smaller empires were the Golden Horde on the steppes of southern Russia and the Balkans, the Mongolian-Chinese Yuan Empire, and the realm of the Ilkhans in western Asia. A revolution in China in the 1300's ended the Yuan dynasty and restored Chinese rule in the form of the Ming dynasty.

The great Timur, or Tamerlane, a descendant of Genghis Khan, combined some Mongol empires and extended his rule over much of Asia in the late 1300's. A descendant of Timur named Babur established a powerful Mongol state in India in 1526. Babur's realm was called the Kingdom of the Great Mughals. The term Mughal comes from the Persian word mughul, meaning a Mongol. A Mughal emperor, Shah Jahan, built the beautiful Taj Mahal in the early 1600's. The British destroyed the Mughal kingdom in the 1700's.Mongol Empire was a system of extortion, especially in Russia, where they did not rule directly. Tribute in slaves, gold, horses, and chattels was collected every year by the Horde at specified locations. Russian princes were expected to show abject submission to the Khanate. In China where they encountered a superior culture, the Mongols simply assimilated that culture while imposing a superior class, the Mongol rulers, over the native Han Chinese.

Russia

The State and forme of their government is plaine tyrannicall, as applying all to the behoofe of the prince, and that after a most open and barbarous manner. For as touching any lawe or publique order of the Realme, it is ever determined of before any publique assemblie or Parliament bee summoned. Giles Fletcher, **Of the Russe Commonwealth**, 1591.

The history of Russia has been driven by the conflict between weak 'european' and strong 'asiatic' influences and can be simplified into five periods.

800-1100	Kieven
1200-1400	Mongol
1500-1917	Muscovite
1917-1991	Communist
1991-?	Federation

Kievan Russia was founded by Scandinavian mercenary/traders who during the same period conquered Scotland, Ireland, Eastern England, Normandy, Spain, and North Africa. In Russia they established landed estates, adopted Orthodox Christianity, and traded in slaves (the word derives from Slav) and chattels with Constantinople and Venice. The rulers were mainly traders and regarded the Slavic population as a labor force to which it was only marginally connected. Located in the steppe region, Kievan Russia never enjoyed security.

It fell easy victim to the Mongol hordes that invaded from Asia during the 12th and 13th Centuries.

Mongol invasion was the formative influence on Russia. It introduced 'asiatic' standards of rule and conduct. For 300 years Russians were abject subjects to the Mongol horde and assimilated the racial and cultural patterns of their rulers. The ruthless character of its government and the slavish behavior of the ruled toward their rulers became a Russian trait often remarked by Western travelers.

Muscovite rule by Tsars was patterned on the Mongol rule. Tsars were absolute rulers and all Russians were 'slaves' to the Tsar. His rule was law. The pattern was developed by the Dukes of Muscovy in the 1300's and by Ivan Grozny in the 1500's. Later in the Romanov dynasty certain superficial Westernizing influences were sanctioned by Tsar Peter but he mostly consolidated the absolute rule established earlier.

Communism was a ***second Mongol invasion*** of Russia in that it reestablished the 'asiatic' character of the nation's heritage. Lenin was part Mongol by blood, Stalin was a Georgian, Trosky a Jew. Communism did not change the Tsarist and Mongol heritage, it simply perfected absolutism into totalitarianism by abolishing all private property and privacy. It turned away entirely from 'Western' traditions. Total individual insecurity joined with total dependence on the state for livelihood, created conditions under Stalin as abject as the Mongol rule.

This was the experience of Russians until the corruption of Soviet rule and the *nomenklatura* that began in the late 1950's.

Federal period begun in 1992 appeared at first to be a change from traditional Russia social and state practice toward a Western democratization but has remained a 'gangster' state run by the KGB (now FSB) mafia that took over rule of the Soviet Union in 1982. Democracy does not come naturally to the Russian people. Political freedom and self-determination have never been important in a state that regards itself as surrounded by enemies. Further, the tradition of rule by a small minority that exploits the majority is so engrained that little social solidarity remains in Russia. Each clique and 'mafia' exploits opportunity without concern for the national good. Corruption and intramural rivalry prevail. The notion of civil society is alien to Russia. In general the heritage of Russia persists to this day and includes the following.

For more than 1000 years, the fundamental characteristic of Russian society is that ***everything is forbidden that is not expressly permitted***, exactly opposite to that of Western, and especially English and American civil society where ***everything is permitted that is not expressly forbidden.*** This difference is so profound and the consequent social, political, economic, and civil development is so unlike ours that the West has until recently considered and described Russia to be, as Winston Churchill said, a *"mystery wrapped up in an enigma"*. Nothing is further from the truth. Russia and its history and culture are entirely intelligible and explicable once the underlying structure is understood.

The second difference between the West and Russia is that ***unanimity, not consensus, is the basis for governance.*** Even in Novgorod, considered to be the most "liberal" city state in medieval Russia because it was closely associated with the German based Hanseatic League, dissenters were expelled from the city once a decision was made by the ruling council of boyars. It was automatically assumed that dissent was a prelude to disloyalty and needed to be prevented by driving the opponents from the walls of the city. Unanimity under the Tsar was assumed, since all decisions were made by him and were absolutely binding.

The need for unanimity means that any change in Russian policy is preceded by a clean sweep by the ruler of all advisors and ministers. In 2004, President Vladimir Putin announced at a news conference just before the March election, in which he received 70 percent of the vote, that he was summarily dismissing all his appointed ministers. This kind of summary dismissal reflected traditional use of authority, which undoubtedly increased his popularity as did his arrest of plutocrats who acquired privatized state assets following the fall of the Soviet system. Failures of government in Russia are attributed to advisors and ministers, never directly to the Tsar, Communist Party chairman, or President. The Tsar was, until the early years of the 20th Century, regarded by the peasants as a defender of their welfare, however misled he might be by those around him. For every person purged under Stalin, another appointed to succeed fully approved the action. Policy or governance is done by ***purge***, usually a clean sweep by the ruler of all advisors and ministers.

A third difference is that society in *Russia is public and collective*, whereas it is *private and individual in the West*. Because the state and society are integrated under the absolute rule and will of the Tsar/leader, there has never been a civil society or rule of law in Russia. Law is whatever the Tsar/ruler decides it is. No matter what legislated or codified laws may prescribe, they are subject of overrule at the will of the Tsar/ruler. Doing business in Russia is notoriously risky because of the absence of laws and regulations, courts in which to apply them, judges and lawyers to interpret and plead, and case law to provide precedents in economic, corporate, and civil law. The fact that there is no civil society or rule of law in Russia (and in most of the non- Western world) is almost impossible for Westerners to understand so rich are we in the results of free association in economic ventures, social and scientific pursuits, private interests and clubs, and sports and leisure activity. Whereas the West considers how individuals live their lives to be a ***private*** matter outside the state, in every other part of the world, the lives of individuals are subject to state or tribal ***public*** authority with no independent rights or protections. The state is ultimately the only association permitted in Russia, and the loyalty to the state of all private associations is suspect.

These underlying authoritarian principles and practices reflect and respond to the conditions that Russia has faced throughout its history. Wedged between the warlike nomads of Central Asia and expanding German, Lithuanian, Polish, and Swedish states, Russia has never had territorial security. Consequently, whether facing Mongol Hordes or Nazi Panzer divisions, the entire society and state in Russia have been on war footing, organized entirely around mobilizing and arming its forces to oppose invasion and secure its borders.

Ivan Kalita (1535), Ivan III (1560), and Ivan Grozny ('the Terrible', 1590) organized the Tsarist State, under which the will of the Tsar was law, no person had any rights against the state, and no person or group of persons had the right to establish organizations outside the state. Formed under and modeled on the Mongol suzerainty of the Golden Horde (1300-1535), it gave the Tsar absolute control over and disposition of Russian people, lands, and resources. Every person in Russia was ultimately a slave of the Tsar, and considered him or herself to be such. As late as the 19th Century, Russian noblemen, when corresponding directly with the Tsar, signed themselves "your faithful slave."

State and society, which is to say public and private, were merged, and society was and remains a function of and within the state. Private associations and organizations, clubs, and interest groups were and remain suspect ***because*** they were private. President Putin moved to restrict entry of foreign missionaries and non-government agencies consistent with this statist view.

Tsar Ivan Grozny created a ***police state*** (variously called Oprichnina, 3rd Section, NKVD, KGB, FSB) within the official state apparatus to spy upon and coerce all members of Russian society. There is no civil society in Russia in which rule of law and due process insure order and civil rights to all citizens. All so called laws and individual rights, property, privileges, wealth and so on are subject to arbitrary seizure or cancellation by the State/Ruler. Courts serve the State in carrying out its orders through mock legal procedures in modern times. Secret police were essential to prevent subjects from forming civil associations that might challenge state rule. Setting subject against subject to divide and rule is the pattern of Russian government. This pattern of state organization continues to this day in various forms, sometimes overtly tyrannous, sometimes indirectly authoritarian. The Russian people accept, expect, and support this kind of rule and vigilance from their ruler.

Added to his secular authority was the position of Tsar as successor to the Emperor of Byzantium and the Patriarch of Constantinople. The dual role of divinely anointed and politically absolute ruler continued with variant excursions into "politically correct" forms of Westernizing enlightenment under Peter, Catherine II, and Alexander I. Stalin, a more traditional and effective leader uninterested in Western opinions or institutions, pursued the goal set by Ivan Grozny by integrating the Russian people in totalitarian slavery. As patriarch of the Communist international movement, he also enjoyed a quasi-religious status.

Peter the Great (1679-1720) established the modern Russian State. He organized society in 14 *"chin"* or ranks to which everyone in Russia belonged. The chin defined the role, salary, uniform, and status of each subject, and each subject was entitled to a position and salary at the level for which they were qualified. In effect, everyone was an employee of the state.

In broad terms, there were three principal ranks: the Tsar and his immediate family; the nobles who provided military and state service in return for their estates and serfs; serfs who were bound to the land and subject to the absolute rule of the landowners. Urban subjects presented a confusing and unruly group, organized in chin but freer to establish businesses and industries. Most industries in Russia were founded in the 19th Century by freed peasants who grew enormously wealthy, founded many theaters and art galleries, and sponsored emerging writers.

After a thousand years of absolute, and under the Soviets totalitarian rule, Russians find authoritarian government reassuring and are lukewarm toward Western democracy. No one but a Tsar/Leader is believed to pursue the overall interests of the people, and the comfortable if somewhat exiguous guaranteed position and salary of government employment provided by the Soviet Regime predisposed the majority of Russians to state economic as well as political control.

A 2001 survey by the Russian Institute for Social Research found that fewer than 7 percent of Russians believed the current Russian Constitution served as the foundation of the Russian State or the basis for rule of law in Russia. By the year 2050, an authoritarian government will be accepted and perhaps even voted in by the Russian people. This government will not be a threat to its neighbors because the demographic conditions and economic organization of Russia cannot support an aggressive policy toward the outside world.

Another comparison is worth mentioning. In 1921-1923, Lenin introduced the New Economic Policy (NEP) which opened the faltering Soviet Union to Western corporate investment. Engineers from American and European corporations (General Electric, General Motors, Fiat, etc.) led projects to build truck and automobile factories, dams and hydropower, and industrialize the broken economy. Russia once again (Italian architects, not Russians, built the Kremlin and the St. Basil Basilica in Moscow and most of St. Petersburg in the 16-18th Centuries) invited Western entrepreneurs to create an economic system that later helped them withstand Nazi invasion. Since 1991, Russia again has invited foreign capital to develop its shattered economy. There is no reason to assume however that Russia will remain open to foreign capital in the future. Stalin terminated the NEP policy once its advantages had been realized and replaced it with domestic 5-Year Plans that were inefficient but subject to total control and secrecy. A Russian government may again begin squeezing and eliminating Western capital influences once the post-Soviet economy is developed.

China

From 1978 as a result of Deng Xiao Ping's policy of opening China to the West, China developed into one of the most economically successful nations lifting more than 900 million Chinese from rural poverty to industrial 'middle class' living standards. Possible only because the United States took on the role of protecting world trade and open markets so all nations could develop their economies to achieve prosperity without fear of military threats from formerly dominant nations. The breakdown of this liberal international trade system began 2018 as Russia resumed aggression and economic 'warfare' with Europe and China began expanding and threatening its neighbors. The sharp decline in Chinese population as a result of Mao's one child policy has led to a point where Chinese population is in irreversible decline and Xi Jing Ping's hostile foreign policies *vis a vis* the United States have resulted in drastically reduced Western investment in and trade with China.

The economy is approaching collapse as foreign investment and trade gradually ends. This disaster is concealed by the regime as accurate census or data collection on the economy is no longer sought and instead they publish fictional data and public reporting that suggests a thriving economy. For example, accurate census data is no longer sought. Claims of 1.4 billion people conceal the fact that population is declining and is already less than 1.1 billion.

The Communist Party (CCP) is not concerned with the economic progress and rising standard of living of its people. It pursues an ideological agenda of reducing Western influence on the Chinese people and an aggressive foreign policy whose principal objective is conquest of Taiwan and Siberia east of the Urals. In August 2014 Xi Jing-ping signed an agreement with Russia that allows for extensive Chinese infrastructure, agriculture and mining development in Russia. Russia since the Ukraine war is dependent on China for revenue from oil and gas sales and this agreement is a Trojan Horse to increase the already substantial legal and illegal Chinese moves into Siberia on resource extraction projects. Xi Jing-ping wants to weaken Russia by providing limited support to keep the Ukrainian invasion going until Russia can no longer support the war and is so weak as to be unable to resist China's take over Siberia east of the Urals by the target date of 2049. A policy adopted in August 2024 by the CCP.

Ambitious aggressive foreign moves are likely to be hampered as public unrest increases and youth unemployment and closing of businesses deprive youth of their chance for a successful future. Collapse of the regime is a possibility given the irreversible decline economic and social.

This is tragic. China freed of the CCP can rely on the Chinese strong work ethic, high average intelligence, and very high personal motivation to succeed. Freed of the CCP and releasing this aptitude for capitalist economic development, a prominent role of China in the world economy would certainly be possible. No foreign population is more compatible with American values. The large and successful Chinese population in the United States is the most easily assimilated immigrant population outside Western Europe. Even now there are close ties between Chinese business and government leaders and the United States. They commonly send their sons and daughters to universities here. Because China has a historically pacifist and pragmatic tradition, there is a good chance that absent the CCP the rise of China to international prominence can be accommodated peacefully. China has severe limitations that will curb its ambitions. Despite extraordinary economic growth since 1980, millions of rural Chinese are outside the magic circle waiting to get in. Local unrest and violent protest over poor living conditions and corrupt government is pandemic throughout China, though concealed so far as possible. Rising expectations in the face of declining opportunity will increase pressure on the Communist regime.

The most characteristic Chinese cultural artifact, the Great Wall of China, began construction in 200 BC and sections were later added and rebuilt. It extends from the Yellow Sea to the province of Gansu in North-central China and its many sections and branches cover about 4,000 miles. Chinese history is a sequence of invasion, civil war, conquest, and liberation but one characteristic predominates. The Great Wall is the most dramatic manifestation of the ***drive for insularity*** that characterized Chinese society from the beginning. The Chinese language is its most pervasive manifestation. Although the Great Wall was penetrable, the Chinese language resists all but the most dedicated students. Mongol rulers were expansionist and aggressive, but the native Han dynasties tended to hug the borders, defend them, and exact tribute from foreigners but not invite them to settle. One emperor made teaching Chinese language, one of the most deliberately exclusive, punishable by death.

The Song dynasty that began in 960 AD established a system of civil service examinations that completed the shift of social and political power from aristocratic families to officials selected on the basis of talent. The Song dynasty also established Neo-Confucianism which combined the moral standards of traditional Confucianism with elements of Buddhism and Taoism as the official state philosophy, and all later Chinese dynasties continued to support it. Chinese inventions during the Song period included gunpowder and movable type for printing, but the most significant was the introduction of ***early ripening rice*** which made it possible to grow two or three crops a year in the south. The increased rice production helped support the population, which for the first time exceeded 100 million.

Rule of such a vast population was indirect and stratified. No means existed for direct efficient control. Each layer of society, including the peasants, was pretty much left alone so long as tribute/taxes were rendered to the next level. Intervention was rare because every layer wanted to meet the minimum requirements in order to be left alone. And as in Russia, requirements were kept at a minimum. The system for peasants required supplementing income by crafts. A similar system prevailed in Russia. Only with the largely forced introduction of Western industrial textiles and manufactured goods in the 19th Century did the peasant craft system break down in China and Russia, thereby impoverishing the peasant population, with major political and social consequences.

Traditionally, most Chinese lived in villages of 100 to 200 households. Many families owned their land, though in numerous cases it was not large enough to support them. Many other families owned no land. The members of these families worked as tenants or laborers for big landowners and rich peasants. They had to pay extremely high rents-- from 30 to 60 percent of the harvest. In some cases, peasant families were so poor that they became beggars or bandits, or even sold their children as servants or slaves to rich families. Under this system impoverished families developed strong ambition and entrepreneurial spirit, much like French peasants after the Revolution. Because Imperial rule was remote and indirect, this peasant population and its work ethic and family loyalty retained the potential for major economic enterprise if released from State control. That happened for the first time in 1980 under Deng Xiao-ping even though all land is still under the primitive system of communist state ownership.

Only about 13-percent of China's land area can be cultivated. Thus, farmers have extremely little cropland to support themselves and the rest of the huge population. Agriculture accounts for less than 25-percent of China's GDP, but it ranks as the country's largest employer by far. About 60-percent of China's workers are farmers.

Given the huge population, central authority has always been weak and inefficient in controlling China. Power centers led by warlords were common and fragmentation of Empire into north and south, east and west was endemic. Available weapons and means of transportation limited effective control. Even in Communist China, corrupt regional Party overlords regularly abuse their authority. This pattern of uneven control and local abuse limits the actual power of the ruling Party apparatus.

Because there is no civil society, Tongs similar to Sicilian Mafia organizations became a means for organizing the civilian population in urban areas. Tongs ran business, prostitution, opium dens, trade, businesses, public works contracts, and so on, led by a Tong family head and dispensing jobs, housing, financial security to its affiliates in return for loyalty and support. Chiang Kai Chek was elevated by the Yellow Tong in Shanghai. Membership in a Tong was essential for survival of most urban Chinese.

Given this indirect rule and vast decentralized pattern of government and economy, China has always perplexed Westerners. The process for reaching decisions, getting to definite agreement, establishing commitments is entirely opposite to American practice in particular. No Chinese will offend by contradicting. He will agree or appear to agree just to maintain amicable relations. But no Chinese will make a decision independently. Every decision is referred to higher authority or to some collective authority. Agreements are formalities largely to be ignored if one's interests are not served. Contracts are not considered binding, just working propositions. The recent effort to assimilate modern Western business practices in order to qualify for equal membership in world trade organizations has been extremely difficult. There was no business law, banking law or procedures, no civil or business legal system. Even today the state officials intervene in market decisions following the traditional Chinese pattern. Honoring international copyright laws is alien to Chinese traditional practice in which 'borrowing' from the West without paying was common. (Unfortunately, Chinee will lie, cheat, steal or deceive if necessary to gain profit or advantage.) Similar conditions prevail in Russia and to some extent in India, where drug patents are regularly ignored.

Chinese are **xenophobic**. Chinese believe they are a superior culture and race and would prefer to have nothing to do with the outside world. They would like to withdraw into their cultural fortress and will to the extent possible. They are **defensive**, not aggressive so are unlikely to have or at least to pursue territorial ambitions. Recent aggressive moves by Qi Jing-ping are a departure from traditional state policy, which always sought subtle and unobtrusive gains and avoided conflict if possible. Taiwan is a symbolic issue that can be managed, despite the noises made on both sides. China is weak in petroleum resources in particular, and there is no bordering country that could be conquered to provide them. Japan tried to extend control throughout Asia in order to secure industrial supplies. But today no power in Asia is able to make that attempt.

It has close ties with Russia to obtain oil and gas resources, and obliquely supports Russia in its war in Ukraine. That is in pursuit of a hardly reported Chinese policy of weakening Russia and extending Chinese economic and political influence in the former Soviet states of Kazakstan, Uzbekistan, Kirgizstan, Tadzhikistan. China is also infiltrating Siberia east of the Yenesei River which it historically claims as Chinese territory seized by Tsars in the 18th Century. This is taking place *sub rosa*. Putin is well aware of the plan but is constrained to keep quiet about it for the present. In the long run, China's best source of needed land, water, and resources is Siberia not Southeast Asia.

No matter what contracts China signs, such sources are subject to fairly easy interdiction by the United States, which has the most powerful navy and air/missile forces in the world. Most China trade goes through the straits of Mallaca in Indonesia. The United States could close that route and within six months China would face economic collapse for lack of foodstuffs and energy! Allowing China to extend its economic benefits and investments to such Africa and other foreign areas is welcome. It will dissipate their financial reserves in insecure and likely economically unsuccessful commitments and reduce their ability to finance military and scientific challenges to the United States.

The putative potential military threat to the United States posed by a resurgent and nationalistic China is largely smoke screen for military appropriations in the United States. ***The massive Chinese army is a full employment scheme not a military threat***. There is no area but Russia and India where it could be meaningfully deployed. Japan is an island geographically secure and technologically superior to China. No move to develop missile and nuclear threats against the United States would be successful. Such threats would conflict with Japan and Russia before affecting the United States. They would also require huge investments of capital that would deprive the civil sector of growth needed to sustain the huge population. Further, the United States could intervene economically and militarily well before the threat became serious. China has more to gain by peaceful trade than saber rattling. Any threat to access to the United States market would be lethal to

Chinese economic growth. The United States is developing ties with the other mass population state, India, which could easily replace China in manufacturing should that become necessary. This recent turn toward India is just a ploy by the Bush Administration to dampen hostility toward China within the Congress.

America's Special Relationship with China

Little known and hardly remembered, America's special relationship with China has played an unusual and significant role in the history of both countries. In the 19th Century the New England clipper trade developed close family ties between the American upper class and China.

Franklin Delano Roosevelt's father made his fortune (partly in opium trading) and lived in China in the mid-19th Century. FDR had a lifelong affection for China as a result. Correspondingly, he had a lifelong hatred of Japan, which may have predisposed him to the unjust incarceration of Japanese American citizens in camps in Arizona and New Mexico during WWII. It certainly influenced his willingness to give Chiang Kai-shek almost unlimited aid and great power status in the United Nations following WWII.

Henry Luce, publisher of *Time, Life,* and *Fortune* magazines, was the son of a missionary in China and became a dedicated supporter of Chiang Kai-shek. Curiously, the father of Chiang's wife, Madame Soong, had studied at a Methodist seminary in North Carolina in the early 1900's, and later became one of the wealthiest and most influential figures in the Nationalist Party. Chiang 'converted' to Methodism in the 1920's under the influence of his wife. The conversion stood him in good stead in the post WWII period, a period when collections for missionaries in China and federal support for Chiang against the godless communists was vigorously promoted by the Luce press and the religious establishment.

The 'betrayal' of China by communists in the State Department was a favorite theme of Senator Joe McCarthy and the Republican right during the 1940's and 1950's. Secretary of State John Foster Dulles and his brother Allen Dulles who headed the CIA were also sons of missionaries and acquired an anti-Communist zeal as a result. Writers like Pearl Buck romanticized China for Americans, the Eastern Establishment founded and supported many chairs in Chinese studies, and children of missionaries became academics at these colleges and universities and experts on China after WWII. During WWII, the Marine Corps sent a unit to work with Mao on tactics and strategy for fighting the Japanese. As a result, Mao was quite friendly with the Marine Corps and the Corps respected his military capabilities. When Marine units were stationed in Qingdao in 1948, Mao stayed out of the city until they were withdrawn, rather than risk conflict with former friends and provoke the American 'China lobby' to force United States military intervention. Only with the triumph of Mao and the Korean War did the era of close establishment ties <with China come to an end. They have been renewed in recent decades.

China is not or at least need not be a threat to the United States. The close ties between China and the Chinese-American community can be developed and extended. It is true that Chinese are chauvinistic and have their interests primarily in mind. Who doesn't? But their pragmatic and very long view of developments and history eventually may prevail against the futile aggressiveness of Xi Jing-ping.

India

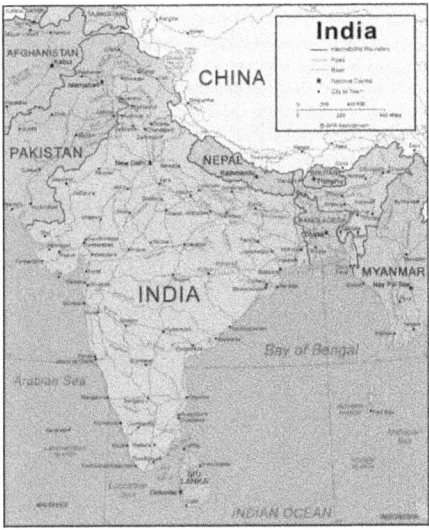

If it didn't exist, India would be impossible to imagine. It has 1.5 billion people who speak more than 1,000 languages and dialects, more or less mutually unintelligible, divided into four major and several hundred lesser, mutually exclusive castes, and practicing Hindu (80 percent) and Islam (12 percent), two violently incompatible religions.

For all the wisdom of the East' that surrounds Western understanding of India, largely based on general impressions of Buddhism, vegetarianism, and Gandhi, India is a miserably poor, repressive, and often violent society. Each state has its own language and pursues policies independent of the central government. Political anarchy is probable as India's population increases to 1.7 billion people by 2050. Unlike China, the central government of India has no means or authority to enforce birth control or any other central policy.

Adding to the potential and actual demographic and social fragmentation, an emergent Militant Hinduism, which matches militant Islam in its retrograde social objectives and even advocates the return of suttee and other Hindu barbarities, is enflaming Islam/Hindu antagonism, the most enduring feature of Indian politics since independence from Great Britain in 1947. The growing conflict between Hinduism and Islam is symbolized by the razor wire fence India has plans to build along the entire border with Pakistan and Bangladesh at a cost of $4 billion. The ostensible reason is that both countries allegedly are infiltrating Muslim terrorists to incite domestic Muslims against the Indian State.

Whatever 'Western' institutions, language, dress, education, technology, and preferences may appear, they are confined to less than 10 percent of the population, while 90 percent share in millennia-old cultural and social practices and abject poverty. Despite economic and technological progress in some provinces and cities, illiteracy remains about 50 percent. An improved living standard for the vast majority is unrealistic because India simply does not have resources or social structure sufficient to provide for the coming population boom. Bollywood and Bangladore mask an underlying demographic powder keg

Abuse of women is of course common. One example is ***dowry death***, assassination or forced suicide of thousands of women for the reason that their dowry was unsatisfactory to their husbands' family, is widespread. In Gujurat province, some 5,600 women were found dead in 2000 (57 percent had been burned to death, 18 percent poisoned, 15 percent died in faked accidents). Society, the police, and the courts quietly sanction such traditions. Use of echograms that revealed the sex of a fetus led to 5 million abortions of females each year. In 1994 the Indian government officially prohibited physicians from disclosing the sex of the fetus. However, that just created a bootleg practice that enriches physicians. The imbalance between females and males affects marriage prospects. By 2020, about 28 million men will not be able to find wives and found a family.

Language and Political Divisions

Regional, language, and ethnic differences among Indians create difficulties for national unity. In 1953, after much pressure on the Indian government, the state of Andhra Pradesh was created for Telugu speakers. In 1955, the States Reorganization Commission recommended the creation of other states based on language. At that time, the state boundaries were those that the British had drawn up. In 1956, most of India's major language groups were given their own states. Additional states based on language were created later. Indian states are organized largely according to language groups, but each state includes people from multiple language and dialect groups. Each state also has its own official language. About three-fourths of the Indian population, mainly in north and central India, speak Indo-Aryan languages (Assamese, Bengali, Gujarati, Hindi, Kashmiri, Marathi, Oriya, Punjabi, and Sindhi). In southern India, which has a fifth of the total population in India, speaks mainly Kannada, Malayalam, Tamil, and Telugu, which belong to the Dravidian family of languages. In the Himalayan region of the northeast and along the border with Myanmar many people speak Kuki, Manipuri, Naga, and other Sino-Tibetan languages. Some groups in the northeast and central areas speak Mundari and Santali, which belong to the Mon-Khmer, or Austro-Asiatic, family of languages.

India's national language is Hindi, one of the Indo-Aryan languages. More than two-fifths of the people speak one or more of the dialects of this language, and at least some Hindi is understood by as many as two-thirds of the population. The study of Hindi is required in elementary and secondary schools in India. English has an official status as an associate national language across India, about 3 to 4 percent of the population speaks English, and much of the nation's official business is conducted in English. It is the common language among educated people and is widely used at colleges and universities.

Caste System

Hindus are organized into social groups called castes or *varnas*. The caste divisions in India originated about 1500 BC when groups of Indo-European Aryans (meaning 'kinsmen' or 'nobles') invaded India, conquered the native Dravidians, and drove many of them southward. They established the caste system, which consolidated and provided religious sanction for their domination of the Dravidians and which remains largely unchanged today. The Brahmans--the priests--were the highest caste and the Shudras (Dravidians) were the lowest. The Brahmans perfected Sanskrit, the language of the Aryans and composed the earliest known Hindu scriptures, the Vedas about 1400 BC. The most important Hindu sacred writings, called the Upanishads, appeared between 800 and 600 BC.

Ancient Hindu texts described the four main castes called varnas. The Brahmans (priests and scholars) were the highest group followed by Kshatriyas (rulers and warriors), Vaishyas (merchants and professionals), and Shudras (artisans, and servants). Smaller castes were called jatis. A person's caste determines his social status. Over time, each caste came to include hundreds of sub-castes which determined a person's place in the community and the occupations he might hold. Altogether, the caste system has thousands of categories.

Although the caste system is officially disapproved and is often ignored in Westernized cities, its influence remains unchanged in rural areas. Each caste is endogamous, practices hereditary economic occupations, often has distinctive marks or clothing, and is usually forbidden to marry or associate with persons of another caste. The caste provides an individual with a secure place in the world, but locks him into an unchanging way of life. Violations of caste propriety are severely punished. It is not uncommon for a brother to murder a sister who involved herself with a man of inferior caste. Gang rape of a girl of inferior caste involved with a male relative is common in order to disqualify her for marriage. Suttee (widow murder) and other practices also grew up around Hinduism and the caste system.

Complicated rules govern contact and behavior between the castes. For example, marriages between people of widely different castes are rare, and the upper castes do not eat with the Shudras. A large group of people--approximately 150 million people-- is considered to be outside the caste system. Known as untouchables, this group has an even lower status than the Shudras. Untouchables have traditionally held the most undesirable jobs, such as the cleaning of toilets and the disposal of garbage. Some upper-caste people believe that they will be polluted by the touch of members of this group.

Although the Indian Constitution grants the Untouchables equal rights and bans discrimination against them in jobs and education, they remain an oppressed group, especially in villages.

Invasion, War, and Civil Anarchy

Throughout its history, India has been swept by invasion, war, political anarchy, and civil violence. From about 455 to 1500 AD, armies from what are now Afghanistan, central Asia, and Iran invaded India, including the Huns from central Asia and Muslim armies from Arabia. In 1206, the Muslim general Qutb ub-din Aybak proclaimed himself sultan (ruler) of northern India and established the Delhi Sultanate. In 1398, the armies of the central Asian leader Timur, also known as Tamerlane, swept over India. Timur sacked Delhi before returning to his capital at Samarkand in what is now Uzbekistan. Mughal (Mongol) invaders took over India in the 16th Century.

English East India Company

In 1600, Queen Elizabeth I of England granted a charter to the East India Company to open trade with India and East Asia. The company got permission from the Mughal Emperor Jahangir, to trade in India and set up trading posts and forts at Bombay (Mumbai), Calcutta

(Kolkata), and Madras (Chennai). During the 1600's, the English became the leading European power in India. By the mid-1700's, little remained of the Mughal Empire as the Marathas and other tribes ravaged much of southern India. The East India Company expanded its trade, increased its political power, and began collecting taxes in some regions. Some Indian rulers refused to agree to the company's terms. At the Battle of Plassey in 1757, the forces of Robert Clive, an agent of the East India Company, defeated the army of the Mughal governor of Bengal. This British victory was the starting point of the British Empire in India, though at that time, most of the country still remained under the rule of Indian princes. In 1774, Warren Hastings was appointed the company's first governor general of India. Growing British interference in Indian customs and religion led to the Sepoy Mutiny in 1857. The mutiny began at an army base in Meerut, near Delhi. Its cause presaged coming conflicts within India and the peculiar religious parochialism that continues to this day. Indian soldiers called sepoys revolted after British officers instructed them to bite open rifle cartridges believed to have been greased with cow and hog fat. Both Hindus and Muslims objected to the order. The religious beliefs of the Hindu sepoys forbade them to eat beef, and the Muslim sepoys could not eat pork! The Indian Rebellion quickly spread from Meerut to the rest of northern and central India. However, the rebels were poorly organized, had few weapons, and lacked good leadership. By 1859, they had been defeated.

The British Raj

In 1858, the British government decided to govern India directly. This direct rule is often called the British Raj, which means 'rule' or 'administration'. Parliament took control of the East India Company's Indian possessions, which became known as British India. In most other parts of India, called the princely, or native, states, the British governed indirectly, through local rulers. In 1876, Queen Victoria of Britain was given the title **Empress of India** by the British Parliament. Indian troops serving under British officers fought the Second Afghan

War (1878-1881). This war helped establish India's boundary with Afghanistan. British India defeated the Burmese in the Third Burmese War (1885). Burma (now Myanmar) then became a province of India. It remained a part of India until 1937.

Indian National Congress

In 1885, a number of Indian lawyers and professionals formed the Indian National Congress. In 1906, several Muslim leaders, encouraged by the British, formed the All-India Muslim League. In March 1919, the British passed the Rowlatt Acts to try to control protests in India. On April 13, 1919, thousands of Indians assembled in an enclosed area in Amritsar. Troops entered the meeting place and blocked the entrance. The British commander then ordered the soldiers to open fire on the unarmed crowd. The shots killed about 400 people and wounded about 1,200. This event, called the Amritsar Massacre, proved to be a turning point.

By 1920, Mohandas K. Gandhi had become a leader in the Indian independence movement and in the Indian National Congress, which had become the most important Indian political organization. Gandhi persuaded the Congress to adopt his program of nonviolent disobedience. Gandhi asked Indians to boycott British goods, to refuse to pay taxes, and to stop using British schools, courts, and government services. In 1940, the Muslim League demanded that a new country be carved out of India for Muslims. The name Pakistan, which means 'land of the pure' in Urdu, came to be used for this proposed nation. According to Muslim leaders, India was to be for Hindus and Pakistan for Muslims.

The British declared early in 1946 that they would grant India independence if Indian political leaders could agree among themselves on a form of government. The Muslim League declared August 16, 1946, as Direct Action Day. On that day, Muslims held nationwide demonstrations calling for the establishment of Pakistan. Bloody rioting broke out between Muslims and Hindus in Calcutta. Similar violence later occurred elsewhere in India.

Kashmir and Chronic Conflict

In 1947, Indian and British leaders agreed to partition the country into India and Pakistan. India became an independent nation on August 15, 1947. Pakistan had become an independent nation the day before. Partition was accompanied by more violence and bloodshed. More than 10 million people became refugees, as Hindus and Sikhs in Pakistan fled to India, and Muslims in India fled to Pakistan. About half a million people were killed in Hindu-Muslim riots. Pakistani Muslims launched an invasion to take Kashmir by force, and Pakistan laid claim to the state. Kashmir's ruler responded by seeking India's protection and by making Kashmir part of India. The war between India and Pakistan lasted until 1949.

Border disputes between India and China erupted into armed violence in October 1962, when Chinese forces swept into northeastern India. In November, the Chinese pulled back, and a cease-fire took effect.

In early 1965, fighting broke out along the Pakistan-India border, but Shastri and President Muhammad Ayub Khan of Pakistan quickly agreed to a cease-fire under UN supervision. There were many violations of the cease-fire, and later that year, Pakistan and India fought over Kashmir. Once again a UN-sponsored cease-fire took effect.

In the early 1980's, a militant Sikh movement grew in the Punjab. The leaders of this movement claimed that the Sikhs suffered from widespread discrimination. They wanted a separate state only for Sikhs. Some Sikhs carried out acts of terrorism and violence against people who opposed the movement. Sikh militants occupied the Golden Temple in Amritsar, the most sacred Sikh shrine. In 1984, government troops attacked the temple. The leaders of the militants died in the fighting. Many Sikhs were angry that their shrine had been attacked, and two Sikh members of Indira Gandhi's security force assassinated her in October 1984. The assassination touched off riots in which several thousand Sikhs were killed.

In the late 1980's, Muslim groups in Kashmir began to hold demonstrations against Indian rule. Many received the support of the Pakistani government. In 1989, the demonstrations turned violent. Since then, thousands of people have died as a result of clashes between Indian military forces and the Muslim groups. In 1989 and 1990, violence between Hindus and Muslims erupted over the status of a mosque in the town of Ayodhya in the state of Uttar Pradesh. In 1992, Hindu extremists destroyed the mosque. This action led to violence between Hindus and Muslims in many areas of India.

A number of ethnic separatist groups emerged in the 1980's and 1990's. They included the United Liberation Forces of Assam, which called for independence for Assam, and the Bodo movement, which favored autonomy for the region inhabited by the Bodo people. In 1993 and 1994, violence broke out, mainly in Manipur, between Nagas wanting independence and Kukis, who also live in the region. The clashes left hundreds of people dead, and many villages destroyed. In 1999, Indian troops clashed with Muslim guerrillas who had established positions on the Indian side of the truce line in Kashmir. India claimed that the guerrillas included Pakistani troops, but Pakistan denied that its troops were involved. Pakistan and India nearly reached the brink of nuclear war in 2002, but tensions eased eventually. From this brief survey it is clear that India could enter a period of civil unrest and possibly war with Pakistan, another country with surging population and few resources. The fact that they both have nuclear weapons presents a threat to the region and the world at large. However, the growing economic presence of American corporations in Bangladore and other developing parts of India has added restraint to the mix. Rather than lose the increasing investment and commitment of US business in India, the government has committed to peaceful resolution of conflicts with Pakistan. A similar decision on that side of the border bodes well for short term peace at least. Nevertheless, the population explosion in India will disrupt any easy or peaceful resolution of domestic foreign issues in India.

Japan

Until 1945, Japan had never been conquered. An island inaccessible by land and made up mostly of mountainous terrain, Japan's population was concentrated in the arable narrow plains near the coasts. As a result, the population was easier to organize and mobilize and the country was easier to defend against invaders whose only approach was by sea. Perhaps most important, until the Mongols, no major power wished to invest the money and effort needed to conquer this relatively small country of limited wealth.

Given its island security, Japan could develop without outside interference. This insular advantage meant that the Japanese became one of the most homogeneous populations on earth. No immigration or major settlement of foreign peoples occurred within Japan, so a strong sense of racial identity and superiority developed early. Japan is not essentially defined by any indigenous cultural or institutional heritage. Its culture and institutions were largely imported. Japan's binding characteristic is its racial consanguinity, which allows the Japanese to adopt any foreign cultural or institutional form without altering their fundamental social cohesiveness.

Despite its insularity, Japan is one of the most adaptable civilizations in world history. Japan twice voluntarily adopted a foreign culture virtually lock stock and barrel and completely transformed its institutions, without conquest: The first time in the 6th through 9th Centuries by assimilating Chinese culture and institutions, and the second time in the 19th Century by assimilating Western culture, institutions, and industrial economy. The Japanese early proved willing to introduce foreign cultures and make them their own. The strong, hierarchical rule of regional clans and the later imperial system made such introduction easier and efficient because approval by the clan heads insured compliance throughout the clan and throughout its subordinate guilds, peasants, and slaves. Strong vertical power structures in Japan made changes relatively quick, total, and efficient. Buddhism was introduced from Korea in the late 6th Century, and Chinese culture and imperial political organization were introduced in the period 650 to 800 AD. Chinese written characters were adapted to create the written form of the Japanese language.

Another characteristic of Japan is its ability to maintain ***forms of authority*** in the face of changing social and political ***power relationships***, much like England another island power. During the Kamakura period, 1185-1333 AD, Japan created its distinctive feudal political system in which the Emperor and his court resided in Kyoto as a largely symbolic ruler while a feudal military dictator called Seiidai***shogun*** ('barbarian subduing great general') exercised real power in Kamakura. This division introduced the practice of military rule independent from but not supplanting imperial status, allowing the military ***power*** to pursue policies and funding independent of the imperial ***authority***. During the Kamakura period, Zen Buddhism and a military cult of Zen warrior monks, glorifying the sword, Spartan endurance, and loyalty were introduced. This cult and its practitioners became an arch-type of Japanese culture.

The Mongols provided a test and a confirmation of the racial unity of the Japanese people. In 1274 and 1281 AD, Kublai Khan launched invasions against Japan with a large fleet and nearly 150,000 warriors. Both attacks failed due to the firm resistance on land and at sea of the entire Japanese population. Japan remained independent and outside the Mongol tribute system. Solidarity in the face of an invading enemy, however, did not survive internally. Financial exhaustion and disorder brought about by the invasions introduced a period of civil war, which divided the nation north and south. Clan warfare and civil violence became a constant feature of Japanese society, emerging in especially virulent form during the 1920's, when murder of rival politicians from the four ruling clans led to eventual Army control of the government.

Westernization and Anti-Westernization

The beginning of Westernization, periodically interrupted and resumed, occurred in 1543 AD, when the Portuguese landed in western Japan and introduced Western products and especially the musket, which revolutionized warfare in the island empire. The Portuguese were well-received and established extensive trade, introducing European goods and Catholicism. Buddhism went into decline and Western influences began to transform the culture and organization of Japan. From 1600 to 1868 AD, a repudiation of foreign influence was led by the Tokugawa Shogunate, which established the military capital at Tokyo which became the economic, political and cultural capital of the nation. The Tokugawa Shoguns stamped out Christianity and introduced and to some extent reinvented deeply conservative practices such as the feudal code of bushido and a revived Shinto religion.

In 1609, Dutch traders landed in western Japan but by 1641 the Tokugawa Shoguns had driven English, Portuguese, Dutch and other foreign traders and missionaries from Japan or had severely restricted their activities. Only in 1720 was a ban on study of Europe and the importation of European books removed. In the early 1800's, the debate over whether to open Japan to Western trade and influence resumed in earnest as a result of expanded American whaling in the northern Pacific and extensive Western trade and influence in China. Abuse of American seamen forced to land in Japan led to several attempts by the United States to contact and develop relations with Japan. In 1851, Commodore Perry arrived in Tokyo Bay with a letter from President Millard Fillmore to the Emperor requesting improved treatment for American castaways and access to coaling stations in Japan for the California to Shanghai steamship services. Following considerable debate, the Shogun agreed to meet foreign demands and signed treaties with the United States and Britain in 1854, Russia in 1855, and the Netherlands in 1856. However, the Emperor at Kyoto rejected accommodation with the Western powers.

Meiji Empire

Conflict continued for more than a decade until the Emperor gained complete control of the nation in 1868, beginning the Meiji period, which lasted until 1912. The Meiji ended 700 years of Shogun rule in Japan. The Meiji Emperor Mutsuhito changed his anti-foreign posture. The feudal system and military rule were abandoned and industrialization and Westernization were implemented aggressively. Universal military service was introduced in 1872, leading to a peasant army loyal to the Emperor. In 1889, a new constitution was adopted. The Emperor retained the right to declare war and make peace, and could issue ordinances that had the force of law. A bicameral parliament and civil, commercial, and criminal codes of law based on western models were adopted. In 1890, the first general election was held with 460,000 voters out of a population of 42 million.

The Sino-Japanese war of 1894-95 and the Russo-Japanese war of 1904-05 established Japan as the leading power in the Western Pacific. China ceded Formosa, the Liaotung Peninsula, and the Pescadores, opened treaty ports, and paid an indemnity to Japan. Russia ceded the southern half of Sakhalin. In 1911, Japan annexed Korea. In 1915, Japan presented China with its 21 Demands', which gained economic control over much of China's economy. World War I and its aftermath gave Japan extensive land concessions in China and the Pacific as successor to German treaty concessions lost by the war. The Naval treaty of 1922 gave Japan virtual naval parity with Western powers in the Pacific.

During the Showa Imperial period beginning in 1926, militarism and repudiation of foreign influences gained ground. The army increased in power supported by the peasantry against the moderate urban middle class and capitalists. In 1932, following minor incidents, Japan seized Manchuria and created the puppet state of Manchuko. Japan assumed control of northern China. Assassination of Premier Inukai by military reactionaries ended party rule in Japan and led to a turnover of government to the Army and Navy. Japan announced its withdrawal from the League of Nations effective 1934. Invasion of China began in 1936, and the march to world war culminated on December 7, 1941, the most fateful day in Japanese history.

Following WWII and the nearly complete destruction of Tokyo and other industrial centers, Japan adopted a Western constitutional government, reformed its economic system, and created democratic forms in education and politics. The Emperor remained as head of State but was 'un-deified' in an example of the total flexibility of the Japanese with respect to culture and institutional forms.

Japanese Culture

Japan has a distinguished and unique culture and civilization. Zen Buddhism, the tea ceremony, ceramics, koto music, haiku, gardens, flower arrangement, understated architecture and domestic furnishings, and the like are unique and beautiful products of Japanese culture. Japan is the only society, other than Classical Civilization to provide a justification and social role for suicide.

Japan successfully resisted the most powerful empire, the Mongol, and remained outside the theocratic empire system but adopted an imperial system from the Chinese. It was also different in its almost constant aggression against Korea and China for a millennium: 900--1945. Most theocratic empires engage in limited aggression, preferring to secure boundaries rather than to expand them. Japan is different in part because it has few natural resources with which to sustain its economy. Nearly every major product, especially oil and metals, must be imported.

As its population ages, Japan will face major difficulties. Immigration is unacceptable so labor shortages will be a concern to Japanese industry, although this problem is being solved in part by transferring manufacturing to other Asian countries and by a remarkable robotics industry that replaces human labor in many areas of manufacture and public services. Japan relies on its phenomenal economic power for influence internationally.

In the face of Communist Chinese expansion Japan has retracted its post-WWII policy of passive defense and is expanding a formidable naval and military force that can assure its security in partnership with the United States, its major trading partner. A joint defense alliance between the United States, Japan, Australia, New Zeeland, and Philippines has formed to meet any challenges posed by China, North Korea and Russia in the Asian theater.

PART V

The Heritage of Tribal Societies
Black Africa/Islam/Latin America

Tribal societies are the most volatile and dangerous in the world today. They will provide the source and locale for most world conflicts for the indefinite future. Tribal societies are common throughout the world but the most important are in Black Africa and the Islamic world. Despite the veneer of Islam, Muslim countries are fundamentally conglomerates of tribes that share the basic tribal culture described in Part III. Unlike the Islamic world, Black Africa has no superficially unifying religion or language and has purely tribal societies without pretence to a common religion, language, or heritage.

Latin America is an odd case. It is classified as part of the tribal non-Western tradition because Spain was Arabized during 700 years of Muslim rule from roughly 780 to 1490 AD and imperfectly shares the fundamental outlook of Western Civilization. Spain of course was devoutly Catholic, but its culture and mores and outlook derive from that of Islamic tribal rulers. Oddly, Arabic and Spanish histories share a fundamental event. At the time they forced the Muslim rulers from Spain, the Kingdom of Aragon and Castile discovered America. Gold in the Americas made Spain suddenly extremely rich, based on the slave labor of indigenous Americans. Wealth without achievement or work allowed the Spanish to indulge religious fantasies of being chosen to lead the counterrevolution against Protestantism, fantasies of superiority, and contempt for labor, nature, and foreign societies. Spain sank into a fanatic, sterile version of religious piety and social degeneracy. Similarly, the discovery of oil in Arabia made feckless Bedouin Sheiks suddenly fabulously wealthy and led to delusions of being chosen by Allah and being superior to all other peoples, along with waste of the wealth acquired. Spain shared the Arabic outlook described in this section, which was transferred directly to Latin America.

Africa

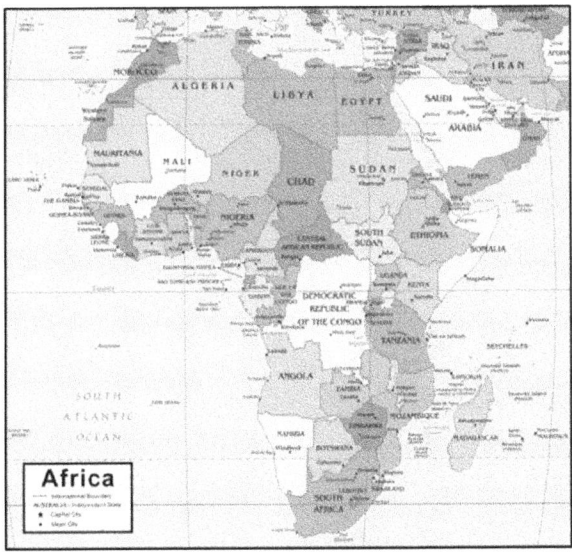

Black Africa is and has been in shambles for decades. Since independence beginning in the 1950's, the pattern of personal misconduct of African leaders and political, economic and social chaos created by their regimes is unvaried, constant, and by now endemic. Although 'colonialism' and 'racism' are still used as excuses for the disastrous condition of Black African States, the passage of fifty years of war and tribal slaughter belies such excuses.

HIV AIDS is simply one more of the self-inflicted miseries besetting Black Africa. In 2003, the total number of AIDS cases in Black Africa reached 29 million, or 70 percent the World total of 42 million. The disease has reached uncontrollable proportions and any attempt to reverse it will be symbolic and largely futile. The irresponsible leadership of Africa is simply unwilling and unable to mobilize local resources for the purpose. Any financial assistance the Western States provide will be wasted and misappropriated, and direct medical assistance would simply be nominal given the number of cases existing and added each year and the absence of any medical infrastructure to treat thousands of HIV AIDS patients. Attempts to publicize the threat and induce Africans to practice "safe sex" or abstinence encounters both the reluctance of Africans and their leaders to recognize the disease at all, and traditional animist beliefs that diseases are caused by spells cast by witches or evil spirits invoked by personal enemies. Since rational analysis and planning and responsible management of public resources for the public welfare are not established practices in Black Africa, the HIV AIDS epidemic is likely to run its course depopulating much of Central Black Africa, where it is most prevalent, over the next 25 years.

Political Irresponsibility

Il y a des héros en mal comme en bien.
Rochefoucauld, **Maximes**

The paradigm of irresponsible leadership in Africa was established by Kwame Nkrumah, who became President of newly independent Ghana in 1958. His personal corruption set the pattern of 'kleptocracy' for the entire Black subcontinent. After nationalizing cocoa plantations, gold mines, even laundries in Accra, declaring a dictatorship, bankrupting the country, appropriating state revenues to pay for his extravagant lifestyle and mistresses, and driving out all opposition to his rule, Nkrumah was overthrown by military coup in 1966 while traveling in Asia (since then, travel abroad by rulers regularly provides occasion for military coups in Africa), which led to the collapse of the cocoa industry and decades of economic chaos.

Many examples followed his lead. In Equatorial Guinea, President Macias Nguema had by 1968 created a 'concentration camp' from which one-third of the population fled across neighboring borders. Only in 1979 was Nguema overthrown and executed by an army coup. In 1976, President Bokassa of the Central African Republic, independent since 1969, declared himself "Emperor", emulating his most admired predecessor Napoleon, and ordered a crown, throne, and ceremonial accoutrements from France for his coronation. He was overthrown in 1979. Hastings Banda, President of Malawi, declared in 1965: *"Anything I say is law. Literally law. It is a fact in this country."*

In 1977, Nigeria, independent since 1960 and the largest (98 million people) African State was described by Obasanjo, head of the military government:

Nigeria is still a place where people are prepared to destroy anything, to cover up any crime, if doing so promotes their economic interest or might.

In 1985, Umaru Dikko, aide to then President Shagari, fled to affluent exile in London after looting the treasury, a pattern followed since by lesser figures who continue to loot oil revenues from the Nigerian National Petroleum Corporation. Billions of dollars in oil revenue (80 percent are purloined by 1 percent of the population) are diverted to private accounts in London and other European banks by corrupt administrators and ruling groups.

The most outrageous example of African political leadership is Edi Amin of Uganda (independent since 1962), whose rise from illiterate noncom to President by coup d'état in 1971 established a pattern envied and emulated by similarly obscure but ambitious outlying tribesmen in other states. Basing his regime on his native Moslem Kakwa tribesmen, a small minority group, he removed and murdered members of the Acholi and Langi tribes, favored by the deposed President Obote. He exiled some 50,000 Asian businessmen, doctors, engineers and other professionals who provided what little social and economic cohesion Uganda had and persecuted the Christian majority (66 percent) in favor of the minority Moslem tribes (West Nile and Nubians). After eight years of murderous and absurd antics, he provoked sufficient opposition throughout Africa, that in 1979 Tanzania "liberated" Uganda. Amin found refuge in Tunisia with Omar Khaddafi and eventually settled in Saudi Arabia, where he found sympathy because of his support of Islam. The rare principled personal example of Nelson Mandala of South Africa turns out to have been no basis for optimism. His ruling party has returned to the graft-ridden cronyism typical throughout Africa. Once the subject of international boycotts and moralizing as the renegade state Southern Rhodesia where white leaders obstructed transfer of power to the Black majority, Zimbabwe, independent since 1980, is now a corrupt, dictatorship with an economy in ruins due entirely to its President Mugabe.

Further examples of similar chaos can be found in Rwandi, where Hutu tribes slaughtered hundreds of thousands of Tutsi minority tribesmen; in Zaire, where tribal warfare has decimated the population; and in Liberia, where President Taylor was overthrown in 2002, after years of corrupt and criminal rule. The evangelist Pat Robertson urged the Bush administration to save Taylor because he was a Christian Baptist, disregarding entirely years of murder and repression under his rule! So called King Mswati III of Swaziland paid E635,000 to provide each of his 10 wives with a BMW, while 1.2 million of his subjects live on $1 a day. The list goes on.

Characteristics of Black African Tribal Societies

These examples show that Black Africa has endemic and, so far, ineradicable social and political problems that make civil society, rule of law, and productive economic growth unattainable. Statements of public policy and news reporting about Africa are uninformed and misleading for many reasons. Commonly, there is little interest in analyzing the underlying structure and behavior patterns of African societies, and there is a universal pattern of overlooking causes which are politically unacceptable, especially in the United States, in favor of the apologetics formulated around "colonialism and the consequences slavery and racism." These shibboleths are invoked whenever the underlying causes of Black African failure are discussed. The truth would put at risk the thriving industry of wasted foreign aid and loans, study grants, contracts for experts, luxury hotel meetings, and consultations and conferences about the African predicament.

Resources provided by African states that are considered vital to Western economies have been available from dictators and corrupt regimes for a comparatively small additional cost in bribes and extortion. A shift by Europe from Russia as a result of the Ukraine war to more manageable African oil states makes any West African regime able to maintain order acceptable. Likewise, any regime that is successfully challenged will be abandoned and the prospective regime supported to ensure continuous flow of resources.

The interests of the local population are of no interest to the ruling group and are not the direct responsibility of the corporations that acquire and develop the resources. This relationship has been misconstrued as neocolonialism because it might appear the corporate interests manipulate the political events in their areas of influence. They do supply revenues through purchase of oil and other resources, but the disposition of those revenues remains in the hands of local authority which pilfers state funds for private use at all levels of government administration.

The fundamental problem is that there is no state or nation, no civil society, and no humanist tradition in Africa on which to build stable, democratic societies. Western dealings with Africa fail largely because they are based on analogies with American experience. None of the assumptions made about Africa by Westerners have any application to actual conditions in Africa. The so-called Western political and social institutions of African states and societies, such as Presidents, legislative institutions, elections, universities, and the like are so unrelated to African reality as to be entirely misleading.

It is difficult to reconcile the great charm and apparent intelligence of Africans, especially those educated in England, France, or the United States and seemingly assimilated to our humanist ideas, with their barbarity, immorality, and even criminality. Why do doctors and other professionals in Africa exact sexual favors from female clients, which is a primary cause of spread of AIDS, especially in Central Africa? Why would a leader as charming, well-educated and well-spoken as Nkrumah steal public funds, flaunt mistresses, persecute opposition leaders, and bankrupt Ghana, the country he led to independence? Why do foreign shipments of grain rot on docks or end up sold the highest bidder by truckers contracted to deliver them to inland areas suffering drought and starvation? Why does foreign financial assistance to combat HIV AIDS and address other medical and social welfare needs end up in the foreign bank accounts of local rulers? Why are ministers charged with public works completely delinquent in discharging their responsibilities? These are not isolated cases or examples. They are the common pattern of conduct in all Black African states. Their opponents, usually calling for reform, if successful, soon engage in the same behavior. Among the reasons for the Black African disaster and total incomprehension and failure of Westerners to understand or deal with Africa include the following.

There are no states or nations in Black Africa

Boundaries of the delineated African States were established by colonial powers at the Congress of Berlin in 1885. They reflect territorial claims of those powers at the time, but have no relation to the tribes and their territories included within the boundaries. Consequently, each state includes numerous mutually hostile tribes and ethnic groups. Commonly one group is larger than the rest, or in places, two or three tribal groups vie for predominance. Invariably each tribe speaks its own language, often unintelligible to the others, further reducing the possibility of common ground.

In Rwanda, Hutu make up 85 percent, Tutsi 15 percent of the population. German colonists so admired the pastoral Tutsi that they gave them authority over the agricultural Hutu. Severe rule by Tutsi aggravated Hutu hostility and by the time Rwanda achieved independence in 1959, the basis for subsequent decades of mutual slaughter was established. In 1993, the Hutu, in a tribal-wide outbreak of blood lust, slaughtered nearly 900,000 Tutsi.

Similar hostilities and outbreaks of genocide between tribes occur in all parts of Black Africa. In each state, one tribe achieves predominance within the formal political system. The leaders then eliminate rival tribes from agencies and other positions of power. The excluded retire to their tribal homelands and plot a return to power. President Mugabe of Zimbabwe comes from the ruling Shona tribe (77 percent), while leaders of the excluded Ndebele tribe (17 percent) form an opposition from their homelands in the eastern part of the State. In Nigeria, the Muslim Hamitic Fulani/Hausa tribes of the north long raided black Igbo tribesmen of the eastern tropical forests for slaves. The black Yoruba tribes of the west also raided Igbo for slaves. The civil war surrounding Biafra's (read Igbo) declaration of independence in 1967 was typical of the engrained tribal hostility in Africa. Such rivalry extends to all parts of Black Africa.

Another problem is that tribal homelands usually occupy land on either side of so-called national borders. Overlaying a map of States with a map of tribes makes this dramatically clear. Consequently, when a tribe is excluded from state governance by another tribe that assumes control of the State apparatus, the excluded tribe mounts an opposition and insurrection supported by fellow tribal members in adjacent states. This "balkanization" of African tribes is the fundamental reason why no existing state in Black Africa, with the exception of Botswana, where Tswana tribe makes up 97 percent of the population, is viable.

Further, few states in Africa meet any criteria for statehood. Most have resources and populations so limited that they are unsustainable without foreign aid. They produce little of what they consume. Foreign aid and loans invariably are expended by the ruling tribal leaders on weapons to arm their militias used to repress opposition tribes and on the boondoggles of statecraft, embassies, residences, travel, and foreign bank accounts. Leaders of most states are unable to defend their borders, much less maintain order throughout their territory. Often they control only areas within their Dal homelands.

There is no concept of humanism in Black African culture

A more fundamental reason for the failure of Black African states is the lack of a humanist ethic and tradition. Tribal outlook is exclusive. African tribes have no terms comparable to Western terms for 'humanity', or any notion of a common humanity that transcends different ethnic backgrounds and culture. Tribal solidarity applies only to members of the tribe. People outside the tribe are not considered human or worthy of any consideration. They can be kidnapped, killed, enslaved, or especially under current conditions, ignored, excluded, and deprived of State benefits without compunction. This total disregard for human suffering or the well-being of fellow Africans accounts for the astonishing bestiality of African intertribal slaughter.

Rulers have no concept of responsibility for public welfare

Ruling groups have no concept of responsibility. Positions within the state are simply vehicles for personal aggrandizement. A minister of government is concerned mainly with skimming funds for his personal account, usually safely held in a bank in Europe. All employees practice the same graft, its extent depending on the relative position and power of the person involved. The idea of public service is nonexistent, since all positions are coveted mainly because they offer the opportunity to extract bribes and kickbacks.

There are no individual rights in Black Africa

Individuals do not exist in African culture. Each person is defined entirely as a member of a tribe. Whatever personal rights or consideration he may enjoy derives entirely from membership in a tribe. The most important fact about an individual African is his tribal affiliation. Anyone who becomes an outcast or leaves the protection of his tribe is fair game for all forms of exploitation.

The future of Black Africa

Given the deeply imbedded tribal social outlook and animist religious beliefs, much of Black Africa may slowly disintegrate into tribal warfare. There is no unifying principle around which all Africans can unite. African political leadership is made up of self-serving profiteers and opportunists. The Western-educated minority has developed to perfection the rhetorical smokescreen needed to dupe uninformed Western publics and governments into supporting endlessly futile aid programs.

Islam

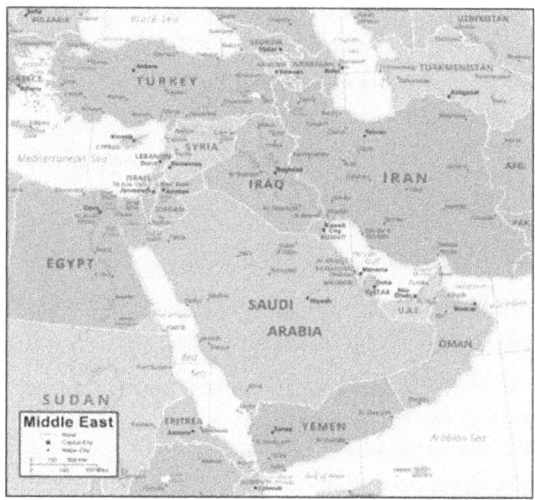

Islam is totally unlike Christianity and Islamic society is totally unlike Western society, which makes understanding the Muslim world nearly impossible for people of the West. For example, every assumption we make about standards of fair play, morality, truth, shared sense of community, and humane conduct are unknown, are in fact considered weak, contemptible, and even ridiculous, in the Muslim world. Islam began as a Bedouin tribal religion, and rather than transforming that society, it reinforced the most retrograde tribal influences, such that Islamic society remains tribal in culture and outlook to this day.

Christianity evolved from its Hebrew origins to become a universal religion that served as the foundation for Western civil society, something entirely alien to Islamic tribal society. Jesus, born into Israeli tribal society, was anti-tribal in his teaching, preaching forgiveness and the golden rule, love and charity for neighbors, and peace and goodwill to all. Interestingly, the word "love" (which translates the Greek word *agape* used by Paul in Corinthians I, 13) does not appear in the Qur'an.

Claims by apologists that Islam shares the moral and ethical teachings of Christianity or Judaism simply are not confirmed by the history and practice of Islam. Under the close scrutiny of mainly British and Americans, the Muslim world has superficially cleaned up its act. For example, Saudi Arabia finally 'abolished' slavery in 1972 (although de facto slavery continues). But the status of women cannot be resolved because Islamic tribal society considers women to be chattel (although stoning or beheading of adulterous wives is now kept to a minimum).

Tribal societies are founded on principles of dishonor and revenge, which require taking every possible means (however dishonorable they might appear to people of the West) to avenge an insult or injury to a member of the tribe. As Nawab Bugti a clan leader in Baluchistan said in 2006: *What is better than seeing your enemies driven before you and then taking their women to bed?* Murdering women, children, and other defenseless victims is not considered dishonorable, is in fact considered admirable in the Muslim world, where taking advantage of a weak or defenseless opponent simply makes good sense. Muslims have no concept of "fair play", a notion they consider absurd so far as one gives up an advantage, assumes an unnecessary risk, for no corresponding advantage or gain.

Islam is uniquely suited to provide 'religious' sanction for personal neuroses and psychoses. Arabs are full of anger, rage and hate because of their upbringing in Bedouin derived tribal society. Raised to develop willfulness and egoism within their family setting, they are subjected as adults to humiliation and subordination in the Islamic world at large, which their superiors impose on inferiors as a means of showing their superiority.

Hence, lifelong resentment and hostility are embedded in every Muslim, and revenge is his sole satisfaction and objective in life. Instead of faith, hope and love, they have anger, rage and hate, which intensify the desire for revenge common to all Islamic tribal groups. Islam requires very little of the 'faithful' and provides much scope for personal and tribal resentment and revenge.

Any interpretation is possible by any Imam, Ayatollah, or individual who claims to be a Mahdi, such as Osama bin Laden. Islam makes no mention of forgiveness, brotherly love much less Paul's faith, hope, and love, the very foundation of Christianity. Because the differences between Western civil and Islamic tribal society are so great, and because the Islamic/Arabic outlook threatens to be a source of world disorder for the indefinite future, a clear understanding of the origins of Islam and the Arabic outlook is of enormous importance. No successful policy to deal with Islamic terrorism, the direct product of the Islamic faith, can be developed without such understanding.

Muhammad and the Origins of Islam

Muhammad ibn Abdallah ibn Abd al-Muttalib was born in 570 in Mecca (a trading post along the caravan route between Syria and Yemen) within the Bedouin tribal society of Arabia. Muhammad belonged to the Banu Hasim clan of the Quraysh tribe. The Quraysh were bandits who preyed on trade caravans, and theft, murder, feuds, tribal wars, idol worship, and exposure of female children were common in Bedouin tribal society. Muhammad's grandfather was keeper of the Ka'bah stone and temple in Mecca, which was dedicated to the worship of Allah, the ancient Semitic God.

Arabs were influenced by the Hebrew *Torah.* They believed that the Ka'bah temple was originally constructed by Adam and reconstructed by Abraham (who was not considered to be a Hebrew) and his son Ishmail, from whom the Arabs believe they descend. Abraham set the Ka'bah stone in a wall of the temple and it was revered by Arabs as a holy relic. It was the destination of annual pilgrimages by tribes throughout Arabia, and a source of income for the Quraysh. At the time of the birth of Muhammad, the original monotheistic worship had been corrupted by a number of tribes who placed Bedouin pagan idols in the temple as well. Muhammad worked in the caravan trade as a camel driver and merchant and apparently had "visions" throughout his life. During this period a number of monotheist Arabs called Hanifs had rejected idolatry for a purified vision of One God. This group influenced Muhammad.

Beginning in 610, he received divine revelations imparted in discourses with the Angel Gabriel, called The Recitation or Qur'an. They continued for two years before he began to communicate them to his wife Khadijah, and others of his family.

His teaching began in Mecca and spread slowly against much resistance by Quraysh and other tribes. Muhammad allegedly drew on Hebrew and Christian teachings and included the Torah, Psalms of David, and Gospels as holy books of Islam. Abraham, Moses, and Jesus were respected holy precursors, but Muhammad is considered to be the last and greatest Prophet. Jews and Christians had gone astray by corrupting scriptures and worshipping Jesus as God. Muhammad restored the original Semitic religion of Abraham by worshipping One God. Islam means submission, absolute submission or resignation to the will of God.

Because the evangelical style of the Hebrew texts directly influenced the language of Muhammad, the moral, ethical, and religious teaching of the Qur'an has a biblical ring. What most surprises a Western reader are the Bedouin tribal outlook, beliefs, and practices reflected in the Qur'an, which make Islam a tribal, not a universal, religion and constitute the main obstacle to modernization of the Islamic world.

Qur'an and the Teachings of Islam

Muhammad was illiterate, but probably learned of the Hebrew sacred texts from his grandfather and regularly met Jews and Christians in the course of his extensive trading activities. The Qur'an consists of Muhammad's dialogs with the Angel Gabriel, which convey the word of God. The scattered transcriptions of his sayings made during his lifetime were finally compiled during the second Khalifate of Umar and set in final form during the third Khalifate of Uthman (644-56).

The Qur'an necessarily is repetitive, since it includes scattered accounts of Muhammad's sayings over more than 20 years. It is arranged roughly by length (longest to shortest) of the pronouncements, rather than in their chronological order, which was impossible to determine. The Qur'an is a random mixture of exhortation, rhetorical riffs characteristic of Old Testament prophetic style and admonitions to women (including one directed at his wives) to obey their husbands, along with descriptions of paradise. [Qur'an 66:1-4 Hafsah, one of Muhammad's wives, caught him having sex with a Coptic slave from whom he had promised he would separate. Hafsah told 'A'ishah, another of Muhammad's wives, and Muhammad obscurely reproves Hafsah for conspiring against him.]

Whatever claims may be made for the beauty and moral elevation of the Qur'an, they must refer to the original Arabic. Translations indicate nothing that rises to the beauty of the Psalms, the ethical scope of the Ten Commandments, the moral fervor of Isaiah, the noble humanity of the Sermon on the Mount, the sublimity of Paul's sermon on faith, hope, and charity in Corinthians I. Compared to the ardent and inspired passages of the Old and New Testaments, the Qur'an is rhetorical and uninspiring.

But religious teaching does not require literary excellence or spiritual loftiness if it presents humane guidance for the human passage. In this respect the Qur'an is especially perplexing. None of the standard commentary (based on alleged untranslatable nuances and complexities in the Arabic dialects) that attempts to dismiss or wish away the sources of this perplexity is convincing, since we have the plain words of Muhammad himself. Among the most disturbing elements of the Qur'an for Westerners are Islamic Paradise, the role of women and marriage, the lack of sacraments as we understand them, and the ambivalent attitude toward nonbelievers.

Paradise as bordello

Paradise (or Hell) in the eschatological sense is the destination of the believer after death, a direct consequence of resurrection and eternal life under good or bad conditions. Christians describe paradise as a mostly sex-free (despite resurrection of the body) indeterminate state of spiritual ecstasy contemplating the presence of God. Both men and women enter the Christian paradise, but no particular activity or setting other than "many mansions" is described. Hell and its horrors are more vividly described in secular and ecclesiastical Western texts, perhaps because the terror aroused by Hell was more likely to motivate sinners to good behavior than any anodyne description of Heaven ever could. Avoiding the worst is humanly a more persuasive argument than contemplating the best.

Islam is quite different from Christianity. In Islam, only male believers are resurrected for the afterlife in Paradise. Motivation to belief and orthodoxy is incited by descriptions of a Muslim paradise that the Christian paradise can't match in detail or seductiveness. Muhammad describes paradise many times in the Qur'an, repeating the rewards to be enjoyed with almost pornographic relish. His description matches the fantasy of every Arab male adolescent: slaves to do the work, endless food and wine, beautiful compliant women ("dark-eyed, virgin, bashful, high-bosomed, loving"). A few excerpts from the Qur'an give the general idea.

> *As for the righteous, they shall be lodged amidst gardens and fountains, arrayed in rich silks and fine brocade. Yes, and we shall wed them to dark-eyed houris. (44:49-52)*
> *Fruits we shall give them, and such meats as they desire. (52:18)*
> *Therein are bashful virgins whom neither man nor jinee will have touched before. Virgins as fair as corals and rubies. (55:47-61)*
> *There shall be virgins chaste and fair. Dark-eyed virgins sheltered in their tents whom neither man nor jinee will have touched before. They shall recline on green cushions and fine carpets. (55:63-76)*

> *They shall recline on jeweled couches....and theirs shall be the dark-eyed houris chaste as hidden pearls. We created the houris and made them virgins, loving companions for those on the right hand: a multitude from the men of old, and a multitude from the later generations. (56:13-19)*
>
> *Their's shall be gardens and vineyards, and high-bosomed maidens for companions. (78:31-33)*

A rather pathetic attempt by Muslim scholars to mitigate this impression by translating *houris* as 'raisins' is somewhat belied by the term 'high-bosomed'. Such rewards for the faithful made recruiting easier, playing on Semitic obsessions with sex and virginity, desert privation and oasis abandon, and the descriptions of brocade and silks show the hand of the experienced merchant.

Making endless sex the ultimate reward paid off. Centuries later a Shi'a Ismaili sect called Assassins (Crusader corruption of the word *Hashshashin*) allegedly drugged candidates with hashish then put them in garden with maidens who fulfilled their every fantasy. When awakened they were told they had experienced the joys of Paradise available to those who die in the service of Allah. Most were understandably eager to join. They learned how to carry out assassinations (which often included suicide), focusing on the kill in total disregard of personal safety or escape. They learned how to use dagger and poisons and methods of disguise to infiltrate the enemy camp. Much of this sounds like Al-Qaeda, and this form of paradise may be, however banal, the principal motivation of suicide bombers today.

Obsession with female virginity (the only value women have as persons because it is the only guarantee of patrimony), strict confinement of women (women never associate with males on social occasions or appear in public with males other than members of their family), and dress codes that prohibit any display of physical charms (the Burkha is a fantastic Islamic contraption that conceals a woman entirely) contrast with the sexual fantasies, obsessions, and frustrations of Muslim males, for which the Qur'an offers prospective, albeit post mortem, relief. An after-life of continuous copulation with beautiful women helps assuage the frustrations caused by refractory conditions in real life that thwart the libido of Muslim males. They enviously watch the wealthy who can create this paradise on earth, which is what the oil Sheikhs do whenever they leave their homelands and in private at home. Of course, males everywhere have such proclivities, but an afterlife of endless fornication is a reward unique to Islam.

Women as Chattel

The Islamic treatment of women is appalling. Many Muslim women step forward to extol the joys of polygamy, seclusion (purdah), denial of education and personal freedom and growth, but Westerners remain unconvinced.

Women do not share the prospect of Paradise in Islam, and no alternative venue to accommodate their needs is described or promised in the Qur'an. Muhammad may give women more consideration than they enjoyed in traditional Bedouin society (he strongly opposed exposure of female children, a common tribal practice), but the overall impression is that they are chattel, of higher value and importance than property and livestock, but not by much.

Women may look forward to a life of subordination, obedience, submission, especially sexual submission (*'Women are your fields: go, then, into your fields whence you please.'* 2:228), and silence. The superiority of men is a fiat of heaven. *Men have authority over women because God has made the one superior to the other and because they spend their wealth to maintain them. Good women are obedient. (4:34-36)* The most charming of the many proscriptions placed on female behavior comes in Qur'an 24:30: *Let them not stamp their feet when walking so as to reveal their hidden trinkets.* Perhaps the spirit of rebellion had a life of its own under the burkha.

Islamic Marriage

Be to me as my mother's back.
(Bedouin declaration of divorce.)

Bedouin traditionally perform intercourse from behind. The only female absolutely forbidden to an Islamic male is his mother, hence the reference.

In Christianity, only monogamy is permitted, and marriage is a sacrament, joining a man and a woman in an indissoluble union of love in the presence of and blessed by God. Marriage as a religious sacrament has played a major role in humanizing Western society. It reflects the equal dignity of women with men in the Christian plan for salvation. Whether an individual marriage lives up to the Christian ideal or not, the positive influence of the ideal has been incalculable. Islam, in contrast, considers marriage to be a secular contract of no religious significance. Further, women have no religious significance in the Qur'an. Women are not considered to be equal to men and are not destined for Paradise, so marriage is mainly for procreation of sons and the personal enjoyment of the male. Wives are referred to by the name of their eldest son, for example Mother (Umm) of Mansour, indicating both her role and importance. (Sadaam Husein's 'Mother of All Battles' derives from this practice.) In the Koran, the prophet recommended that believers confine themselves to no more than four wives at a time, but he placed no limit on the number of slaves and concubines. Other than recommending some decency toward wives and female slaves, women are accorded little significance in the Islamic canon.

Of course women have no say about whom they marry and are disposed of by the male patriarch for the advantage of the clan or tribe. Unfortunately, marriage brings no security. Divorce is easy for the male, a matter of renouncing the wife in the Mosque four times. The only constraint might be the need to maintain some favorable relationship with the wife's clan. Because only the well-off can acquire a large number of wives to display their superior position and gratify their sexual appetites, most Muslim males practice serial polygamy, marrying five or six times in a lifetime.

Islam has no Sacraments

Unlike Christianity, Islam has no sacraments. A Christian sacrament brings the individual believer in direct communion with Christ/God. The Catholic Church established seven sacraments: baptism, confirmation, Eucharist or communion, penance or confession, extreme unction, ordination (for priests), and marriage. They are characterized mainly by the individual's communion with Christ mediated by the priest, which makes all the sacraments a personal communion that is witnessed by the priest or by the priest and the congregation. Protestantism altered the sacraments, but the sacramental principle remained.

Islam is a religion of absolute submission (the meaning of the word Islam) to the all-powerful Allah. This submission requires five duties: statement of belief in one God, prayers five times daily, donations to charity, fasting during Ramadan, and pilgrimage to Mecca once in a lifetime.

The relationship to Allah is generic rather than personal and, in some sense, irresponsible, since it focuses on submission to fate rather than individual character and responsibility. This call to obliterate the will and submit to fate inclines Muslims to collective hysteria rather than individual growth and responsibility. In contrast, Christianity does not wish to obliterate the individual's will, rather it engages the individual's free will to join with God in conscious effort to achieve salvation and make a better world.

Unbelievers

Islamic spokesmen have developed a complicated apologetics for dealing with Western concerns about the teachings of Muhammad regarding unbelievers. They emphasize that Jihad is not holy war, but rather a 'quest for personal virtue and enlightenment'. Passages in the Qur'an that raise concerns are never to be interpreted as written, no matter how clearly written they may be.

1. *Believers, do not make friends with any but your own people. Unbelievers will spare no pains to corrupt you. They desire nothing but your ruin. Their hatred is evident from what they utter with their mouths, but greater is the hatred which their breasts conceal. (3:118)*
2. *Let not the unbelievers think that they will ever get away.... Muster against them all the men and cavalry at your command, so that you may strike terror into the enemy of God and your enemy....(8:59)*
3. *Believers, make war on the infidels who dwell around you. Deal firmly with them. (9:123)*
4. *He forbids you to make friends with those who have fought against you on account of your religion and driven you from your homes or abetted others to drive you out. Those that make friends with them are wrongdoers. (60:7)*
5. *The unbelievers are your inveterate enemies. (4:97)*
6. *Believers, make war on the infidels who dwell around you. Deal firmly with them. Know that God is with the righteous. (9:121)*
7. *Make war on them (unbelievers) until idolatry shall cease and God's religion shall reign supreme. (8:36)*

Unfortunately, the text seems to speak for itself. The hostile intent of Islam toward unbelievers remains a lurking threat in the back of the Westerner's mind no matter how much is made of the peaceful and nonviolent intentions of the Prophet. This is not to say that the West has not expressed aggressive and hostile intentions toward Islam. Perhaps the best summary of this standoff is *Qur'an 11:121-122: Say to the infidels: 'Do whatever lies within your power, and so shall we. Wait if you will; we too are waiting.'*

Whatever the correct interpretation, the Qur'an does offer considerable incentives to those who are prepared to fight and die for the faith, perhaps eagerly given the reward in view.

> *Never think that those who were slain in the cause of God are dead. They are alive, and well provided for by their Lord. (3:169-170) As for those who are slain in the cause of God, He will not allow their works to perish...He will admit them to the Paradise He has made known to them. (47:3)*

Spread of Islam and the Arabic Outlook

> *Do not split up your religion into sects, each exulting in its own beliefs. (Qur'an 10:33)*

Although Muhammad claimed to build upon the teachings of Judaism and Christianity and to borrow ethical values from both, the humanizing elements of Islam have never had much influence on the way Muslim tribal society actually works. Islam spread the Arabic Outlook of Bedouin tribal tradition throughout the Muslim domains. This Outlook predominates, from Morocco to Pakistan and Indonesia, wherever Islam prevails. The Arabic Outlook also influences Spain and Latin America to the extent that Spain adopted many aspects of the Arabic Outlook during the 700 years of Muslim occupation. A summary of its main characteristics follows.

The Arabic Outlook is tribal. Tribal organization centers on the tribe, clan, or extended family group. The tribe is patriarchal. The head of the tribe controls all wealth and property and makes all decisions, including decisions about marriage. Tribal societies usually are polygamous. Each male has as many wives and concubines as his station requires and his means allow. Women are regarded as chattel. Women unrelated to the tribe and ineligible for marriage are considered fair game to be exploited sexually and economically. Women members of the tribal family are sequestered to prevent contact with males outside the family group. Tribal societies are also patrilocal. Married couples live with the husband's father. Marriage is often endogamous, in which marriage of first and second cousins is practiced to preserve the integrity of the tribe.

The cohesive force of Islamic tribal societies is **revenge**, which gives each member a socially patterned vector for relieving deep personal frustrations and anger against outsiders. Each member of the tribe or clan is required to avenge any dishonor to any other member of the clan. Alliances with other tribes and clans may occur, usually as a way to gain advantage over a common adversary. Such arrangements are always temporary and dissolve when the advantage of one or the other party is no longer served. Tribal society focuses only on its own interests and has no interest in or concern for people outside the tribe. Cooperation between tribal societies or clans lasts only so long as advantageous. The reason is that the unifying principle of revenge in tribal society is no substitute for the power of solidarity common to civil society.

Islamic tribes never developed a higher form of unity such as the State. Loyalties are always tribal, personal, and parochial. That is why despite great wealth and the talents of their people, Muslim States have failed to develop cohesion and sustained cooperation to pursue their mutual interests. This is the great advantage Israel has in confronting a vastly superior number of hostile Muslim states. They have no sense of solidarity.

Islamic marriages are endogamous whereas Western marriages are exogamous. First cousins are allowed to marry *(Qur'an 33:50)*. The genetic disadvantages of inbreeding are somewhat mitigated because few brothers and sisters, uncles and aunts, have the same mother. Women must wait to marry until a male cousin decides whether or not he wants to marry her. A brother has the option of marrying his brother's widow.

In the Arabic Outlook, women are regarded primarily as breeders of sons and instruments for sexual gratification, not full human beings who deserve the opportunity to grow and develop their own talents and fulfill their own hopes and aspirations. They are not considered equal partners by their husbands, or as life companions who share love and respect. All social occasions are between men. Women do not mix socially with men and are confined to the company of women. Depending on their wealth and circumstances, Arabs have multiple wives. Rulers commonly have a dozen or more. Most Muslim men marry only one wife at a time, due to the expense involved in keeping several wives, but five or six wives over a lifetime is not uncommon, in addition to regular extramarital escapades. Arabic men do not attempt or seek mutual sexual gratification with women and have no concern for a woman's need for love and affection. Bedouins traditionally perform intercourse from behind, a purely physical act of pleasure for the male, lacking intimacy, caring, and mutual affection.

This degraded view of women typical of the Arabic outlook has had disastrous effects. It reinforces the regressive social and personal conditions typical of Arabic/Islamic states today. Wives live with their husbands' family. The mother-in-law rules the new wife, who has no rights or property to protect her. This humiliating situation is mitigated only when she bears her first son, the only important function she performs. Sons are the only unqualified relationship women have, and they consequently seek to indulge them in order to retain the attachment. Arabic males are raised to develop willfulness, egoism, and violent temperament. They are 'spoiled' by constant maternal and paternal admiration. No discipline is applied, since cultivating will is required to compete in Arabic society and is the principal objective of male child raising.

Arabic men are therefore entirely egocentric, have no concern for anyone but themselves or at most their own tribe, are incapable of sustained commitments or steady application to work, acknowledge no limits to the expression of their pleasure or frustration, and are subject to extreme violent behavior when thwarted. Examples abound. In 1951,

Saudi Prince Mishari bin Abdul Aziz, aged nineteen, attended a party given by British vice consul Cyril Ousman. A disagreement developed, the Prince left the party, returned with a gun, and proceeded to spray bullets into the Ousman home, killing Cyril. His wife was pensioned off by the Saudi royal family. In 1975, Prince Faisal ibn Musa'id shot his uncle King Faisal because the King had imposed a travel ban on him following a series of notorious drunken and drugged escapades in the United States where he attended a number of colleges for short periods. Such emotional instability is typical of the Arabic personality. It is also expressed in bouts of extreme religious fanaticism. Musa'id's brother had been killed following an attack on a television station which he sought to destroy. Following a period of dissipation in Europe he suddenly got religion and advocated extreme austerity and a purified Islam. Such irrational changes in temperament are common among males formed in the Arabic outlook.

Arabic men have no concern for people below them in society, and have complete contempt for honest labor. They readily abuse workers and laborers, have no respect or concern for people outside their tribe, and little enough for those within their tribe. Fathers exploit sons and daughters, and they in turn are expected to do the same to those under them. Arabs have no concern for the environment, for nature, or for wildlife. They consider God's creation as simply available for their use and enjoyment with no intrinsic value or higher purpose. All these destructive attitudes and behaviors are typical of the tribal Arabic Outlook and prevail today throughout the Islamic world. Saudi Arabia, Bahrain, Kuwait and the United Arab Emirites are tribes, not states, and are run as personal fiefs of the ruling families and clans, despite the flags and paraphernalia of nation states.

The orgasmic fantasy Paradise of Islam, like the debasement of women, also has a drastic retardant effect on the Islamic world. Islamic society trains Muslim males to be willful, egotistical, and violent in asserting their desires and whims. In effect, they never mature. They are indulged as children to display temper and assert their will against others. They are also sensitive to any slight and are quick to take offense. As adults confronting a world indifferent to their preferences, they are humiliated when forced to fawn on male superiors who have been raised as they have. Resentment, desire for revenge, and long-range conspiring to get even and improve their opportunities are rampant among males in Muslim tribal societies. With so many frustrated egotists running around, much of their resentment is vented on women, children, social inferiors, animals, the environment, and religious enemies.

War, Murder, Schism: Islam and the First Khalifas

The first two decades of Islam following the death of Muhammad established the pattern of murder, war, and tribal conflict that has prevailed in Islamic society to the present. Schism, murder, and intertribal warfare became endemic in the first century of Islam. This is partly because Islam, from the start was spread by warfare not persuasion and was used to secure supremacy of the Prophet's Hashemite tribe over other Bedouin tribes. Successors to the Prophet, the Khalifas, also used Islam to gain supremacy for whatever tribe they belonged to.

Muhammad was a member of the Quraysh tribe of the Bedouin Banu Hashim clan in the Hejaz region of what is now Saudi Arabia. When he died in 632, consistent with ancient tribal tradition, the sheikhs and tribal elders met to select a successors or Khalifa, from within the Hashim clan. The Khalifa became ruler of Muslim believers because there was no separation between religion and state. The Khalifa usually assigned secular administrative duties to a Vizier and military duties to an Emir.

As more distant Bedouin clans fell away from the faith in the absence of Muhammad the first Khalifa Abu Bakr led his armies against the recreants in the first Jihad, or holy war, and eventually defeated all the enemies of Islam in Arabia. Flushed with success, and mounted on camels that gave them speed and mobility they then conquered Damascus in Syria.

The second Khalifa Umar ibn al-Khattab succeeded Abu Bakr in 634. He conquered Iraq Persia (636), Jerusalem (640), and Egypt (646). The turning point came with the death of Khalifa Umar, who was murdered by a Persian slave. Uthman ibn Affan of the Umayyad clan was selected as the third Khalifa. He promptly remove all Hashemite clansmen from authority and placed members of his own clan in control. Civil war was temporarily averted when Khalifa Uthman was murdered by a son of Abu Bakr (the first Khalifa and a Hashemite). Ali ibn abi-Talib, who had married the Prophet's daughter Fatima, became the fourth Khalifa in 656. Tribal strife resumed when Ali moved to replace all Umayyad officials with members of the Hashim tribe. Muawiya, head of the Umayyad clan refused to give up his governorship of Syria, and civil war began in earnest.

The first fundamentalist sect Khawarij, similar to the Wahhabi sect of present day Saudi Arabia, formed around Muawiya. Khawarij sought to purge Islam of impurities, declared Uthman and Ali traitors, advocated punctilious observance of the Korean, and called on all Muslims to join a Jihad to imposed Islam on Unbelievers. Irresolution on the part of Ali, whose primary base was in Iraq, led to disillusionment with his leadership within the Hashemite clan and he was murdered in 660.

Muawiza then declared himself Khalifa, moved the headquarters of state from Medina and Mecca to Damascus, in Syria, and announced that his son Yazid would succeed him. Thus the Umayyad dynasty was established, which conquered North Africa and Spain (710) with help from Berber tribesmen, and threatened France until Charles Martel held the line at Tours in 732, eventually leading to their withdrawal from France. Muslims in Iraq remained loyal to Ali and founded the Shi'a sect.

In 749, the Umayyads were overthrown by the Abbasids, a Shi'a faction that became Sunni once in power. They founded the city of Baghdad, Iraq, and moved the central government of the Islamic world from

Damascus. In 761, Abd al-Rahman, an Umayyad survivor, established an independent Emirate in Cordoba Spain. Three of the first four Khalifa were murdered. In 680, Husayn, Ali's son and the grandson of Muhammad, was brutally murdered along with his son by Umayyad forces at Karbala in Iraq. Commemoration of his death is the most solemn event in the Shi'a calendar. To provide a Christian analogy, it is as if Matthew murdered Mark, John murdered Matthew, Peter murdered John, and Paul murdered Peter.

Islamic Law

Islamic law is the principal subject of study in the Muslim world, unlike Western Universities where a broad curriculum offers a wide range of subjects and presents heterodox views. In Islam, each school seeks orthodoxy and conformity, not originality. Several schools of jurisprudence or legal systems were developed. All are based on differing interpretations and emphases of Islamic law in the Qur'an, the Hadith, and the lives of the Prophet and his Companions. Sharia, or Islamic law, is the sum of all these legal systems. The principal schools were the following:

Hanafi, developed by Abu Hanifah, derived and codified rulings in five categories of human action: the forbidden, the disapproved, the permitted, the Sunna or voluntary virtuous, and the mandatory. These provided the basis for legal arguments by Islamic legal scholars before a *qadi* (judge), or for obtaining *fatwas* (religious rulings of an imam) based on the fundamental texts of Islam. Hanafi is considered the most tolerant school of Islamic law and is followed in Turkey, the Balkans, Central Asia, Chinese Turkestan, Afghanistan, Pakistan, and India. ***Malikis,*** based on legal traditions developed in Medina by Malik ibn Anas is followed in Muslim Spain and North and West Africa. ***Shafi'is,*** is based on the Hadith and use of analogy. This school, developed by Muhammad ibn al-Shafii, a student of ibn Anas, prevails in Egypt, the Arab states of the Middle East, the Kurds, and Muslims in the Indian Ocean and Southeast Asia.

Hanbalis, developed by Ahmad ibn Hanbal, is based on fundamentalist theology and stresses use of authentic Hadith in preference to analogy. This school dominates the Arabian Peninsula.

Differences between the schools include determining when Ramadan begins. Hanafis accept the testimony of two male witnesses or one male and two virtuous women who observe a new moon as sufficient to confirm the start of Ramadan. If clouds obscure the sky, one such witness suffices. Malikis accept the word of two Muslims of good morals, regardless of sex. Shaf'i require only one honorable Muslim man. Hanbali accept the word of one honorable man or woman. Punishments also differ by school and by region. Such picayune distinctions indicate the introverted character of Shaf'i require only one honorable Muslim man as witness. Hanbali accept the word of one honorable man or woman. Punishments also differ by school and by region. Such picayune distinctions indicate the introverted character of Islamic 'law' as compared to the West, which is based on the great system of Roman Law, European common law, and the Renaissance revisions of these systems.

Mysticism

Muslim mysticism, known as *Sufi*, developed in 12th to 14th Centuries, perhaps influenced by Mongol and Turkish invaders. Its practitioners were widely revered for their holy quest for divine love, sainthood and union with God. The Mongols conquered Baghdad in 1258 and converted to Islam. Under their rule *Sufism* developed throughout Central Asia and several Sufi orders were established. *Qadiris* formed around 1100 consists of disciplined, strict practitioners of the codified Sunna, were fighters on behalf of the faith, but also preached by example. *Rifa'is* formed by an Iraqi around 1200 practiced body piercing, cutting the flesh, swallowing burning coals, and handling poisonous snakes as ecstatic affirmation of faith, practices derived from Mongol shamans.

Naqshbandis established in the late 1300's are strict Sunnis and became famous for their popular preaching, devotion to *Sunna* and *Shariah*, and their warlike courage in defending Islam. *Bektashi* are *Shi'a* and known for heterodox practices such as drinking alcohol. They gained influence under the Ottoman Turks, and adopted Turkish as a devotional language instead of Persian or Arabic.

The Turkish conquest of Constantinople in 1453 was a supreme triumph for Islam, but under the Ottoman Turks, the focus of the Islamic world shifted unrecognizably to North Africa, Central Asia, Anatolia, and India and to sustained conflict with European nations in the Balkans. Arabic Islam fell into obscurity and backwardness. The reconquest of Spain in 1492 somewhat offset the loss to the West of Constantinople. The Turkish naval defeat at Lepanto in 1600 and military defeat before Vienna in 1656 began the reconquest of Christian territory from the Turks over the next two centuries. This set the stage for the resurgence of Arabic fundamentalism beginning in 1750.

Mullah, Mosque, Madrassa

The practice of Islam is focused on the Mosque, headed by a Mullah trained in the teachings of Islam who leads prayers and preaches sermons on Friday. The mosque is the center of social life. Contributions of alms required by the Qur'an are given to the Mullah for distribution to the needy and deserving. Friday prayers and a sermon by the Mullah are attended by the faithful. The community commonly accepts the Mullah as a guide and leader and follows Mullah or Ulema fatwas (legal rulings and pronouncements based on interpretation of the Qur'an) without question. Islamic schooling consists of study at a Madrassa where the Talib (student) completes the following course of study taught by an Ulema and Islamic scholar well versed in the teaching of the Qur'an: *Learning the Qur'an by heart*; *Interpreting the Qur'an*; *Islamic jurisprudence*; *Islamic law*; *Life and sayings of the Prophet Muhammad*; *Spreading the word of God*; *Islamic philosophy*; *Arabic language*; *Mathematics*.

This is only the form of education in most of the Muslim world. It is more religious indoctrination than learning. Lacking any central authority, Islamic Mullahs (or Ayatollahs in the Shi'a sect) and Madrassas vary in quality and have considerable latitude to develop independently. Many rural Madrassas are rudimentary affairs. Some are major institutions, like the Haqqania Madrassa in northern Pakistan, which offers high school to Master and Ph.D. degrees in Islamic studies and enrolls several thousand Talibs (the name adopted by the Taliban). Haqqania Madrassa trained many of the Taliban in Afghanistan and was a recruiting ground for Pakistani fighters for the Taliban.

Because Westerners assume an Islamic Mullah corresponds in role and ministry to a Catholic Priest or Protestant Minister, Mullah pronouncements (fatwas) can come as a considerable shock. Mullah Omar of the Taliban authorized a two-hour massacre of opponents in 1996 as fully sanctioned by the Qur'an. (It went on for two days.) Wahabbi cleric Yusuf al-Qaradawi in Qatar, issued a fatwa in 2001 declaring that suicide bombing is martyrdom, not suicide, and supported the Taliban against the United States in Afghanistan. Saudi Wahabbi Mullah Sheikh Saad al-Buraik in April 2002 preached murder of Israeli men and rape of Israeli women. Mullah Muqtada al- Sadr, an Iraqi Shi'a, conspired in the 2003 suicide bombing assassination of Ayatollah Mohammad Baqir al-Hakim, a revered Shi'a cleric, because he was willing to cooperate with the provisional coalition government set up by the United States after the defeat of Saddam Hussein. As we shall see, such pronouncements are fully in character with the practices of Islamic society.

Tribal Islam

Rival Bedouin tribes sought the Khalifa as a means to enrich their members, not to govern with and for the benefit of believers. No sense of common interest, mutual respect, and spirit of compromise ever developed in the Muslim world. This is due to the Arabic outlook that dominated the society and the tendency of Islam to reinforce rather than counter the worst tribal characteristics within the Islamic world.

For example, some Hashemite refused to accept the Umayyads when Khalifa Ali was murdered, believing that the succession should fall to Husayn, the son of Ali and Fatima. They formed the Shiat Ali (followers of Ali) sect, which eventually took root in Persia and now represent 50 percent of the population of Iran. Shiites make up only 15 percent of Muslims today, but they number some 60 million believers. They are led by an Ayatollah (Imam equivalent), or teacher, considered infallible because their teaching came from Allah through Muhammad to Ali. The 12th Imam Muhammad disappeared in 878 and is expected to return before the end of the world as the Mahdi.

Shiites, considered as the radicals or fundamentalists of Islam, eventually split into more than seventy sub-sects. One sub-sect formed around the belief that it was the 7th Imam Ismail, not the 12th, who was the Mahdi or Expected One. Another sect was formed in Persia from the Ismaili group just before the first crusade. The sect known as Assassins in the West claimed the right to murder anyone who stood in its way. They trained suicide squads of young men ready to kill and die for the faith. Shiites have always been able to form death squads of young believers ready to die for the faith, such as the Hezbollah in Syria and Palestine.

The greatest number of Muslims (85 percent) are Sunni who follow the Sunna or "path" set down in the Koran and the Hadith or sayings and acts of Muhammad. Sunni and Shiite are normally irreconcilably opposed, as during the first Crusade when Sunni Syria and Shiite Egypt were played off against each other by the Christians until Saladin briefly united the opposing factions to drive off the Christians.

Saudi Arabia and Wahhabism

The most momentous event in modern Islam occurred in the 18th Century with the simultaneous founding of the Saudi dynasty and the

Wahhabi sect. This marked the beginning of militant Islam, which led to al-Qaeda and 9/11. Modern Saudi Arabia was founded in 1747. Muhammad ibn Sa'ud of the A Sa'ud family of the Bani Hanifah tribe which ruled the Najd region of what is now Saudi Arabia joined with Muhammad Ibn Abd al-Wahab of the Al Sheikh family of the Banu Tamin tribe to form the nucleus of the present state of Saudi Arabia. Wahabbism, an austere, radical, intolerant, and violent sect formed by Muhammad as-Wahab, claimed to return Islam to what he believed was its uncorrupted and true belief at the time of the Prophet and the first Caliphs. It was partly a rejection of Turkish political rule and domination of Islamic teaching. But it was also a tribal rejection even of the Prophet, celebration of whose birthday was anathema to Wahabbism. In effect, Wahabbism sought to reinvent Islam as a religion of the Nadj tribes and to eliminate influences of other tribal leaders of Islam, including the Hashemite Muhammad himself. Wahabbism reinterprets tradition and rejects all other influences and schools within Islam, including Sunni, Shi'a, Sufi, and other sects and authorities. Wahabbis are fanatical purifiers of what they perceived to be corruptions of Islam, such as Shiism, Sufism, the schools of law, commemoration of the birth of the Prophet, revered sites and buildings, and methods of decorating and designing mosques. They reject any association with nonbelievers and especially with corrupted Muslim sects. Wahabbis, joined with the ruthless Sa'ud tribal leaders, began a conquest of the Saudi Arabia which eventually, under Ibn Saud, became a protectorate of Britain. By 1932 he had control of the all the territory and the Kingdom of Saudi Arabia was proclaimed.

The Saudi state consists of the rule of Sa'ud family and the Wahhabi cult, which controls all aspects of private and public life, although Wahabbism makes up only 40 percent of the Muslim population of Saudi Arabia. Only tribal allies from Najd have a role in the government and security apparatus of the State. All other tribes are ruthlessly repressed, even to the point of forced conversion to Wahhabism, which is currently being imposed on the eastern Shiites, who are suspect because of their co-religionists in Iran and nearby Iraq.

Discovery and development of the world's largest oil reserves, located in the Shiite eastern province enriched the Saudi ruling group beyond their most fantastic dreams. As the sponsor of the most violent Muslim sect, the Saudis have funded Wahabbi proselytizing throughout the globe. Saudis sponsored Wahabbi terrorist resistance groups in Palestine, Kashmir, and Afghanistan. Wahhabi infiltrate Muslim communities worldwide. Their objective is to drive traditional Muslims (Sunni, Shia, Sufi, etc.) from mosques and place Wahhabism in control. This has been done in Russia, Europe, the United States, Latin America, and throughout the Muslim world.

Wahabi Infiltration of the United States

In the 1980's, the Wahabbists established themselves in the United States, taking control of mosques by using their inexhaustible source of Saudi funds from the Islamic Development Bank, and by establishing lobby groups and front organizations to influence government and public opinion and raise funds for terrorist groups. (Wahabbis within the San Diego mosque provided accommodations for several months for two of the 9/11 high-jackers.)

Front organizations include the Muslim Public Affairs Council, the Council on American-Islamic Relations (strong supporter of Hamas), the American Muslim Alliance (which distributes literature denying the Holocaust occurred), and the Islamic Society of North America, which enforces Wahabbism on the 1,200 officially recognized mosques in the United States. Subsidiary groups include the Islamic Circle of North America, the Islamic Association for Palestine (a supporter of Hamas), American Muslims for Jerusalem, the Muslim Public Affairs Council, and the Islamic Institute. The Holy Land Foundation for Relief and Development (HLF) was founded in 1989 and headquartered in Texas with branches in other cities.. It served as a fundraiser for Hamas and the other groups until President Bush shut down the HLF in 2001.

The Saar Foundation, founded in Northern Virginia by Suleiman Abdul Al-Aziz al Rahji member of one of Saudi Arabia's richest families, also raised funds for Wahhabi extremist groups. Wealthy Saudi's are the main support for extremism, including Osama bin Laden. Saar is connected with Khalid bin Mahfouz, former financial adviser to the Saudi royal family and ex head of the National Commercial Bank of Saudi Arabia, who backed Osama bin Ladin and the Muwaafaq Foundation which was an arm of the bin Laden terrorist organization. The World Assembly of Muslim Youth office in Annandale, Virginia, was headed by Abdula bin Laden. This organization is an organ of the Saud clan and funds Wahhabi terrorism. The International Institute of Islamic Thought and the Graduate School of Islamic and Social Sciences are also Wahhabi organizations.

Teaching Terroism

Wahhabi madrassas (religious schools) in Saudi Arabia, Pakistan, Indonesia, and elsewhere cultivate virulent hatred of and promote violence against Jews in the United States, and the West, as well as traditional Muslim sects. For example, the Wahhabi cleric Sheikh Saad al-Buraik in April 2002 preached in Riyadh: *Muslim Brothers in Palestine do not have mercy or compassion toward the Jews, their blood, their money, their flesh. Their women are yours to take, legitimately. God made them yours. Why don't you enslave their women? Why don't you wage jihad? Why don't you pillage them?* Sanctioning murder of Jews and others is common practice, and these madrassas are the source and inspiration for suicide bombers and recruits to militant Islamist groups like al-Qaeda and Hamas worldwide.

Saudi Royal Family

Saudi Arabia is now ruled by descendants of the Saudi King Abdul Aziz, who had forty seven sons from some twenty two different wives, plus as many daughters from an even more extensive collection of concubines. Today the Al Saud family' amounts to nearly 20,000 (joining the Al Saud with the Najd Al Sheikh, Thunaiyan, Sudairi, and Jiluwi families of comparable status), including the large number of 'Crown Princes', all requiring palaces and incomes to support their eminent status. The vast wealth from oil reserves is distributed within the family with no external review and no public accounting.

The leading members of the royal family were the Sudairi Seven, sons of Ibn Sa'ud and his favorite wife Hussah bint Ahmad Sudair. These include King Faud born 1921, Prince Sultan (Minister of Defense) born 1924, Crown Prince Abullah born 1923, Prince Salman governor of Riyadh, and Prince Nayef born 1933. Younger candidates for the throne include Prince Turki (son of the Sudairi King Faisal now deceased) born in 1945 and chief of foreign intelligence until he left that post after September 11, 2001, probably because of his close ties to Osama bin Laden, and Prince Bandar, born in 1950, son of Crown Prince Abdullah and who serves as Ambassador to the United States. Prince Meqran governor of Medina and Prince Meshael have become notorious and hated for their not infrequent orders for brutal flogging of Saudi citizens, a practice no less utilized by other Princes.

Succession is usually by seniority by consensus, since it reduces internal disputes and preserves the order required to keep Saudi family rule secure, unlike most of the Saudi Kings in the 18th and 19th Centuries who were murdered by their brother or nephew successors. Crown Prince Abdullah, a relative progressive and non-Wahhabi traditionalist, successor to King Fahd. Abdullah would like to reduce the influence of Wahabbists, a risky enterprise.

Persian Gulf States

Other oil states of the Persian Gulf are strongly influenced by Wahhabi views and members of their ruling families support al-Qaeda. Bahrain is ruled by the Sunni Al Khalifa family. Half the 300,000 population is Persian Shiite in origin, so constant vigilance is required to detect conspiracy against their rule. The Al Khalifa family controls the military and police, and all oil revenues, which are disposed of as family property.

Kuwait is ruled by the Sunni Al Sabah family. Kuwait has a native population of 562,000, of whom 20 percent are Shiite. Nearly 800,000 non-Kuwaitis, of whom 20 percent are Shiite also live in Kuwait. The Al Sabah family controls the police and security forces as well as all oil revenues. Tribal families also rule in Omam, Qatar, Abu Dhabi, Dubai, Shariya and other Emirites in the Persian Gulf. Succession by murder within the ruling families is not unusual. In Abu Dhabi, where the Al bu Falah dynasty of the Bani Yas tribe has ruled continuously since the 1760's, 8 of the total 15 Emirs during that period have been assassinated. In Shariya, Sheik Sultan assumed power in 1972 after his brother Khalid had been murdered by his cousin and the former ruler Saqr ibn Sultan. In 1995, Crown Prince Hamad bin Khalifa ath-Thani ousted his father Emir bin Hamad ath-Thani. The Prime Minister is Abdullah bin Khalifa ath-Thani, which suggests the limited candidate pool for top leadership positions in that Emirate.

Qatar, which provided bases for military operations in Iraq and is also the home for Wahhabi cleric Yusuf al-Qaradawi, who issued a fatwa in 2001 declaring that suicide bombing is martyrdom, not suicide. He also said he supported the Taliban against the United States in Afghanistan. The Arabic news network Al-Jazeera is based in Qatar.

Oil and Society in Arabic States

These parasitic tribal units live on oil revenue, which provides very high per capita income requiring little work in return. The Arab contempt for labor and work requires that thousands of outside experts and common laborers be imported to keep their economies running. Arabs, corrupted by the fantasyland funded by oil, are now unfit for sustained effort of any kind. They serve as nominal heads of national industries and collect appropriately outrageous salaries, but hire experts from abroad to do the technical and scientific work required to run their oil industry and other essential enterprises and utilities.

In Saudi Arabia, some 80,000 American and British keep the oil fields operating, while early 80 percent of the common labor force is immigrants, many from Asia. Most immigrants are treated like, and all are certainly regarded as, slaves (slavery was officially abolished in Saudi Arabia in 1972).

The main business of the Saudi 'family' is to deal with petitioners from all over the Islamic world, strategically placing gifts, bribes, and loans so as to neutralize possible opposition to their rule. They are the principal financiers of terrorist groups, including al-Qaeda, an offshoot of the Wahhabi Islamic sect. Wahhabi mosques have been built with Saudi money throughout the Islamic world.

The Wahhabi mosque in Saudi Arabia trains cadres of Islamic fundamentalists, using texts from the Koran which explicitly incite murder of Israelis and Infidels, of whom the West seems to be the primary target. Members of the Saudi family deny any role in funding the Wahhabi sect or supporting their teachings, yet nothing has been done to limit their most extreme incitements to violence.

The Koran does contain militant and violent language directed against infidels that could be interpreted as encouraging slaughter of unbelievers. Since Arabs have no objective sense of honesty in dealing with infidels and nontribal members (much less within their own group), all statements and promises designed to reassure the West are considered simply means to attain one's own ends. Denials and protestations are largely window dressing. If accepted, this simply intensifies their contempt for the West, so easily duped as to forego direct intervention to protect itself. All Western acts of generosity, moderation, and good will simply amuse Arabs inured to lying and violence as reasonable and preferred means to their ends.

Contempt for the West is universal in the Arabic world. The Saudi's buy everything they desire, produce nothing, and believe that the enormous wealth fortuitously provided by enormous oil reserves simply proves their superiority over all foreigners. They are debauched in private, but this is of no consequence so long as appearances are maintained.

They frequently visit European capitals where they can employ entire cadres of prostitutes and purchase or rent elegant residences to indulge themselves.

Reports of the scandalous behavior of Saudi princes recur in the Western press, but the ruling family controls the media in Saudi Arabia where such reports are never seen. To quote David Pryce Jones: *A handful of absolute despots oppress and attack with every available stratagem all those within reach. The rich and strong mercilessly bully and exploit their inferiors. Fathers subjugate wives and children. From the proudest power holder down to the humblest family, all are engaged in pillaging whatever they can for themselves, or at best for their tribe and religion, rather than considering the public interest and constructing the commonwealth. Politics in practice is reduced to the black arts of applied force, and in any emergency, of terror. In all relationships, domestic, private and public, internal and external, violence is therefore not only customary but also systematic and utterly impervious to piecemeal reform or amelioration. (The Closed Circle, p. 402)*

Freedom VS. Equality

Latin America

I had seen and yet see no prospect that they would establish free or liberal institutions of government. They are not likely to promote the spirit either of freedom or order by their example. They have not the first elements of good or free government. Arbitrary power, military and ecclesiastical, was stamped upon their education, upon their habits, and upon all their institutions. Civil dissension was infused into all their seminal principles. War and mutua destruction was in every member of their organization, moral, political, and physical.

Secretary of State John Quincy Adams, **Diary,** *1821.*

Latin America is included here because Islamic culture pervaded Spain prior to its conquest of Mexico, Peru, and the rest of the continent. Latin America is divided into four principal classes:

1. *Property-owning Europeans of mainly Spanish descent who control some 95 percent of the wealth and dominate the church and military.*
2. *Indians and mestizos (mixed race) who generally live in poverty in both cities and rural areas.*
3. *Middle class academics, lawyers, and businessmen who have little themselves but often hold political office as representatives of various parties that represent large economic interests.*
4. *Inflated army overstocked with officers from both upper and middle classes and a few from the labor class. The armies have no one to fight but domestic enemies of ruling parties and juntas and are poorly trained.*

Governments in Latin America are kleptocracies. Even the much touted populist regime of Hugo Chavez in Venezuela is organized to provide kickbacks and payoffs from the national treasury to friends and supporters. Onto the class pattern established by the Spanish conquest of Central and South America is superimposed the Arabic outlook of the ruling Spanish elite, which they derived from the 700-year Muslim rule of Spain. The much touted 'liberation' of Latin America from Spain by Simon Bolivar was simply a successful effort to prevent Spain from mitigating exploitation by the dominant land owning class. Bolivar liberated them from control. The Arabic outlook is what makes Latin America most like the tribal societies of the Islamic world. It includes:

1. *Indifference to other classes of society and the welfare of the poor.*
2. *Wasteful personal use of wealth by the property-owning class rather than investment in ways to improve the economy of the nation.*
3. *Endogamous class-centered social practices including marriage of first cousins.*
4. *Willingness to kill members of any group that tries to change the system of exploitation.*
5. *Drug cartels that control large areas in Mexico, Columbia, and other states.*
6. *Endemic corruption in politics, business, and social relations.*

The Catholic Church for a time reinforced class exploitation in Latin America. The upper clergy were appointed from the ruling class while the local priests came largely from the illiterate peasantry they served. Since WWII, the Church has reformed entirely in order to improve the well-being of all people in Latin America. Nevertheless, the wealthy class remains in control of resources. This would not necessarily be bad, in fact it is necessary to have some means of accumulating capital for development. But the ruling class in Latin America accumulates capital, then places it in European and United States banks safely out of reach of potential revolutionaries. Capital for development is borrowed by Latin American states from the United States and European banks, even though private capital generated and owned within Latin America is abundant and sufficient were it available there.

Reform might be possible if the lower classes and the middle class acted responsibly. But the lower class has adopted the negative and destructive Arabic traits of their rulers, broadly described by the term ***machismo***, the degradation of women and the futile pursuit of virility through violence toward women. The middle class has adopted the exploitative attitude of the ruling class. Instead of representing a progressive movement to reform and improve conditions in Latin America, the middle class exploits positions in the government for self-advancement and financial gain. Bribes for services are standard practice in governmental agencies, and public contracts and other financial dispensations are arranged through cronyism and kickbacks.

Political rhetoric means nothing. Political leaders throughout Latin America well understand that political power is used primarily to enrich oneself and ones kinship group. Since WWII, Presidents of Mexico have averaged $1 billion in personal wealth skimmed from public funds, favors, and kickbacks over the course of their terms. This money usually is transferred to Swiss banks, and Mexican presidents often retire to Europe in order to elude any chance of financial accountability.

Such practices extend throughout the society. The armies are incompetent, poorly trained, and absurdly oversupplied with overpaid officers and generals compared with the enlisted ranks. All positions are sinecures for friends and kinship groups. Police are largely timeservers who exploit their position to extort money from the public. They are commonly available to the highest bidder and have consistently cooperated in drug smuggling as have most major politicians.

Reform in Latin America will be slow, easily reversed, and encounter the engrained negative traits pervasive in the Region. Some states, perhaps like Chile, have emerged from the military coup-driven political system to develop economic and political structures more like those of America and Europe. Reversion to populist/fascist regimes is always a threat however. But only economic development will extend to the vast impoverished mestizo populations a higher and decent standard of living.

Part VI

International Issues

The foregoing topics provide a framework for understanding the 'news' about international situations. The test is to match what has been said in this book to what is happening. Choose the explanation given here or elsewhere that makes most sense to you. But do not make assumptions such as 'that couldn't be true' or 'that is not possible'. Remain completely open to the truth however strange it may seem at first glance. And do not 'trust' blindly any source simply because you think it is authoritative or you prefer to believe it. Experts are particularly unreliable. The media, governments, interests, lobbies, advocacy groups and others are so biased or uninformed about underlying conditions that much conflicting information and opinion is passed on as serious inquiry or analysis. Most of it is irrelevant and misleading. And federal administrations and politicians are especially prone to doctor the truth or conceal it.

Three international issues are particularly controversial because so many interests are manipulating media and public understanding of them for their own purposes: the role of the United Nations, world economic competition and the so-called oil crisis.

United Nations and International Order

The United Nations is a product of and target for confused views about and unrealistic attitudes toward power, many of them shared by and originated in America. Power determines and insures order in the world. The United States is the most powerful nation in world history. Yet we have an inadequate understanding of the nature of power because we exercise it pretty much without opposition. Power has never in recent times been applied to us successfully simply because there is no state or combination of states that could seriously challenge us, although in Vietnam we experienced how our power **applied to others** may be defeated. The defeat was only possible because the full power available to the United States was not applied. Our elected officials are especially ignorant of power and its use. That is why our foreign policies since 1950 have been disastrous. Having great power and lacking a clear understanding of the nature and limits of power and how to use it, we are disappointed at times by the indifferent results we achieve in our efforts to influence other nations. The United Nations often is the focus of this frustration.

Power and Security

The main product of power is security, which for a state is a condition in which no external power can prevent or obstruct actions by the state. The United Nations, in itself powerless, presumably is intended to guarantee the security of all nations. Therefore, any security it obtains for its members is a product of power combinations of individual member states. International security results when the actual distribution of power between nations is recognized as true by all or most states, and no state attempts to alter the arrangement, because all states accept the existing situation as optimum, even if it is not entirely or even substantially what each would prefer. Crises occur when a nation or combination of nations challenges the current consensus on power distribution. Resolution of a crisis can be achieved in three ways: *persuasion, payoffs, or coercion* to obtain compliance or agreement. Ideas, money, or guns are the principle instruments of power and are usually applied in that order.

The United Nations began in 1945 with 50 member states and now has 191. The Security Council of the United Nations has 15 members, five of them permanent (United States, China, Great Britain, France, and

Russia) and ten of them rotating members. The Security Council, as its name implies, decides on matters of international security including peace missions, sanctions, and emergency aid. A permanent member can veto a decision of the Security Council. The General Assembly, made up of all members having equal representation, decides what programs to implement and allocates financial resources by majority vote. In broad terms, the General Assembly is most concerned with economic and social issues, mainly income redistribution as between the 'have and have-not' nations. The permanent members of the Security Council are concerned with political and security issues, such as nonproliferation of weapons of mass destruction and regional political stability.

Most United Nations States are unsustainable

What is politely ignored is the vast disparity in power within the United Nations. More than two thirds of the member states, mainly in Africa, Southeast Asia, parts of Central and South America, and the Western Pacific, do not meet the minimum criteria for being recognized as a state. Maintaining embassies and the paraphernalia of statehood is a severe burden on citizens of most of these so-called states. They are unable to defend their borders or maintain internal order and do not have the economic and natural resources required to develop industries, agriculture, and energy and transportation infrastructure to a level that would provide economic sufficiency or parity with other states. Most do not have integrated populations united in support of national interests. In Africa this is especially common. Nigeria is an egregious example. A kleptocrat state run by tribal/militia overlords to convey oil wealth to partners and supporters is unable to maintain order even in the critical eastern oil region. In 2006 the eastern oil region Ijaw tribe attacked oil installations (and forced a reduction of 10 percent in output) demanding an increase in its share of the revenues, yet their putative leader, Diepreye Alamieyeseigha, former governor of the state of Bayelsa, skimmed revenues diverted to that state to support his high lifestyle. These nominal 'states' are consulted, deferred to, placed on international commissions, and their representatives are appointed to major international agencies as if they had power comparable to the viable states within the United Nations.

Power in international relations is based ultimately on force. Wealth is irrelevant. Unless a nation has the arms sufficient to withstand or overcome an opponent, it is essentially helpless in the face of any aggression by that opponent. Some states use money to bribe peace from hostile powers.

Attempting to disarm and declare nonviolent principles in carrying out international relations is noble but disingenuous. All international order has to be guaranteed by whichever states are militarily able to enforce it.

Local conflicts, mostly in Africa and the Islamic fringe states, present endemic challenge to world order. United Nations peacekeeping forces cannot deal with the genocidal wars in Africa. Involving NATO troops is folly, certainly involving US troops is. *The United States should not become directly involved in any conflict in Africa or the Islamic world.* All the wringing of hands over the Hutu genocide of Tutsi in 1993 or the Darfur genocide in 2006 is pure public relations for Black votes in the United States. Under no circumstances should we have got involved in these endless tribal disputes.

Global Economic Competition

Following WWII, approximately two-thirds of the world population subsisted outside the capitalist economy of developed industrial States. The United States, in order to shore up opposition to Soviet expansion, committed its naval power to ensure safe ocean transport and trade worldwide. Small states before unable to protect their commerce now could develop industries and markets without the expense of military means to protect such commerce. By 1960, the defeated industrial powers Germany and Japan rejoined the United States and the rest of Western Europe to make up the world capitalist industrial economy.

Other States provided raw materials to the developed. World supplies of oil, industrial metals, and food products were abundant and could easily supply the developed economies.

Of particular importance for maintaining this advantageous situation was the self-exclusion of Soviet Russia, Maoist China, and Socialist India from international competition for capital, markets, and resources. All three preferred the insular and self-sufficient economic policies typical of the theological empires from which they derived. They bought grain and sold raw materials to raise foreign currency from time to time, but they did not seek to compete in the world capitalist market system. All three accepted low productivity and standards of living for their populations in return for ideological consistency and the economic advantage and political control of the ruling elite.

All this changed between the rise of Deng Xiao-ping and Chinese capitalism in 1976 and the fall of the Soviet Empire in 1991. China had suffered a number of economic disasters under Mao and had been brought to economic and social ruin by the Red Guard revolution of 1967-1973. Deng Xiao-ping, in an act of statesmanship unparalleled in Chinese history, reversed Maoist ideology (while using familiar Communist jargon) by opening China to foreign capital and investment and most importantly to domestic entrepreneurship. The political collapse of the Soviet Empire left their industrial and raw material sectors open to foreign investment as the only way to reestablish stability. As a result, both Russia and especially China entered the world capitalist system to compete for markets, capital, products, and resources on an equal footing with Japan and the Western States.

The economic balance of post WWII so advantageous to the West, which held for nearly fifty years, has ended. Unfortunately, the culture of waste and extravagance developed in the United States over the same period continues to determine expectations. The United States may be facing a period of progressive declines in standard of living as the competition for resources increases. Correspondingly, the agricultural sector of the US economy could enjoy unprecedented profitability as billions of Asian consumers compete for our food products.

World Oil Reserves

The most obvious subject for future resource competition is oil. Since 2006, fracking has eliminated United States need for foreign oil imports and we are now basically energy independent. In contrast, China as the second largest consumer of oil worldwide is entirely dependent on oil imports to run its economy and is vulnerable to cut off of oil supplies, especially through the Gulf of Mallaca in Indonesia. Estimates of petroleum reserves vary in reliability and are revised periodically. There are three trillion barrels of known and recoverable existing oil reserves. Iraq and other Gulf states have potential for new oil field discoveries once exploration intensifies. Russia can double its current recovery if outdated technology, which gets only 20 percent of existing Russian reserves, is replaced with advanced technology. Azerbaijan and Kazakhstan have estimated reserves of 70 to 80 billion barrels. Other areas have great potential for new discoveries. Lack of refining capacity has been the main cause of recent shortages. Constructing new refineries and improving existing refineries will bridge the conversion from oil to other sources of fuel.

Latin America has about 120 billion barrels of petroleum reserves, or 12-percent of the World total. Venezuela and Mexico are the largest producers. Other Latin American countries with important petroleum deposits include Argentina and Brazil. Venezuela has the largest reserves in the region, about 47 billion barrels. Huge deposits of heavy oil lie north of the Orinoco River in eastern Venezuela. The other major oil region in Venezuela is the Lake Maracaibo Basin in the northwestern part of the country. Although a republican form of government was established in 1959, corruption and attempted military coups recur. The population is 75-percent urban, a concentration of underemployed poor that leads inevitably to regular street demonstrations and occasional violence. The state-owned oil industry, nationalized in 1975 with compensation to private owners, once run as independently of political disputes and as reliably as such disputes will allow, now is in ruins under the populist regime of Hugo Chavez. Venezuelan supply will likely remain unreliable and social unrest will occasionally threaten short-term dislocations. Mexico has the second largest reserves in Latin America, about 51 billion barrels. Most of Mexico's reserves lie in the eastern part of the country, chiefly in the states of Campeche, Tabasco, and Veracruz, along the coast and in the Gulf of Mexico. The petroleum industry is operated by a government agency. In 2018, Mexico, Canada, and the United States ratified the free trade agreement which provided elimination of trade barriers and increased trade, investment, and political stability that will make Mexico a reliable source of petroleum for the indefinite future.

North Africa has about 42 billion barrels of oil, or 4-percent of the world reserves. Most of the oil is in Libya, Algeria, and other countries in northern Africa. Libya has the largest reserves, about 23 billion barrels. Algeria produces large quantities of natural gas and petroleum, chiefly from fields in the northeastern part of the Sahara region. Total reserves amount to about 9 billion barrels. Relative stability makes Algeria a likely reliable source of oil.

Black Africa has about 32 billion barrels of oil reserves, amounting to 3 percent of the world total. Black African oil comes mainly from Nigeria, one of the potentially most unstable states in Black Africa. Independent since 1960, Nigeria, 357,000 square miles and 98 million people, is the largest African State divided into 36 internal states made up of three principal tribal groups: Muslim Hausa and Fulani (29 percent) in the North; Yoruba (21 percent) in the West; and Igbo (18 percent) in the East. A number of smaller tribal groups, including the Ijaw (10 percent), are dispersed between the three largest tribes. In 1967, the Eastern Igbo Eastern region, where the main oil reserves are located, seceded to form the Biafran Republic. In the ensuing civil war, nearly

1 million Igbo were killed, before the "republic" capitulated in 1970. Misrule, corruption, political assassination, and military coups have been regular features of Nigerian political life. The major tribes remain hostile to each other, and the situation will likely grow worse. In 2002, the twelve Muslim northern states adopted the strict Islamic legal code of Sharia and their trend toward radical Islamic doctrine will likely lead to future conflict. Billions of dollars in oil revenue are regularly diverted from the nationalized oil sector to private accounts in London and other European banks by corrupt members of the ruling groups, so the prize of political control is nearly irresistible.

Middle East has about two-thirds of the world's oil, about 660 billion barrels. Saudi Arabia has about 260 billion barrels, or about a fourth of the world's reserves. Most of Saudi Arabia's petroleum lies in areas along the Persian Gulf. Iran, Iraq, Kuwait, and the United Arab Emirates each have about 10 percent of the total world petroleum reserves. These States were discussed in another section.

Europe, including the Asian part of Russia, has about 7-percent of the world's oil supply. Russia, with about 48 billion barrels, has the largest reserves in the region. Most of these reserves lie west of the Ural Mountains, although there are several large oil fields in Siberia. The only other major European reserves, which amount to about 14 billion barrels, are beneath the North Sea. These reserves belong chiefly to the United Kingdom and Norway.

Asia, excluding the Asian part of Russia and the Middle East, has about 40 billion barrels of oil, or 4-percent of the world's reserves. About half these reserves lie in China. China's largest oil field is at Daqing northeastern China. Other major Chinese deposits lie on the Shandong Peninsula and in the province of Xinjiang. Indonesia, with about 5 billion barrels, has the second largest reserves.

United States and Canada have about 31 billion barrels of oil reserves, which amounts to 3-percent of the world total. The United States has about 25 billion barrels, mostly in Texas, Louisiana, California, Oklahoma, and Alaska. US reserves substantially increased by fracking oil produced from shale in Pennsylvania, New York, Colorado, Wyoming, and Texas. Canada has oil reserves of about 6 billion barrels.

Mineral Resources

Supplies of critical mineral resources such as chrome, cobalt, manganese, vanadium, platinum and diamonds will grow scarcer as industrial demand and world competition deplete reserves. Black Africa, the politically most unstable area in the world, controls a significant portion of world reserves of these minerals. The United States imports 100-percent of its chromium from South Africa and Zimbabwe, which have 98-percent of the world reserves. The United States imports 86 percent of its cobalt from Congo, which has nearly 75-percent of world reserves. Cobalt ore also occurs in Azerbaijan, Finland, Kazakstan, Russia, Zaire, and Zambia. South Africa has 73-percent of world platinum reserves, and Black Africa overall has 40-percent of vanadium reserves and 33-percent of chromite reserves. China, South Africa (31 percent), and Ukraine (53 percent) produce most of the world's manganese, followed by Brazil and Gabon. The ocean floor, especially in the Pacific, has large deposits of manganese nodules but recovery requires advanced deep sea mining technology. The United States, which has few deposits of high-grade manganese ore, imports about 75-percent of the manganese that it uses. Vanadium is found chiefly in Finland, Russia, and South Africa. Africa has the largest reserves of industrial diamonds. The Democratic Republic of Congo exports 24 million carets annually, Botswana 19.8 million carets, and South Africa 10.7 million carets.

United States and World Economic Competition

The United States faces the greatest economic transformation since the industrial revolution began two centuries ago. Since 1780, beginning in England and the United States, the application of water, oil, electric, and atomic energy to manufacture goods and provide services has transformed economic production and standards of living. Productivity has increased 1000-fold, and financial, as opposed to landed wealth of enormous proportions has been created. Initially, wealth was concentrated in the hands of the proprietor class and standards of living were low except for a small percentage of the population. The United States was an exception from the beginning because it had vast areas of productive agricultural land that insured a comparatively high standard of living for all its citizens and tended to keep the country predominantly rural rather than urban. The United States remained under-populated until late in the 19th Century, and labor was therefore relatively scarce and could command higher wages. Where low wages prevailed, workers could simply move on to new industrial areas where demand and opportunity were greater. Many immigrants before the Civil War were from rural areas of Britain and Europe, motivated to acquire land for growing crops and qualified to manage a farm. They could become independent farmland owners, but they depended on urban bank and industry credits to purchase farm equipment, fuel, fertilizer, seed, and transportation to markets. The large volume of farm production tended to depress prices, while prices of industrial goods purchased by rural communities (whose production could be readily controlled by John Deere, Caterpillar, International Harvester, and other manufacturers) tended to rise.

By the 1880's, this price squeeze had erupted into a rural Populist Revolt and the Grange movement to organize farmers against predatory banks and railroads. The movement attacked banks for extortionate interest rates and railroads for extortionate transportation costs. It favored using silver as well as gold for the monetary standard in order to increase money supply.

At the same time, a revolt of urban industrial workers was underway. Beginning in the 1880's, immigration of dominantly urban proletariat from southern Europe and Eastern Europe introduced a workforce unable to take advantage of vacant public farmlands in the West. The urban immigrants were more likely to be tied to industrial employment, and the large number of urban settlers made labor cheap and readily available. Standards of living in cities were low and wages always lagged behind rates of inflation. There was no job security and unemployment and layoffs were common. The Labor Movement to unionize for collective bargaining and negotiate better wages and working conditions began at roughly the same time as the Populist Revolt to improve credit terms available to farmers and raise prices for farm goods.

The industrial and banking interests of the East and Midwest were able to use the North-South divisions of the Civil War to keep Southern and Northern farmers from joining in one party to influence this economic trend, and they were able to excite the antipathy of rural areas for urban alien, immigrant industrial laborers to divide the electorate and dominate national and most state governments. In 1897, William Jennings Bryan, representative of the Populist Movement and to some extent the labor movement, was nominated to the Democratic Party and ran on a cheap silver ticket opposing the "Cross of Gold" but lost the election when the rural north voted republican.

Beginning in the 1880's, the main issue in American politics became ***distribution of wealth.*** The industrial and financial establishment was able to dominate the debate and win elections until 1933 by dividing farmers north (Republican) and south (Democrat) and rural (Republican) and urban (Democrat) labor. In the Depression, farmer/labor coalitions were formed in northern states to support the economic reforms of Franklin Delano Roosevelt and the Democratic Party.

Since 1945, all elections have centered on the condition of the economy. The surge of prosperity, home ownership and consumption since World War II has progressed with occasional setbacks, called downturns and recessions, associated with the business cycle. Destruction of advanced economies during WWII gave the United States an unprecedented advantage. The United States had the wealth to purchase resources worldwide without competition from other industrial powers at extremely low prices. It also had enormous pent up buying power in the general population, due to wartime saving. Further, invention and innovation were and remain primary economic drivers in the United States economy. Enormous investment and consumer spending continued to drive the economy to new levels of prosperity, and wealth was more widely distributed, depending on the level of economic activity. In 1990, the incredible advantage enjoyed by the United States following WWII was amplified by the collapse of the Soviet Union, which simply fell apart under the economic stress of the microchip revolution led by American high technology.

Recovery of the European and Japanese economies in the 1950's did not adversely affect the United States. It created markets and added political stability in areas severely devastated during WWII. The Soviet Union remained a third world nation in every respect but militarily, sustaining a high level of armaments and missile and space technology at the cost of the civilian sector. But this pattern of imposing minimal living standards to support military defense and security of the state was long accepted by Russians.

Beginning the 1970's, Europe and especially Japan began to compete in US markets providing automobiles and consumer technology goods. The increasing market share of Japanese autos reduced employment within the United States initially but was offset in the 1980's by the trend to establish foreign auto assembly plants within the US. Toyota, BMW, Mazda, Honda and others manufacture auto lines within the US, usually in partnership with domestic companies that purchase shares in the Japanese and other foreign companies. Japan, Taiwan, Malaysia, and South Korea eventually came to dominate the computer component manufacturing sector. NAFTA shifted jobs south to Mexico, where assembly of cars, computers, consumer electronic products (such as vacuum cleaners, laptops, stereo equipment) from parts made in Asia is a current trend.

Telecommunications via the worldwide web has revolutionized labor markets in the medical, financial and business services industries. Domestic outplacement of jobs began in the 1990's. Skilled workers abroad, especially in India, can perform technical services at much lower cost. India has made this shift abroad possible because its educated citizens are fluent in English, the lingua franca of India. Combined with computer, high tech, business, medical and scientific training equal to the United States, India can provide such services at salaries much below US levels. Technical services completed overnight can be transmitted the following morning from India to the American client.

Another fundamental change is from permanent in-house employment to contract outplacement. When telecommuting became feasible in 1990, many permanent full- time workers began to work at home a few days a week.

Employers eventually concluded that many administrative services (shipping, facilities maintenance, bookkeeping, personnel records, etc.) could be contracted out, saving pension, benefit and other costs. Many of these jobs could also be contracted abroad. This change in labor markets is not necessarily a bad trend. Prosperity and jobs in Mexico improve their domestic prospects, reduce pressure to immigrate illegally to the United States, and raise standards of living south of the border. This in turn can increase demand for US made goods and services as income and savings rise in Mexico.

Such improvements in foreign employment and economic growth also provide strategic support for peaceful resolution of international disputes. Development of high-tech industry by IBM, Microsoft and others in the Bangalore region of India, one of the most highly developed educational and technical areas in the world, has affected the international policy of the Indian government. During the "atomic" crisis of 2000 between India and Pakistan, the American companies warned that they would have to move their operations elsewhere since remaining under the constant threat of nuclear disaster was unacceptable. The Indian government decided reaching some accommodation was of much greater importance. Correspondingly, Pakistani government officials, influenced by US assurances of financial assistance, saw the advantages of high-tech economic development within their equally qualified labor market, and have also moved to end or at least moderate the disagreement.

Natural Resources and Economic Growth

By definition, such resources are finite. Discoveries of new, sizable deposits of molybdenum, platinum, cobalt, chromium, titanium, and other industrial minerals and of oil and gas reserves are infrequent. The earth has been scoured for such resources. Oceans are a prospective source. Large ocean floor sources of scarce manganese and other industrial metals have been discovered and require mainly new technology to bring them in volume and economically to the surface. Offshore oil drilling now pumps Caribbean oil from wells drilled some 2 miles below the surface. In 2004, oil companies began to reduce their estimates of remaining reserves. British Petroleum reduced their estimates by 20 percent. Most countries outside the developed circle consume small fractions of resources compared to the major powers which helped maintain the low-cost high standard of living enjoyed in the United States since WWII. The United States consumes 40 percent of world resources and has less than 5 percent of world population.

PART VII

Western Intellectual History

The foundations of Western Civilization are no longer taught in American schools. Consequently, Americans have little perspective on world history much less current affairs. If we do not understand what made western civilization and why it is superior to all others, we cannot be persuaded that saving it is the most urgent objective of United States policy. Part VII outlines our intellectual heritage, Part VIII reviews the history of the United States (which also is no longer taught in any coherent way), and the Part IX reviews why and how Western Civilization must be saved.

Introduction

Four basic facts of human existence lay at the beginning of religious speculation. First the division of the world into male and female, second the division of the observed universe into earth and sky, third the relationship of man to the forces or gods that created and govern these phenomena, and fourth birth and death and the fact that we do not know where we come from at birth and where we go at death.

The division into male and female involves issues of fertility, life cycles, and the very question of food, shelter, and survival itself. **Fertility** as the universal force of nature was associated with women and birth. The certainty of maternity compared with the uncertainty of paternity affected the status of women in all societies.

The division of heaven and earth presented questions of primacy, of higher and lower, of the source of power, and cosmic forces. The clarity, drama, and awe-inspiring beauty and terror of the sky, during the day and at night, was so great as to induce wonder and fear, feelings that inclined religious belief toward propitiation and dread. Death, human mortality in a world that seems to go on forever, created existential dread and raised questions of how to prepare for the voyage to the 'other side'. Birth raised questions of where we come from, how we are renewed as a species even though we die as individuals, and what to do with the newcomers in our midst.

Through time, hunter gatherer groups developed systems of belief to account for the mysteries of fertility, the life cycle of birth and death, the beauty and abundance of the earth, and the arbitrary and overpowering force of seasons, winds, natural disasters, diseases, and other calamities. Religions centered either on the earth and an earth mother in control of birth and seasonal renewal or on the sky and a powerful sky god in control of lightening, storms, weather, seasons. The earth-centered religions were polymorphous, emphasizing fecundity and procreation, and had many levels of divine manifestation including myths, legends, and stories to explain natural phenomena. The sky worshippers tended to emphasize power and physical force, male dominance and competition, and regarded war as a means to individual immortality.

Horse and Camel

Two revolutions in land transportation transformed the political and cultural landscape of the Eurasian heartland and the Mediterranean. By 3000 BC, the horse was sufficiently domesticated by Indo-European tribes of the Eurasian steppes that it became a reliable means of transportation. The only comparable revolution was the invention of the internal combustion engine at the end of the 19th Century. The horse gave power and mobility to invading tribes sweeping off the Caucasian plains into the settled areas of Mesopotamia. The culture of the horse greatly reinforced the Indo- European male god and patriarchic cultures. An equally dramatic revolution occurred in the Arabian desert by 200 AD when the camel was domesticated as a reliable means of transportation in the arid lands of the Middle East and North Africa. In many ways the camel is the more extraordinary animal. A camel can carry 500 pounds 25 miles a day and go for weeks without water and much longer without food. Islam was spread by camel.

Religion

Religion originated in three prehistoric cultures that incorporated different interpretations and combinations of these primary elements. ***Indo-European*** nomadic cultures of the Eurasian grass lands; ***Neolithic*** garden cultures of the uplands and valleys in mountainous inland regions of the Mediterranean Sea especially, the Alps, Balkans, Anatolia, Iran; ***Semitic*** pastoral tribes of Arabia and the Fertile crescent.

Indo-Europeans worshipped sky gods, had patriarchal social organization, were warlike from about 10,000 BC, and evolved a culture that sought immortality through distinction in battle. War became a constant activity of Indo-Europeans especially after they domesticated the horse around 3000 BC. Indo-Europeans tended to be rationalistic and anthropocentric, to evolve abstract concepts, and sought understanding and clarity through polarizing of phenomena, a disposition due perhaps to the influence of vast dramatic skyscapes that contrasted with the endless flat grasslands of their environment. Indo-Europeans comprise the Greeks, Hittites, Aryans, Celts, Germans and Nordics among many other smaller groups. They moved from bronze to iron weapons during the period 2000 to 1000 BC and were constantly invading the agricultural theocratic empires of the Fertile Crescent and the Indus Valley throughout that period.

Neolithic garden cultures were matriarchal, worshipped the Earth Mother and fertility goddesses and gods, organized their lives and thought around fertility, evolved elaborate mythologies to explain the flora and fauna around them, and tended toward non-rational thinking mixing animal and human forms in their gods and myths. They invented agriculture around 8000 BC, later developed domestication of livestock, invented the kiln and pottery, originated domestic housing made of brick, wood, and tile, and lived in relatively permanent settlements, moving only as their cultivated soils became exhausted. These cultures were the basis for theocratic empires along the Tigris and Euphrates River basins in Mesopotamia, and along the Nile in Egypt.

Semites worshipped sky gods and eventually invented monotheism based on notions of one eternal Godhead. They had patriarchal social organization, were warlike, but unlike Indo-Europeans, emphasized ethical absolutes, had an almost phobic obsession with purity and cleansing, and evolved a *dualistic* view of the universe in which absolute good and absolute evil were in mortal combat for the souls of men. They were other-worldly, regarding the flesh and the world as domains of evil. They were especially fearful of the female influence as a source of pollution and sin. The Hebrew myth of creation, although correctly rendered as "created he them", thereby making human pluralism and equal value for women the foundation of human society, nonetheless reflected a pervasive gynophobia in the myth of the Fall from grace. Gynophobia probably derived from the uncertainty of paternity, a special obsession in Semitic tribal cultures.

Where nomadic tribal cultures conquered agricultural areas, the latter cultures often assimilated the beliefs, myths, and legends of the conqueror. This earth/sky, female/male *polarization* was mixed as Indo-Europeans periodically invaded or settled among the agricultural societies of the Mediterranean basin and the great river basins of the Near East. The jumble of gods and beliefs created by Semitic incursions is recorded in Biblical accounts. The merger of Earth Mother mythology and lore and Indo-European sky religion is eloquently described in Homer, the founder of Classical Civilization.

The earth-centered religions of the islands, coasts and highlands of the Mediterranean and Aegean Seas and the Near East were sandwiched between two sky worshippers, the Indo-Europeans in the grasslands of the Caucasus and the Semites of the grassland and deserts of Arabia and North Africa.

Grassland Indo-Europeans evolved patterns of thought based on *polarity*, whereas desert Semites evolved patterns of thought based on *duality*. The more benign environment of the northern grasslands, the vast skies and endless horizon of the steppe, the relative abundance and variety of plants and animals, and the great beauty and drama of skyscapes and storms, combined to produce a less severe, more inclusive view of nature, and a hearty and simplistic view of gods and men.

Semitic Dualism

The desert Semites confronted an extreme and merciless environment that disposed them to extreme, right-or-wrong, life-or-death views of nature, God, and man. Their propensity for religious rhetoric and daydreaming probably derived from staring at the endless dunes of the great desert, with its sparse, barren, and unwelcoming environment. Semitic religion posited one God, emphasized the unseen over the over the seen, observed piety and rituals associated with cleansing from impure thoughts and contacts, severe moral and dietetic codes, and fanaticism in propagating or defending the one true faith. Tolerance was never a feature of Semitic religion or culture.

Semitic dualism divided reality into antipodal elements that are totally dissimilar, incompatible, eternally hostile, and are commonly interpreted morally as either good or evil. Heaven and earth, body and spirit are not regarded as complementary and equally good and worthwhile. The earth is a place of deception, illusion, deceit and evil, whereas heaven is unchanging, pure, and the only realm in which truth can appear. The spirit is trapped like prisoner in the body, which is blind, unable to perceive truth, and deludes and betrays the spirit by its appetites and desires.

Indo-European Polarity

Polarizing Indo-Europeans divided reality into extremes that are compatible and complementary. Separation of elements is necessary to order, but all elements are needed and valued. Moral values are matters of degree, and often the good is a product of balancing or mixing extremes. The most typical Indo-European view of the creation of the world comes in Ovid, where no intrinsic evil exists, only **disorder** that comes when elements are inappropriately mixed and the **order** that comes when the colliding elements are rightly separated.

> *Ante mare et terras et, quod tegit omnia,*
> *caelum unus erat toto naturae vultus in orbe,*
> *quem dixere Chaos…Sic erat instabilis tellus,*
> *innabilis unda, lucis egens aer, nulli sua*
> *forma manebat, obstabatque altis aliud,*
> *quia corpore in uno frigida pugnabant clidis,*
> *umentia siccis, mollia cum diris, sine pondere*
> *habentia pondus.*
>
> Ovid, Metamorphoses I

Aristotle provides an example of the typical Indo-European polarizing approach when he defines moral character in his **Nichomachean Ethics,** where Virtue is the mean between extremes, as in the case of fear. Reasonable fear is appropriate. However, cowardice occurs when the coward fears to excess what the rash man pretends not to fear at all, whereas the courageous man fears to the extent that the facts justify and acts to confront the situation without denying or exaggerating the basis for reasonable fear.

Zoroaster and the Spread of Dualism

Organized warfare between large clans appears to have been invented in the 10th millennium BC. The first prehistoric gravesites that include large numbers of men with arrowheads imbedded in their skeletal remains occur in the Ukraine and Egypt during this period. There is some speculation that late Magdalenian clans from southwestern France migrated eastward attacking as far east as Greece and Egypt. Around 9500 BC, Greek tribes managed to curb their advance. Climatic changes during a warming cycle in the 4th glacial period that began around 9500 BC and extended to 7000 BC, led to rising sea levels and the destruction of most settlements along the coastlines of the Aegean and Mediterranean seas.

This unsettled and warlike period produced religious beliefs that glorified warrior gods such as Mithras. But the destruction and insecurity organized warfare caused in the late Neolithic societies, and the natural disasters caused by rising sea levels, led to a pervasive desire for an alternative. Coincidentally, at this time domesticated plants and stock husbandry had been invented and perfected in the uplands of Iran and Mesopotamia bringing about the greatest revolution in human history advanced by the first religious revolution in history.

Around the year 6500 B.C. (according to Plutarch), Zoroaster (Zarathustra) formulated the first modern religion based on peace; moral rectitude, and stewardship of creation. Zoroaster (Stargazer), descended from the Indo-Iranian branch of the Indo-European family, was born in the northwestern part of present-day Iran. He was in some way affiliated with the Magi, a priesthood associated with Zervanism, in which Ahura Mazda (Light) and Ahriman (Darkness) were twin sons of Zurvan (God of Infinite Time). They worshipped fire and water and also included a heritage of Mithra and warrior worship. Zoroaster may have begun as a priest of Zurvanism, but later reformed the religion to purge it of warrior worship. He postulated the path of Asha, Right Order, and men were to restore belief in the sanctity of the material world and work with the creator to achieve its perfection through husbandry.

Cultivation was a form of worship: *"He who cultivates grain cultivates righteousness"*. (Vendidad III) Individual virtues centered on Vohu Manu (Good Thought), Asha (Right Order), Haurvatat (Immortality), Ameretat (Wholeness or Integrity), and Armaiti (Right Mindedness or Humility) through which each individual could achieve the likeness of the divine Ahura Mazda. Each individual is free to choose between the path of Asha and the path of Druj (Deceit). In the beginning God created the world as good, but the world was marred by Druj, which penetrated all parts of creation. Men have the opportunity to take responsibility for the fate of their souls and the world by working as God's helpers to perfect the world. At the end of time the Saosyant (the Savior) will bring an ordeal of fire in which evil will be destroyed and the good will remain unharmed.

Armed with a new technology (domesticated plants and animals plus pottery and some metalworking) and this new theology, and using irrigation, fertilization, cattle breeding, the upland agriculturalists converted other Neolithic tribes to planting and settlement in towns throughout Mesopotamia, Anatolia, Greece and the Balkans. This led to substantial increases in population, city life, and trade, all initially promoted by Zoroastrian beliefs that spread with the new technology.

Zoroaster did not establish a priesthood, but it appears that the Magi incorporated his teachings, which were passed on by oral tradition. The Magi were the first astronomers and remained important as fortunetellers and interpreters of the planetary and stellar system. Over several millennia, the teachings of Zoroaster acquired a sinister interpretation (perhaps under the influence of Semitic dualism) in which heaven and earth, good and evil became absolutely separate, mutually hostile and incompatible realms (the one good, unchanging, and true the other false, impermanent, and evil) which were locked in mortal combat until the end of time. This dualism was later adopted by Pythagoras and Plato in order to defeat the democratic and scientific outlook of the sophists and other supporters of democracy in the Greek polis.

The theocratic empires that formed around 3000 BC developed formal beliefs and rituals as expedients necessary for ruling large, dispersed populations. They combined many gods in a jumble of legends and creation myths. Concepts of good and evil evolved mainly around requirements for strict adherence to rituals and practices needed to appease the gods.

Given the dual orientations of sky gods and earth gods, it may have been inevitable that concepts of good and evil developed around the challenge that earth mother religion might pose to sky god machismo. Around 750 BC, Iranian Magi (adapting the teachings of Zoroaster) propounded a dualist theory in which heaven represents light and good and earth represents darkness and evil. All truth is in heaven, evil and illusion is on earth. By extension, this simple division, already latent in the Indo-European and Semitic sky god religions and the earth mother religions of the Neolithic agricultural societies, became a vector for religious fanaticism and political reaction.

Eventually the human body and human soul were placed in conflict. The body is a prison in which the soul was temporarily confined. The body and the earth became evil, and soul and heaven became good. In Greek philosophy, Plato elaborated this theme. Body senses cannot know truth. Only the mind/soul through contemplation and logical discourse can come to truth and enlightenment. He postulated that heaven was of different nature than earth and followed different laws. Only the wise men who turn from the world of the senses are worthy of rule. The principle that the cause is always greater than the effect led to such absurdities as reverse evolution.

Such dualism served the political objectives of the land and slave holding classes challenged by democracy and budding science and comparative rationalism. In the argument of **nature versus convention**, Plato defended the innate nature of slavery, merit, and aristocracy against sophists who argued more scientifically that all human beliefs, relations and institutions are simply customs and conventions that are not innate, immutable, or absolutely true, but are subject to choice and change. Platonic dualism eventually defeated emerging science and dominated Classical Civilization to its end, contributing substantially to the defeat of democracy and the dominance of the landed slave owners. Dualism remained the primary heresy in Christian thought, despite the biblical statements that Yahweh made the earth and called it good, and the Council of Trent declared the resurrection of the body as a foundation belief of the Christian religion. Augustine to a lesser extent and Luther and Calvin to a great extent adopted the dualism of Zoroaster. Puritanism extended the dualist fallacy to the English middle class which achieved its somewhat diluted social expression in 'Victorian' England.

Theocratic Empire

Four river civilizations (Egypt, Mesopotamia, India, and China) were based on an agricultural economy that relied on annual flooding to deposit rich sediments on the floodplains suitable for growing sizable crops. They developed similar political structures for ruling large numbers of people.

A divine ruler, descended from a god, was the keystone of the system, serving as direct mediator and guarantor of divine favor. Each civilization evolved a cosmology, beliefs, and rituals needed to ensure the loyalty of widely dispersed large populations working the land. The divine ruler was supported by a priesthood that established and maintained the ritual, beliefs, and ceremonies needed to ensure the favor of the gods and the annual cycle of fertility on which the economy depended. In Mesopotamia this class achieved remarkable advances in mathematics and astronomical observation, but they were not interested in science, innovation, or knowledge per se.

The entire system sought stasis and unchanging conformity to established belief and rituals. Any deviation was regarded as an apostasy to the gods that could lead to disaster. They ascribed disasters that occurred under natural conditions to some breach of the established belief system and made suitable sacrifice to amend the situation. A bureaucracy of clerics able to write and keep records was an established part of the system. A "middle class" of artisans, traders and the like provided for mundane needs of the governing class. Finally, a military commander and army were required to defend the static and vulnerable river states from depredations by outlying nomadic tribes. This was the hierarchy usually amounting to less than five percent of the population that ruled over the mass of laboring peasants. Because the river states accumulated wealth and required resources, especially metals, unavailable within their own territories, extensive trade routes linked remote sources of such materials over remarkable distances. Cultivation required the labor of a large population to build and maintain irrigation structures, plant, tend, and harvest crops, and maintain tools and storage facilities, keep records and build structures, including temples, palaces, and the like.

Homer and the Founding of Classical Civilization

Homer's ***Iliad*** is the sublime culmination of Indo-European culture and the foundation and source of Classical Civilization. No work from any culture compares in significance simply because the ***Iliad*** was the first of its kind and because everything that followed finds its source and inspiration in Homer. Homer invented metaphor, the astonishing literary device of using examples of tangible natural events or objects to describe the intangible events of the mind and soul. As for example comparing the perturbation of mind before battle with the breaking of waves on rocky cliffs or the use of the properties of one object to describe another, such as describing the sea as *'wine dark'* or *'dawn's rosy, red fingers'*. Through more than 2500 years of repetition Homer's metaphors have become shopworn, but their original and subsequent effect is immeasurable. Only Shakespeare compares with Homer in that both created a new language for expressing the depth and range of human experience. Shakespeare's is more profound but Homer's made Shakespeare's possible.

Homer lived sometime around 900 BC in the Ionian Islands of Greece along the western shores of the Anatolian peninsula. He spoke in the aftermath of the Doric Greek invasion, which shattered the remnants of Mycenaean Greek culture, the culture of Agamemnon, Menelaus, and the Trojan War. This culture was archetypically Indo-European. A warrior class sought immortality through great deeds in war. Such immortality was assured by bardic poetry that gave accounts of battles and the exploits of heroes. Such bardic poetry exists in all Indo-European cultures, Celtic, Germanic, Nordic, and Aryan.

A number of characteristics of this culture are significant for the entire course of Western Civilization. ***Beauty, not truth, was the founding experience of Classical Civilization and its culture***. The great poetry, sculpture, theater, music and architecture of Greece reflected their obsession with the beauty of the world, personal beauty, as well as beauty in word and deed. Greek citizens vied (*agon*) with each other to excel, which inspired a nearly anarchic individualism that was barely held in check by ostracism, enforced exile for the political crime of hubris (prideful excess). Greek love of beauty was impartial, extolling great deeds of foes as well as friends, Greek and barbarian, alike, although Greeks were scathing in their criticism of the tastes and culture of barbarians.

Greek culture favored the seen and heard over the unseen. Color, light, beauty, savor, vigorous exercise, games and competition, life on earth in the here and now was the greatest state of being. Health and wealth were prerequisites for the life of freedom of course. Gods and men were similar physically but the gods enjoyed immortality. Men could achieve immortality through great words and deeds and live in the Elysian Fields where a life much like the good life on earth would continue. Hell was a valley of incorporeal shades destined to an empty afterlife in disembodied condition.

Freedom was enjoyed only in the public realm of the polis, where persuasion, not force prevailed. The Greek understanding of freedom is entirely alien to our contemporary view. For the Greeks, the necessities of life and the coercion imposed by metabolism were intrinsically slavish. Labor required as raw energy to provide food and goods was slavery, and all who labored with their bodies were slaves. Freedom required an individual to have the means to establish a household to supply his **needs** so he would be free to enter the public realm of *freedom*, the polis where he engaged with others also freed from necessity.

All work and labor was slavish, and slavery was both necessary and essential. Private life in the household was intrinsically slavish, since it ministered to the life needs of the master and the members of the household. Women were not free or admitted to the public realm because they engaged in the labor of reproduction in addition to household tasks. The basis for homosexuality in Greece was that only association between free males was considered the basis for love, whereas association with women was considered merely necessary and not between equals. The influence of notable women like Xanthippe wife of Socrates and Roxane mistress of Alexander the Great did not alter the prevailing condition of women in Greece.

Greeks prided themselves on their freedom and the polis. They constantly contrasted their anthropocentric culture and free city states with the Asiatic barbarians whose massed populations lived as slaves and worshiped animal gods. The Greeks commented constantly on the differences between their anthropocentric gods, free and rational way of life and the bestial panoply of barbarian gods and the mass, regimented populations of their empires.

Plato and the Decline of Classical Civilization

Errare mehercule malo cum Platone...quam cum istis vera sentire.
Cicero, **Tusculum Disputationes I**, 39-40
The more I read him, the less I wonder that they poisoned him.
Thomas B. Macaulay on Socrates

Despite the unique greatness of Athens, fratricidal wars between the Greek city states led to political chaos and eventual ruin and loss of freedom first to Sparta and then to Philip and Alexander of Macedon. The wars were between presumably liberal allies of Athens and the conservative allies of Sparta. This political context largely determined the last great invention of Greece: philosophy. ***Truth, ideas, and the unseen, not the world, beauty, and the seen, were the founding experience and only reality of Greek philosophy.***

As in the arts, the formal study and understanding of the world and its phenomena originates with the Greeks. All science, mathematics, logic, and argument derive from this original Greek achievement that occurred between 600 and 250 BC. The most notable and influential Greek philosopher is Plato who lived from 428 to 348 BC. In his dialogs, which give accounts of symposia in which Socrates discusses with friends many philosophical questions. Plato expounds a theory of knowledge and politics that eventually dominated Greek and Roman culture and stultified Classical Civilization. His influence was so elegantly pernicious that the entire ruling class accepted it and no serious challenge was made to it. It departed entirely from Homer and the original ethos of Greek Civilization. In fact Plato turned Homer on his head, reversing every aspect of Indo-European culture that Homer represented. Plato also departed from the founding experience of Greek philosophy: truth. He replaced truth with a priori theories in order to undermine the experimental and impartial search for knowledge of the world and men.

Plato was directly influenced by an alien worldview that had developed in Asia Minor. By 750 BC, Zoroastrianism had assimilated the ethical-absolutist elements of Semitic religion into a theory of radical dualism. Earth and the body are evil, Heaven is good. They are totally opposed and incompatible. Good and evil, Heaven and the world, God and Satan are in mortal combat and only true believers will be saved. Integration of Zoroastrian radical dualism into Greek Indo-European polarizing forms of logic and thought occurred in the Western Mediterranean not long after. Pythagoras (590-520? BC) formulated the theory that the Earth and the Heavens are of two entirely different natures and substances. Earth is a place of illusion, irrationality and error. Heaven is the source of the rational, the true and the good. Truth is absolute, unchanging, and rational and is revealed only through mathematics and dialectic reasoning. (When one of Pythagoras' students discovered that *pi* is an irrational number, which showed that reality is irrational, he was driven from the fold.)

But deeper political forces were at play in the case of Pythagoras. The Delphic Oracle had become a widespread intelligence operation favoring the aristocratic land- and slave-owning classes against the democratic and free-thinking Sophists and democratic groups. When living in Crotona, Pythagoras formed a brotherhood of local aristocrats, lived in monastic seclusion, practiced vegetarianism, studied mathematics, and promoted Pythagorean theories. Eventually the local democrats grew suspicious of the group and killed them around the year 400 BC.

What the aristocratic party needed was an ideology that formulated the belief and objectives of the conservative cause. Plato provided this ideology a century after the death of Pythagoras. Plato adopted radical dualism from the teachings of Zoroastrianism as had Pythagoras. His motive was political, not intellectual, and he succeeded in arresting the development of science and free inquiry in the Classical world altogether. Plato was particularly hostile toward the Sophists who argued that everything is convention not nature and that there are no absolute values or beliefs.

Plato reversed Homer in the allegory of the cave. For Homer the world was real, and the afterlife was unreal. For Plato, the world is unreal and the afterlife and things unseen (ideas) are real. The heavenly bodies represent a world of perfect unchanging truth as opposed to the changing and unknowable confusion of the material world. Truth is fixed, eternal, and unseen. The world is changing and mortal and not worth knowing. Sense perception is deceived and unreliable. Only rational deduction through thought can lead to truth. Experiment and observation of the material world produces only confusion and deception. Truth is in the fixed sky of ideas not in the temporal world. Even knowledge was simply remembering what had been known but forgotten. Ideas are imbedded in the mind and are real whereas their shadowy representations in the world are untrue and unknowable. Knowledge is the result of memory and reasoning not of experience and observation. None of this is metaphysically or otherwise true. It is simply a hypothesis about the nature of the world and the relation of thinking to it.

Finally, Plato imposed the ultimate test of Greek logic, that the cause is always greater than the effect. This unproved proposition was the foundation of Platonic philosophy and enforced a hierarchical worldview. It reached its absurdity in his theory of 'evolution' from highest to lowest beings. Plato's hierarchy reversed the traditional Greek/Indo-European worldview. He put contemplation and thought, which are directed at the unseen, at the apex of human faculties, in place of action and speech, which are directed entirely at, only become manifest in, and are concerned entirely with the unmediated interactions between men. Plato, as part of the aristocratic Pythagorean conspiracy against the democratic elements of Greek City States, advocated in his dialog **The Republic** a static state, ruled by a divinely enlightened ruler, who makes all decisions. The state suppresses innovation that might upset the eternal cycle established by the divine power, which is an analog of the Egyptian Empire commonly mocked by Greeks. Particularly insightful is Plato's admonition regarding music: *For a change to a new type of music is something to beware of as a hazard of all our fortunes. For the modes of music are never disturbed without unsettling of the most fundamental political and social conventions. It is here, then, in music that our guardians must build their guardhouse and post of watch. Republic IV, 424c-d.* [Note: Similar alarm attended the rise of Rock and Roll in the 1950's]

Perhaps the most pernicious claim of Plato was that human and social differences are natural and innate not conventional. Slavery was innate because the slave had a slavish nature. The best should rule because they are superior by nature. The wisest of all should be the ruler of the State, and all the rest should simply carry out his edicts. The clear objective was to establish an absolute state in control of all aspects of society and based on a caste system decreed by nature, not unlike the system established in India by the Hindu Brahmins. Plato also proposed eugenics as a way to keep the population of the State in the hands of the best: *The best men must cohabit with the best women in as many cases as possible and the worst with the worst in the fewest, and the offspring of the one must be reared and that of the other not, if the flock is to be as perfect as possible. And the way in which all this is brought to pass must be unknown to any but the rulers. The offspring of the good they will take to the nurses… but the offspring of the inferior or defective they will properly dispose of in secret so that no one will know what has become of them. Republic V, 449d.*

Hitlerian eugenics at its source. As a result of Plato's theories, Western intellectual development occurred within the following hierarchy of human activities:

- ***Contemplation*** and thought, considered the highest activity, which required stillness and cessation of all action in order to contemplate ideas and meditate upon them.

- ***Action*** and speech, which only occur **between** men and are the existential prerequisite for stories about individuals, whether heroes or ordinary men, that can be told. The story reveals who the person was and what he did. Without deeds ***and*** words, no story can be told. All literature and history, all fiction and nonfiction, depends on this primary human capacity for speech and action, which reveal a unique persona about which a story can be told.
- ***Work***, which removes material from nature to create objects that make up the 'world' of things which men inhabit and which relate men to each other in an objective world of objects that can be seen and commented upon. The world provides an in-between of durable objects to which we can all relate and about which we can offer our 'viewpoint'. Sharing viewpoints helps us build a commonsense understanding of reality'. Without a world to unite and separate us there would only be the unreal swings of unseen moods, feelings, and thoughts unanchored to objective worldly objects and events.
- ***Labor***, the metabolic exertion of the body needed to perform the most basic cultivation of soil, processing of food, and gestating of new life, as well as the functions that sustain the life of the body.

Thought does not require an author, which is why Socrates never wrote down his musings and was unconcerned about future fame. His was authentic thinking, unlike the fame mongering of later philosophers. ***Action*** requires speech to reveal who the doer and speaker is in order that a story may be told. None of the other activities requires speech, and none of the other activities requires that one know who performed the activity. Only the human revulsion at futility makes it necessary for the maker of an object to identify himself, however, this revulsion and this need have nothing to do with making objects. It has to do with the human capacity to speak and act, and therefore the capacity to reveal who one is and to begin new courses of action, and to organize and cooperate. ***Work*** creates the world in which we live, including homes, tools, public buildings, books, statues, furniture, and the like, all of which make up the material culture of a society or civilization. The purpose of these objects is to **endure** not to be consumed, so they can provide a stable, lasting, common world in which human life can make sense. The purpose of work objects is to create and furnish a world that stands between man and nature, and their greatest quality is **durability**, which can withstand the slow, inevitable wearing down of time and use. This is especially true of great works of art, the most worldly objects we know of, that have no 'use' and yet are the most worldly objects because they are not intended to be used and therefore can endure nearly indefinitely if cared for. But their importance derives not from the outlook of the maker, but from the outlook of the beholder. The outlook of **homo faber** is utilitarianism, in which the value of everything is determined by what use it is 'good for'. **Labor** produces objects for consumption, like bread and other food, or is itself consumed as in personal services or common labor needed to maintain the world. It is the least worldly activity, since it produces no durable objects, and its services and 'products' are consumed immediately or very soon after they are 'produced'. There is no duration, only an endless cycle of consumption, production, and consumption ad infinitum. The basic value of labor is life, since life is not possible without labor and life is labor's 'product'. **Homo laborans** is unworldly and incapable of action or speech in the Classical sense, since speech is irrelevant to labor, although songs and rhythmic music makes laboring easier. He moves from appetite to satiation to renewed appetite in an endless cycle devoid of meaning.

But his is the only activity that produces 'happiness', the feeling of wellbeing that follows laborious exertion, enjoyment of the fruits of that labor, and then deeply satisfying rest in order to restore strength and resume labor.

Roman Law

Roman law was the great contribution of Rome to Western Civilization. Its most famous dictum, **pacta sunt servanda**, provided the stability required for maintaining economic and social order throughout the empire. The significance of this legal principle is easy to overlook given the enormous web of contracts and agreements that make up the modern world. The fact that agreements would be enforced made it possible to bind the future as if it were the present, commit resources and organize economic activity over large areas and extended periods of time. This principle ensured a measure of certainty in an entirely uncertain world.

Christianity

Of infinitely greater influence than Rome was the teaching of Jesus Christ. The **secular and political** significance of his teaching is profound. Christ introduced the duty of **forgiveness**, as important in unbinding the past and freeing the future, as **pacta sunt servanda** was for binding the future and creating stability. Forgiveness broke the otherwise inevitable chain of retaliation that characterized tribal societies, freeing them to begin again rather than follow a predetermined path of mutual retribution. It is also the foundation of hope, which is directed at the future. Forgiveness guarantees that the future can be free rather than bound in irreversible determinism. Christ also introduced the concept of **goodness**, one of the most anti- political concepts ever advanced and which destroys political order and relationships wherever attempts are made to make it the basis of policy. Goodness is anti-political because it becomes hypocrisy if witnessed, made known, even when made known to the doer. Goodness splits the conscience and will because one can't **do** good without knowing one is doing good, which deprives it of its goodness and makes it a mere calculation of charity or an example of good works. One cannot **be** good, one can only strive for goodness. Goodness flees from publicity and is defeated by speech. Hence, its extreme anti-political character. Rousseau and the French Revolution attempted to introduce a toxic mimic of goodness into politics with murderous effect. Christian **love** also is anti-political in that it does not seek publicity and is defeated by speech. The same is true of compassion, which cannot be spoken but can only be manifested by gesture or facial expression. When politicians pretend to establish love or compassion as a basis for policy they corrupt the political realm and the very policies themselves.

Christianity broke with the Semitic and Classical traditions in several important ways. Classical tradition regarded immortality through fame as the supreme good, attainable only by a very few. The birth of Christ divided time into an infinite past and an infinite future. Salvation made the world a transitional stage on the way to paradise, but the requirement of good works to achieve salvation raised the significance of worldly achievement. Christianity promised to each individual, eternal life after death. The very distinction between ***immortal*** and ***eternal*** added a universal dimension to thought unprecedented in Classical Civilization, which believed in immortality of the gods but did not believe they were eternal.

Classical civilization regarded women and laborers as unfit for public realm because they performed the necessary and biologically coercive tasks of childbearing and laboring needed to sustain life. Life and the processes needed to sustain it were considered private matters of the household unfit to appear in public. Life in itself was contemptible, and disease and coercion were considered justifications for suicide. No Greek citizen could be tortured or executed, but it was understood that the individual would willingly take his own life if condemned to death by the polis. Socrates took the hemlock and Seneca cut a vein to preserve each his own "freedom" as citizen to dispose of his own life. Christianity made life essential and precious as the prerequisite to salvation, and life no matter how abased was dignified if salvation was the reward. Christianity raised the dignity of slaves, laborers and women, since all had promise of salvation through faith and good works.

Catholic Church

Christianity is the only sacramental religion. All religions have rituals, sacred texts, and places set aside for worship. Only Christianity has sacraments that directly join the believing individual and God. Baptism, Confession, Catechism, Marriage, Eucharist, Investiture, and Extreme Unction involve the presence of god in the life of the believer.

Christianity, most importantly, reconciled the Semitic and Indo-European divisions with the Earth Mother religions by raising the dignity of the earth and human body. Yahweh created earth and called it good. Christianity promised the resurrection of the body and the life everlasting. Performing good works on earth was a prerequisite for salvation in Heaven. This created a ***worldly*** commitment that had enormous consequences for human dignity and eventually the pursuit of science in Western Civilization.

A further distinction instituted by the Catholic Church around 1150 was the sacrament of marriage. Marriage in all cultures had always been a secular contract of importance only when prominent families were involved. The early Church considered it a remedy for concupiscence but remained somewhat contemptuous of those unable to remain celibate. This ambivalence remained through the dominantly monastic centuries of the Church. Reassertion of the Earth Mother tradition began in the 12th Century, its greatest manifestation being the Gothic Cathedrals, nearly all of which were named for **Notre Dame**. Further, Chivalry, romantic love and the poetry that celebrated that love were invented in Western culture. Mariolatry, the return of the feminine to dignity within the Christian world, also led to a reappraisal of marriage, raising it to a

sacrament equal to the other sacraments involving a holy union sanctioned by God. This parity of male and female within the marriage bond was imperfectly realized in law and society, but it did assert the commitment of Christianity to a higher standard.

Protestantism

The Plague that began in 1350 and killed one-third of the population of Europe intensified pessimism and religious fanaticism. Combined with

Mariolatry and the increasingly corrupt and disordered management of the Papacy, which became a political pawn in the struggle between the Holy Roman Empire and France, the Indo-European polarity of Celtic, Germanic, and Nordic peoples of northern Europe reasserted itself, leading to the revival of Manichean heresy, greater emphasis on the Old Testament, and alienation from the Romanized states of Italy, Austria, and France. In England, the Tudors (Wales) readily split from the Papacy, as did Luther in Germany and Calvin in Geneva. The split between Nordic Mythology and Classical Mythology occurred along geographic lines, with France internally split between Huguenot Protestants of the western part of the country and the Catholic central and southern parts of the country.

In Western Civilization, attempts to introduce elements of the theocratic state were made from 1500 to 1700 in the form of "divine right of kings". Such theories were eventually discredited, but in Spain the close relationship between the Emperor Philip II and the Catholic Inquisition came closest to recreating a static, theocratic form of empire evolved between 5000 and 3000 BC.

The cycle established by Male/Female, Heaven/Earth polarization continues through history to the present. The key indicators for the Female/Earth centered factors has been the status of women, the relative freedom of scientific inquiry, and the presence of democratic tendencies in the society at large.

Return of earth/sky, skygod/earth mother conflict occurred during the Reformation, when Semitic dualism revived, especially in the teachings of Calvin. Predestination, sin, salvation only of the elect, eternal damnation, were all derived from the teachings of Zoroaster combined with the logical absolutism of Plato and Pythagoras. The obsession with purity, cleansing, and female corruption eventually took form as Puritanism, entirely alien to the teachings of Jesus, which included a God of Love, brotherhood and mutual concern, and the like. Luther was nearly as lunatic as Calvin but was personally earthy and appealing. He rejected good works as essential to salvation, relying entirely on faith, a bias derived from the Platonism of St. Augustine, the namesake of his monastic order. The fanaticism inspired by these increasingly dehumanized religious tenets finally began to abate in the 18th Century with Quakerism, Methodism, and Unitarianism in the United States and England. Religious fundamentalism especially characteristic of the more fanatical traits of the Semitic dualism remains a threat to world peace. Wahabbism, started in the 1700's, has led to al-Qaeda and other murderous fundamentalist Islamic groups throughout the Arab/Islamic world.

The Rise of Science

Modern experimental science developed out of the "school of suspicion" that arose once Galileo proved by observation that the Earth rotates around the Sun. Proving that the world is not as it appears and that our senses are in fact deceived by appearances launched a search for the reality hidden behind appearances that has produced the most profound transformation in human history.

God became a ***dieu trompeur***, more mysterious and unintelligible than ever. The epistemology of Plato seemed vindicated. Yet this simply meant that if we cannot know the truth it is all the more important that we ***be truthful***. The apparent dilemma was of short duration. By the 17th Century, experimental science began to develop a body of knowledge that led endlessly forward. The foundation discoveries of Newton, development of the calculus, beginnings of chemistry and physics provided an indication of a much more profound and majestic order of creation. Founding of the Royal Society for scientific research established the principle of total truthfulness, unbiased research, and collective endeavor. Science was temporarily misapplied to debates over the existence of God and the validity of religion in the 19th Century, but by the end of the 20th Century, that naïve matter vs. spirit and similar formulations were irrelevant. Science is cured of any claims to provide arguments against the existence of God.

Rousseau and the Corruption of Western Thought

Jean-Jacques Rousseau (1712-1778) is the most important and most deleterious influence on modern Western history. He inspired and embodied the worst aspects of the French Revolution, and his ideas, attitudes and feelings underlie every modern intellectual innovation and political movement, including socialism, communism, psychology, sociology, progressive education, ethical and cultural relativism, and collectivist and behaviorist theories and political movements.

Rousseau is much less influential in Great Britain and the United States. The American Revolution derived from entirely different ideas and occurred under totally different economic and social conditions, and both Britain and the United States were immune from the pernicious influence of Rousseau and the French Revolution for most of the 19th Century. The enormous gap between the political experience of continental Europe and that of Great Britain and the United States largely dominates the history of Western Civilization in the 19th and 20th Centuries. In the course of the 20th Century, Rousseau's ideas gradually seeped into America through intellectuals influenced by European academics and their theories. Beard's study of the American Revolution published in 1907 began the general corruption of rational, objective standards in the 'social sciences' taught today, which is directly attributable to Rousseau's influence. That a self-pitying, chronic whiner, who failed every relationship he engaged in and betrayed every trust he committed to, should have had such influence can only be attributed to his remarkable gift for formulating and expressing his thoughts and, more importantly, feelings. Some of the most pernicious notions ever expressed are rendered in some of the most elegant French prose ever written. Rousseau was a charming and disarming intellectual villain. Rousseau introduced three concepts that both transformed and subverted Western society and culture: Subjectivity, Totalitarianism, Victimism.

Subjectivity refers to Rousseau's discovery of intimacy and the inner world of feeling and thought that provides a refuge from the scorn and indifference of society. His was a rebellion of the heart against society, not against the state.

The discovery of intimacy as an independent realm of experience led to the vast expansion of moods and feeling expressed in poetry, the novel, and especially in music and later in movies. Appropriately, he was a great novelist, and both a composer and musicologist. He invented a new method of musical notation. His musical works include essays on music, an opera called *The Village Soothsayer (Le Devin de Village)* in 1752, a highly respected Dictionary of Music in 1767, and a collection of folk songs entitled *The Consolation of My Life's Miseries* in 1781. Rousseau extended the subjective realm to every aspect of life. In education he advocated in *Emile* a subjective approach based on the child's 'interest' and pace of learning versus memorization and authority. Rousseau favored the *subjective* as against the *objective,* which eventually led to a permissive view of social behavior and a loss of common sense and objective standards in academic work, where any point of view might be taken as equal to any other. Such Relativism derives from the radical subjectivism of Rousseau.

Totalitarianism refers to Rousseau's proposal of the 'general will' as the only lawful basis for government. This theory precluded a conjunction of different interests and groups under a constitution. The public good can only be represented by a unanimous expression of ***will***, and this ever-changing will, not permanent and stable ***law***, should govern the state and society. This in turn introduced the idea of enemies of the state, since any party or social group by definition pursues its particular interest not those of the general interest.

Only by repressing the personal and adopting the general interest can the individual be saved, politically. The notion of a loyal opposition to a 'general will' was unthinkable since will is indivisible, although it may be paralyzed by indecision. The public good is one and indivisible, not the sum of many parts. The ruthlessness underlying the concept of 'general will' was revealed in the French Revolution by Robespierre, who was precursor to the totalitarian regimes of the 20th Century. When Robespierre adopted the general will of les enrages of Paris, their interest became the will of the state, and all other classes were enemies and executed accordingly.

Victimism refers to Rousseau's theory that society is evil, and individuals are born free and good but are enslaved and made evil by society. Instead of being born in sin, men are born innocent, and evil is in society. The innocence and suffering of individuals versus the ruthless exploitation and indifference of society became the seedbed of multiple political and intellectual movements. This theory introduced pity into public affairs with disastrous effect. Unlike compassion, which binds an individual with the suffering of another individual, pity is a generalized feeling applied to humanity as a whole or to a group or class. Because individuals are victims of society, groups can be identified as collective victims of other groups. The entire culture of class warfare and class victims was introduced by Rousseau and led to Marxism and the various perversions of 'social justice' and psychological interpretations of criminal and other antisocial behavior that remove any responsibility for behavior or condition from the 'victimized' individual or class. In Rousseau's peculiar world, hypocrisy was the greatest crime, because in the hypocrite, good appearance conceals the corrupt intentions of the heart. This led to a game of shadows as layers of appearance were explored and exposed and in which political confessions preceded executions with regularity.

Stalin carried this conundrum to its logical conclusion by assuming that all individuals have thoughts that are self-interested and not related to the general good, and any or all individuals may be persuaded to 'confess' crimes they didn't commit because who committed them is not subjectively relevant. All are criminals as a class and because it is impossible to prove sincerity. Any avowal is subject to accusations of hypocrisy beyond disproof. In this radically subjective world, there is no reality or any way to demonstrate that what one feels or thinks is true or real, because there is no witness but oneself. Given this radical isolation, contrary to the objective and rational views of the American revolutionaries, the French Revolution unleashed two centuries of political murder in Europe.

Darwin, Marx, and the Triumph of the Life Process

Darwin and Marx revolutionized the Western tradition by turning Plato on his head. The revolution can be summarized as a reversal of the foundation principle of Greek logic that ***the cause must be greater than the effect***. Although Hume had challenged the idea of cause and effect, finding only sequent and antecedent, but no cause and effect, Darwin proved through evolution that the cause can be less than the effect. Evolution reversed the hierarchy of Platonic values. Marx also reversed Plato by making labor the creator of all values, not thought or contemplation. In his theory of class conflict, he embodied the French Revolution and the implications of Rousseau's thought, wherein the innocent many who labor are exploited by the guilty few who do nothing. Placing labor at the center of all values, made necessity and life, not the world or fame, the driving force of mankind. Life and its processes are necessary and compelling, so there is no place for freedom in Marx's view of mankind.

Progressive Education in the United States

John Dewey introduced Rousseau to American public education. Progressive educators thought that traditional education should be reformed. Famous progressive educators of the 1800's included Francis Parker and G. Stanley Hall. In the early 1900's, John Dewey became a well-known spokesman for progressive education. Progressive educators tried to reform elementary school methods in several ways. They thought teachers should pay more attention to the individual child and not treat all children alike. Progressive educators believed that children learn best when they are genuinely interested in the material, and not when they are forced to memorize facts that seem useless to them. Children should learn by direct contact with things, places, and people, as well as by reading and hearing about them. Thus, elementary schools should include science laboratories, workshops, field trips, art studios, kitchens, gymnasiums, and gardens. Progressive educators believed this procedure would develop the child's physical, social, and emotional nature as well as mind.

In addition, progressive educators stressed greater freedom, activity, and informality in the classroom. They believed that children learn better when they can move about and work at their own pace. They thought children should gather materials from many sources rather than from just one textbook and should work in groups with other students. Discussion, dramatics, music, and art activities became a larger part of classroom procedures. Progressive education spread more widely through elementary schools than it did in high schools or colleges. Teachers planned individual instruction and centered it on projects, units, or activities rather than the usual courses or subjects. They taught students of different abilities in separate groups. This is partly fine. But as a substitute for actual learning, rather than 'experience' it is disastrous. Public education in the United States is now a captive of educational theories derived from Rousseau and teachers colleges and unions that enforce established progressive educational theories. The system is failing American parents who instinctively want discipline, traditional standards, and intellectual achievement.

Christopher Lee Bowen

The Dark Side of Western Civilization From Calvin to Hitler

Western Civilization was founded on several traditions, including Christianity and the teachings of Jesus. The early church consisted of 'democratic' gatherings of men and women equally sharing the communion of faith. But within two centuries the church was organized into formal clergy and lay believers. Doctrine was established by councils, like the Council of Trent, where many mysteries of the Christian belief were settled. After Rome fell the Church became the only authority in the West, left to encounter the invasions of pagan nomadic tribes from Europe and Central Asia. Millennial expectations seemed to be coming true as the secular world disintegrated. Heresies and psychotic behavior ensued, for example the self-castration of Saint Jerome as a repudiation of the body, clearly contrary to the doctrine of resurrection; Arianism which claimed that Jesus was not divine, though an inspired teacher; Pelagian heresies that denied original sin; and so on. The church came under the influence of the monastic movement, begun in Egypt by anchorites who withdrew into solitary exclusion from society. The church accommodated this move to worldlessness by instituting monastic associations, led by St. Benedict, who formed the Benedictine order, gave it rules, and brought it under church administration.

The dictum of St. Paul that it is better to marry than burn was widely held. Marriage, women and sex were to various degrees anathema and eventually celibacy of the priesthood at large, not just monks, became church practice. Marriage was not yet a sacrament and didn't become so until the 12th Century. Monastic leadership of the church was maintained for more than 500 years. This was a productive form of investment and development as the orders settled, cleared, cultivated and civilized much of France and parts of Germanic Europe. The Cistercian order founded many monasteries that guided various pagan tribes into the church and productive agriculture. Conversion of Clovis in 600 AD brought the Franks into the Catholic Church, providing a military arm for the faith, by 800 extended by Charlemagne to most of Germany as well. The state once again collapsed after Charlemagne and the Church resumed its leadership of Western Civilization. Only in the 900's with the rise of organized kingdoms was secular authority reestablished.

The monastic period began to yield to Mariolatry in the 11th to 13th Centuries. Mary provided the inspiration for most cathedrals (Notre Dame de .....) throughout France and England. This humanizing trend was reinforced by the invention of romantic love, chivalric code, and respect for women, at least in theory. Marriage became a sacrament. The New Testament, Jesus' teachings of love and caring, and the motherhood of Mary softened the message of religion that had relied heavily on invented visions of Hell to persuade the fallen to the faith. The polarizing Indo-European view that included all parts of reality in its spectrum exemplified by Aristotle was introduced into Christian thought by Thomas Aquinas, whose hierarchic views of society and nature provided an inclusive vertical spectrum to his new humanizing view that eventually became the official 'philosophy' of the Catholic Church. Uniting pagan wisdom and church revelation into Western Civilization was his primary achievement.

The Black Plague that began in 1350 altered the 'psychology' of Europe. Nearly half the population died. Only in the 20th Century did we acquire and understanding of the viral and bacterial causes of diseases. In the 14th Century they were considered visitations of an angry God on a sinning world. Although printed bibles were not generally available, it is as if a move from the New to the Old Testament took place: from a Christian God of Love to a Semitic God of Wrath. Flagellation and psychotic self-mutilation, dances of death, mortality, sin, and damnation were common themes for woodcuts, the main graphic means of conveying religious messages to the illiterate. The Old Testament prophets' diatribes against Sodom and Gomorrah, the world the flesh and the Devil, damnation, Hell, and the bleakest view of life and the world prevailed from 1350 on.

As the plague abated this mood passed, especially because the loss of available labor meant that every peasant was extremely valuable. Many fled current masters for more generous new ones. Attempts to force them back into servitude led to Peasant Revolts in Germany and elsewhere. Internal wars, like the Wars of the Roses, as nobles tried to obtain resources by force to maintain their traditional standards of living (and by borrowing from Jewish and non-Jewish merchants) spread death and destruction nearly as efficiently as the plague had done. The middle class in towns emerged for the first time as a major source of funds and wealth and support for Kings against the aristocrats. Discovery of America and gold and silver in abundance enriched Spain and led to inflation in Europe, creating economic chaos in states that lacked Spain's advantage. The corruption of the Italian Papacy now largely purchased by Medici, Borgias, and other wealthy merchant families, came up against a factor in the European heritage that is not easy to explain but is historically clear, relevant, and nearly led to the destruction of Europe, the Germanic tribal tradition.

Rome never conquered the Germanic tribes, so well described by Tacitus. They remained outside the 'civilizing' influence of Rome that reshaped the Celts in France and to some extent in Britain. Germans were recruited for the Praetorian Guard of the Caesars and into the Legions, but the tribes themselves remained independent within the forests of Germany. Tacitus described their elective blood oath leadership, their *furor teutonicus,* their racial homogeneity, their devoted monogamy, their military vigor and personal lassitude. Luther well represented this tradition and rebelled against a different kind of Roman domination much as German tribes had against Caesar. The combination of Germanic schism, middle class insecurity, and trauma of violence since the plague of 1350-1400, provided a phobic emotional complex that reinforced Semitic Dualism, which replaced the teachings of Jesus mainly with those of Calvin in Geneva, and restructured the social and emotional life of Protestant Europe. The Catholic Church also acquired the phobic complex from Spain and the Inquisition, established around the time of the plague, which became an instrument of terror. All Europe became a madhouse of religious fanaticism, psychotic beliefs in witches, sightings of the Devil (Luther threw his ink well at him), and similar unenlightened conduct. The revival of Semitic Dualism, which established exclusive, not inclusive, divisions in the world, was symptomatic in the dominantly Old Testament basis for the Protestant sects.

Calvin is the best 'religious' representative of this disaster. His theocratic state in Geneva, his doctrine of predestination in which nothing a person does can alter his fated damnation, his doctrine of the 'elect' who will be saved and the mass who will be damned, his emphasis on outward piety, conformity, and success as a sign of salvation were especially appealing to the middle class, which was stranded among the remnants of a disintegrating medieval world that despised or ignored them. They were eager to adopt any system that would give them psychic certainty. Puritanism in England and especially Scotland was the result.

Thomas Hobbes is the 'philosophical' representative of the Calvinist outlook, characteristically a product of the Puritan rebellion in England and Massachusetts. His bleak 'war of man against man' reflected much of European experience during the plague, civil wars, and wars of religion. Any political tyranny that could reign in the endless murder and mayhem was welcome. Hitler and Stalin carried out his suggestions and then some 300 years later.

The fall of Constantinople in 1456 added another trend to the mix. As scholars of Greek fled to Italy and northern Europe, a Renaissance based on secular humanism of classical Greece and Rome began its transformation of European culture. Secular enlightenment and sanity competed for supremacy with religious genocide and fanaticism from roughly 1500 to 1945. In America this dualist Puritan madness, following the last burning of witches in Salem in the 1690's, became unbearable and unenforceable. Eventually Quakers and Methodists re-introduced mercy, love and tolerance and the Unitarians pretty much ended any doctrinal vestiges of the original Puritan founders in Massachusetts.

The puritans were pretty much sidelined in England by the established church, the return of Charles II, and the infinite sanity of the Brits. Perhaps the most insidious long-term threat to Western Civilization was the rise of determinism and behaviorism that underlie the collectivist theories of Calvin, Rousseau, Marx, and the social Darwinists that led to Hitler and Stalin. They pervade academic 'thinking' partly as a result of European influences in American schools derived from the experiences of the French Revolution.

Calvin & Rousseau

Calvin and Rousseau form the first pair of determinist influences, oddly both located in Geneva some 200 years apart. Calvin introduced anti-Christian views that fundamentally denied free will, the only basis for Christian redemption. He posited predestination, salvation of the elect already chosen before birth, and damnation of the vast majority, again predestined before birth. Free will, conscience, good deeds, nothing can alter the iron law of divine predetermination. Men are born in sin, are guilty, and most will go to an afterlife of damnation. Just the outside chance that you might be one of the elect might keep you going under this bleak scenario. Certainly, the men of the cloth were especially prone to self-election, which lent fervor to their horrific descriptions of what their gaping audiences faced.

This appalling view of human nature and religion actually gained adherents among the successful middle class in England and Europe, which came to see the aristocrats and the lower classes as most likely to be damned and themselves, with their modest dress (usually black and white), diligent habits of thrift, cleanliness, and work, church going, and respectability appeared most eligible as well. These habits are not to be despised and they contributed to higher standards of personal hygiene, but the inner workings left much to be desired.

Around 1750, Rousseau for various reasons, and in particular to win money in an essay contest, wrote his seminal essay on freedom that began: "*Men are born free, but everywhere are in chains.*" For purposes of brevity, we can propose that Rousseau simply turned Calvin upside down. Rousseau stated that men are innocent at birth and corrupted by society, that they are born free and enslaved by society, that there was original innocence in place of original sin, and original goodness rather than original guilt. The curious reversal placed goodness within individual men and evil in society. By extension, childhood was the time of purist innocence and became a cultural fetish from which the child-centered family emerged. From being spiritually damned the individual became socially corrupt or oppressed. When the French Revolution broke down under the weight and fury of les *enragée*, the street people of Paris and rural poor, immediate application of Rousseau assigned guilt clearly where it belonged with murderous effect. The aristocrats were guilty as a class for oppressing the innocent poor. The damnation of individuals in Calvin became the damnation of classes in Rousseau and later in Marx. Pity of the innocent poor, as a class not as individuals, substituted for Calvin's contempt for the guilty sinner.

Social Darwinism later added a pseudoscientific edge to this growing determinist outlook substituting *natural selection* for Calvinist *election* and *survival of the fit* for *Marx's class warfare*. The respective viewpoints were taken up by the middle class and the 'proletariat' or at least the leaders of the proletariat that formed political parties. The industrial revolution and the huge increase in population in Europe added economic, class, and demographic weight to the emerging determinist class theories.

After the French Revolution a class society system evolved. On the right were wealthy industrialists and petit bourgeois. On the left were haute proletariat intelligentsia and the labor class. The right formed nationalist and anti-Semitic parties (the petit bourgeois needed the Jews to blame for their middling life achievement) while the left formed internationalist ideologically Marxist parties. Nationalism was used successfully in WWI to coerce the working class into supporting the war aims of their governments. The corruption of thought and feeling begun by Rousseau was institutionalized in the Terror of 1792-94 and became the paradigm for European views of revolution and social conflict thereafter. Although the American Revolution was the greatest and most successful political achievement in history, few Americans have any idea why, and their teachers in universities and elsewhere have substituted determinist European interpretations that misrepresent our heritage. The only uncorrupted part of academe is the physical sciences which are the triumph of Western Civilization, although some of their conclusions may be perverted to reinforce the corrupted and misleading doctrines and theories of historians, sociologists, psychologists, economists, anthropologists and the rest.

Fortunately, the United States avoided this European bedlam until after the Civil War because it had vast land resources and natural wealth, a democratic political system and a habit of individual independence and self-reliance. As industrialism developed, Labor unions were formed to improve the conditions for workers in the 1880's and major violent strikes occurred (Pullman Strike of 1887) and European socialist theories were introduced by recent immigrants to explain the conflicts. The ruling industrial elite was able to divide north/south farmers and rural/urban voters until the election of 1932, so no political challenge to their leadership emerged.

Behaviorism

The final factor was the growth of behaviorism in place of freedom as the explanation of human interaction. Various theories of pleasure/

pain driven behavior to explain all human conduct had been developed but the rise of individual 'psychology' in Vienna with Freud and the 'social psychology' of sociology provided seemingly scientific, primarily statistical proofs of the determinist nature of human conduct. Combined with Rousseau or Marx, this led to reinterpretation of crime, even postulating the innocence of the criminal, and various social theories that absolved socially and psychologically 'innocent' victims from the consequences of their actions and responsibility for their current condition. The entire world went on the sick list and remedies for endless ailments and maladjustments were prescribed, all assuming that the person was a victim not a major contributor to his condition. Socializing children, averaging behavior to group standards, treating departure from norms as pathological are examples of the trend.

Concurrent with this darkening intellectual and social trend was the greatest achievement of Western Civilization: secular humanism and science. The Renaissance, while neighbored by fanatical anti-Christian Catholic and Protestant cults, cultivated classical literature and developed universal humanist views of man and nature. This happened throughout Europe. Among the leaders were Copernicus, Kepler, Galileo, Descartes, and especially Newton who provided a unified theory of gravity and motion. In literature the greatest figure of all time, Shakespeare, provided a revolution in how to think and write about human affairs. Music, the greatest cultural invention of the West (music before Palestrina and Monteverdi was a very modest enterprise), has created a world of unsurpassed richness. Architecture, interior design, clothing, variety of food and dining, the entire spectrum of human culture was vastly enlarged, improved and extended eventually to more and more people. Even religion began its return to the teachings of Jesus, once again providing a deeper psychic certainty based on love and community than any of the determinist theories could possibly provide. The greatness of Western Civilization was in overcoming its worst challenges from determinism, Germanic tribalism, and anti-scientific, anti-democratic reaction.

Christopher Lee Bowen

PART VIII

United States: The Last Best Hope

The United States is the most remarkable political and social entity in world history. No other society approximates the military power, social viability, cultural variety, level of individual achievement, personal liberty, economic success, and irrepressible vigor the United States has, except perhaps the Elizabethan age from which we largely derive. The elements that account for this achievement are remarkable, fortuitous, and unique.

The United States began with enormous ***potential*** wealth and resources. Potential is the key word. Spain had acquired Central and South America and explored widely in North America. It discovered rich gold and especially silver mines in what is now Latin America and confined its primary effort to that region. Spain found ***actual*** wealth and already ***monetarized*** resources that could be exploited by Indian slave labor. No effort on the part of the Spanish was necessary in order to obtain immense wealth. A ruling class of Spanish adventurers (aristocrats and commoners) simply took over and ruled the enslaved Indian population and later brought in African slaves when the Indian population was depleted. There were few entire family settlements in Latin America. This was a male freebooter operation and only the ruling class settled with Spanish spouses to enjoy the profits. Simon Bolivar did not 'liberate' South America from Spain. Spain and the church had increasingly placed restraints on exploitation of the native populations and shown concern for more equitable treatment. As a consequence, the established rulers backed Bolivar to separate from Spanish rule in order to retain and consolidate their dominance over the native population. Bolivar's much touted 'revolution' was a pure reaction against any liberalization of policy toward the native Indian and mestizo population which they continue to exploit to this day.

Capitalist Settlement

North America was rich in land, timber, wildlife and pasturage, fisheries, minerals, rivers, lakes and streams and water supply, which required ***people*** and ***capital investment*** to convert resources into actual wealth. Capital was difficult but not impossible to find in England. England had a private capitalist system developed to finance settlement, unlike France and Spain, which relied on the Crown to finance colonization. This reflected the change to industrial capitalism and credit banking that began late in the 17th Century. Most colonies were founded by private joint-stock companies or individuals, which received grants from the English monarch to colonize lands claimed by England. Joint-stock companies, forerunners of modern corporations, obtained funds by selling shares of stock to individuals. The 13 English colonies began as either corporate colonies or proprietary colonies. Connecticut, Massachusetts, Rhode Island, and Virginia were founded as corporate colonies. The other nine colonies were established as proprietary colonies.

In 1624, King Charles I began to convert the colonies into royal colonies. Such colonies were under the direct control of the monarch. By the end of the colonial period, only Connecticut and Rhode Island remained corporate colonies, and only Delaware, Maryland and Pennsylvania were still proprietary. The other eight colonies had become royal colonies.

Corporate colonies had a charter granted by the English monarch to stockholders. An example is the Massachusetts Bay Colony founded in 1628. Proprietary colonies were owned by an individual proprietor or by a small group of proprietors under a charter from the monarch. Some colonists from the Massachusetts Bay Colony later moved away and established corporate settlements in Connecticut, New Hampshire, and Rhode Island. Charles II was restored to the throne in 1660 and granted charters for the colonies of Delaware, New Jersey, New York, Pennsylvania, North and South Carolina, all known as the Restoration Colonies. Some were formed from New Netherlands, which the English seized from the Dutch in 1664.

British Settlers

The greatest need was for people to settle, work, and develop the land and resources. Labor was always scarce in North America until the great immigrations of the mid-19th Century. This combination of immense resources and the constant need for people to settle and develop them required a determined, ambitious, and capable population willing to make the new land a home. Demand for their work and endless available land on the frontier made settlers independent from the start.

The second great factor in the development of the United States was the availability of a substantial number of immigrants from the British Isles. The people of Spain and France (and Russia on the Pacific coast), the only other contenders for occupation of North America, did not have the requisites needed to undertake this task. They came as exploiters in search of easy wealth or as scattered explorers, hunters, and fur traders, rather than in family groups prepared to settle and establish new communities in the New World. Equally important was the radical difference between continental land-based powers and Britain as an island sea power. France and Spain are continental powers whose security in Europe always had priority over supporting and protecting colonies. England as an island had security on land and did not need to expend large amounts of money on armies. She could focus resources on her navy, which was the largest in the world. It provided security at sea, allowing Britain to intervene and colonize anywhere in the world. If challenged abroad by France or Spain, England would ally with the second most powerful continental nation (German States, Russia,

Sweden, Austria, etc.) against the most powerful, creating military threats on land to deter advances at sea against English colonies abroad.

Another important factor in the development of the United States was the culture and level of development of the populations in Europe as compared with Britain. Spain focused on Latin American gold and silver, which required slave labor in the mines. Crops and livestock needed to support the Spanish rulers in Latin America were provided by Indians, usually under Mission direction. The land resources in Latin America were not similar to those in Spain (except for California and parts of northern Mexico), which discouraged settlement. Clearing timber and engaging in hard farm labor was not likely to inspire Spaniards to migrate after years of fabulous wealth without effort. Private settlement was in rancheros that raised cattle for the local market.

The French had other disincentives, including the disinclination of the French monarchy to lose potential soldiers to settlements remote from the homeland. France tended to follow the Spanish pattern of extracting easy to acquire wealth (especially furs) and some naval stores but wasn't focused on colonial settlement of large populations.

A number of unique circumstances made the British population willing, and in the case of the Puritans, their education, motivation, and personal wealth made them able to undertake the enormous challenge of moving families to the New World.

Favorable Foreign Conditions

The United States faced uniquely favorable foreign conditions during and after its founding. **Spain** was not modernized, was in fact mired in fantasy and religious fanaticism, with parasitic dependence on Latin American gold and silver. There was little interest in settlement of colonies. Spain had large nominal colonial land holdings but diminishing power to retain them. **France** also had not modernized. Its economy was still based on mercantilism rather than industrialism, and its domestic administration and economy were based on a sinecure system, which established inherited occupations and froze initiative and innovation. Constantly threatened by land from Spain or Germany, France had in any continental conflict to sacrifice colonial possessions for domestic security. The greatest example is Napoleon who sold Louisiana to raise cash for his continental campaigns.

England was modernized and all-powerful at sea, but had commitments in India, Africa, and the Mediterranean that forced her to ration forces. England's small army forced her to hire German mercenaries to fight in the revolutionary war. England could not devote all its resources to opposing the American colonists, and Canada was always a hostage to the United States should England attempt use of force. England eventually compromised on every boundary dispute with the United States (e.g., the Oregon territory settlement) preferring lucrative investment in American economy to constant military adversary.

Four Folkways

People from four culturally distinct folkways in Britain settled North America: Puritans, Quakers, Cavaliers, and Scotch-Irish. The four were incompatible, often hostile to each other, and extraordinary. They provided the foundation and remain the primary influences on American culture to this day. Each one. will be reviewed in some detail, but it should be noted by way of introduction that all four were persecuted minorities at some time or another in Britain, and persecuted or at least strongly opposed by one another in the United States depending on which was in ascendance.

Puritans who settled in New England came mainly from Anglia (the region of the Danegeld with a strong Scandinavian racial heritage) and areas near London. They were professionals (clergy, lawyers, doctors, merchants) and property owners, many of whom were educated at Cambridge University and provided the principal support for the overthrow of Charles I by Parliament and for the Puritan dictatorship of Cromwell. Puritans had been reviled by Cavaliers and the Crown for nearly a century. Their Calvinist self-righteousness had disrupted the realm and threatened the peace since the days of Queen Mary. In Scotland they were known as Presbyterians and in England as Congregationalists. Settlers from this group felt persecuted under Charles I and organized a Massachusetts Bay Colony to escape Anglicanism and practice their religion. Many Congregationalists were members of Parliament, like Oliver Cromwell, who led the overthrow and execution of Charles I in 1649 and established a Commonwealth. Cavaliers and Puritans (roundheads') fought during the Civil War of 1642 to 1649, and many Cavaliers withdrew to the Virginia colony during the Commonwealth until Charles II was restored in 1665.

Cavaliers and armigerous minor gentry who settled in Virginia, Maryland, and the Carolinas came from Southern England and a few other areas and later supported the Stuart monarchy against Parliament. Their settlements were populated mostly by indentured servants from southern England. Cavaliers supported the Monarchy, bore arms, and had the manners and outlook of aristocracy although many were second and third sons who had no prospect of inheritance. They colonized Virginia and populated the colony with indentured servants bound on average to 7-years labor for passage. The system of indenturing servants started during the 1600's to provide cheap labor for the colonies. Over half of all immigrants to the colonies after the 1630's came as indentured servants. When their contracts expired they were usually granted land on the frontier. Many indentured servants came from the south of England where commoners used to deferring to aristocratic landowners were prevalent, unlike the fractious Puritans and the rebellious Scotch-Irish and English Borderers unsuited to subordination.

Scotch-Irish settlement derived from one of the extraordinary historical coincidences that shaped the United States, the accession of James I to the throne. Elizabeth I had picked him as her successor in order to join England and Scotland under one monarch and presumably establish peace between the two kingdoms. This Union meant that the Scots, an enterprising and brilliant bundle of energy and contentiousness, became a major driving force in the cultural and expansionist policies of the British Empire. James settled Scots and English Borderers in Northern Ireland in the early 1600's to uproot and pacify the Catholic Irish and establish a population loyal to the Crown. The so-called Scotch-Irish drove out or enslaved the Irish and occupied their land. Scotch-Irish who settled mainly in the mountain areas of Appalachia and the South came from Northern Ireland and the border areas of Northern England and Southern Scotland. After years of clan warfare in the Scottish-English borderlands, this population was among the most independent, tough, ornery, and violent in the world. These characteristics proved useful in settling the New World but led to considerable revulsion on the part of Puritans, Cavaliers, and especially the Quakers of Pennsylvania.

Quakers who settled Pennsylvania came from Wales and west central areas of England. They were led by William Penn, leader of the Quaker faith in England. Later they were joined by Pietist and Amish German settlers, recruited by Penn from the Rhineland, who occupied farmland between Lancaster and York and became known as Penn Dutch. Quakers were the fourth persecuted minority to settle the colonies. George Fox, who founded Quakerism in the 1640's, preached the Inner Light of Christ that dwells in the hearts of ordinary people.

The word Quaker was originally meant as an insult to Fox, who told an English judge to *"tremble at the Word of the Lord."* The judge called Fox a *"quaker."* In 1681, William Penn received a charter from King Charles II to establish the colony of Pennsylvania as a haven for the continually persecuted Quakers. While the Quakers governed the colony from 1682 to 1756, Pennsylvania maintained no militia and only a modest police force. They treated the Indians fairly and maintained peace in the colony until the Scotch-Irish who settled in western parts of the state provoked the tribes in the mid-1700's.

A common characteristic of these four folkways was their dislike and contempt for one another. Hostile to each other in Britain, they became even more so in America. The Massachusetts Bay Colony burned at the stake in Boston three Quaker women who came to preach the Quaker message. Quaker conduct was disturbing on two counts: independent women traveling alone came to preach a gospel of tolerance and love alien to the Puritan tradition. The Scotch-Irish who settled in western Pennsylvania pillaged the local Indians and took their land while the Quaker government refused to send troops or provide money when Indians fought back against the Scotch-Irish. The Cavaliers despised the Scotch-Irish as primitive barbarians and the Puritans as regicides and middle class upstarts. The New England contempt for the southern gentlemen found classic expression in Henry Adams' description of William Henry Fitzhugh Lee who was in his Harvard class of 1858:

> *Chance insisted on enlarging Henry Adams's education by tossing a trio of Virginians as little fitted for it (Harvard) as Sioux Indians to a treadmill. One of these Virginians was the son of Colonel Robert E. Lee. Tall, largely built, handsome, genial, with liberal Virginian openness towards all he liked, he had also the Virginian habit of command and took leadership as his natural habit. No one cared to contest it. None of the New Englanders wanted command. For a year, at least, Lee was the most popular and prominent in his class, but then seemed slowly to drop into the background. The habit of command was not enough, and the Virginian had little else. He was simple beyond analysis; so simple that even the simple New England student could not realize him. No one knew enough to know how ignorant he was; how childlike; how helpless before the relative complexity of a school. As an animal, the Southerner seemed to have every advantage, but even as an animal he steadily lost ground. Strictly, the Southerner had no mind; he had temperament.*

As indicated already, settlement by people from four different British folkways (Puritans, Cavaliers, Quakers, Scotch-Irish) founded what became the society of the United States of America. These four groups are distinct and, in many ways, incompatible. Their patterns of thinking and behaving remain the primary influences on American society to this day. Immigrants who arrived from other parts of Europe generally assimilated into the dominant folkway of the areas in which they settled. American history is the product of the interaction and conflict between these groups, and no understanding of our history is possible without an understanding the folkways and patterns of thinking of these four primary groups.

Puritans

Notable Puritans: John Adams, Ralph Waldo Emerson, Harriet Beecher Stowe

Puritans arrived in large family groups with varied skills and endowed with substantial financial resources and considerable ability to organize colonial administration. They created ordered societies ruled by Church elders organized in townships where citizens resided within the town in houses commonly situated closely together. The town itself was centered on the church, town square, and town hall where regular public gatherings occurred. They lived under mutual close observation and believed in community solidarity and the responsibility of each individual to uphold community values. They required church attendance, believed that communal values had priority over personal ambitions, and considered education essential to mature understanding of the Bible and responsible participation in community affairs. They established the first elementary schools, high schools, and Colleges, and were the first colonists to make education mandatory for children to the age of sixteen.

They were deeply motivated by the Old Testament and less so by the New, they had a profound sense of sin that imposed constant self-examination to weed out and counteract the machinations of the Devil. They mitigated their severe approach to religion somewhat by their love and commitment to marriage. However, punishment and "breaking the will" were inflicted on children presumably to discipline and curtail the natural propensity for sin. Although sexual lapses were common in Puritan communities and vigorous reproduction led to very large families, extramarital sex was sternly judged.

By the 1750's, prosperity and growing economic and social exchange abroad and within the American colonies led to a gradual relaxation and eventual dropping of the Puritan religious tradition, leading to the meliorist and benevolent unorthodoxy of Unitarianism. However, the principles of solidarity, social responsibility and activism, public welfare and improvement, and pursuit of learning remained the driving forces in New England society.

Pragmatism, later described and explained by William James at Harvard, rather than theoretical doctrine became a characteristic of the New England region and the Connecticut River Valley, which produced more technological and social innovation than any comparably sized area in history. New England aggressively and outspokenly opposed slavery as its antagonism toward the South increased in the 1830's with the Mexican War. Engrained with the region's tendency to self-righteousness, some New Englanders considered secession.

Cavaliers

Notable Cavaliers: George Washington, William Byrd, Lighthorse Harry Lee, Robert E. Lee

Cavaliers and armigerous gentlemen of Virginia, Maryland, and the Carolinas represented the untormented aristocratic outlook of a class comfortable with assuming authority and accustomed to rule. They had no particular sense of original sin, imminent damnation, or a need for redemption. Driven from England by primogeniture, these mostly second and third sons of aristocratic and gentry families sought to recreate in the New World the conditions of privilege they admired and enjoyed in the Old. They lived on country estates near the lands they owned and cultivated. They gathered at each others' country estates, which usually involved a visit of several days or weeks. They had town houses in Williamsburg where they attended sessions of the Assembly, sold tobacco their main cash crop, and carried out legal and financial business. Except for visits to Williamsburg, they did not live in tight communal settings as in the towns of New England and were hardly subject to the moral supervision and rebuke of a strict and fanatical clergy. Church was High and indulgent, an expression of solidarity with the King and the hierarchical society he represented. William Byrd of Virginia best represents the breed. They believed in natural inequality, the obligation of the upper class to lead and to take responsibility for government and military. They did not despise trade, but they preferred the role of landed gentry, a bias that Jefferson later embodied in his deep suspicion of cities and his belief that all moral merit resided in honest farmers.

Indentured servants, contracted for seven years labor in return for passage and eventual release with a promise of land or a start-up provision, made up the white work force in the Cavalier region. These workers generally contracted individually, and arrived without family, friends or resources, so they were initially entirely subject to the landed gentry. However, the opportunity to head for the hills, daunted only by the hostile reception of Indians living in those hills, made early independence possible but risky. This class eventually became the poor white class of the South. Many of the indentured women supplemented their income by prostitution. Byrd records in his diary a dalliance with the comely wife of an indentured servant who regularly of an evening waited along the road for customers. They were poor, lacked education and initiative and seem to have disappeared into the national woodwork as a class.

Quakers

Notable Quakers: John Greenleaf Whittier; Jane Addams (Hull House); Thomas Biddle

Quakers of Pennsylvania arrived in groups of families under the sponsorship of William Penn and the administrators of the colony. They had secure provision for settlement and received land sufficient to maintain their families. They were welcomed as fellow practitioners of the Quaker belief in humility, gentle grace, love of man, and nonviolence. Hardly views shared by the morally intense Puritans or the morally relaxed Cavaliers. They treated the Indians as equals, dealt fairly with them, and as a consequence experienced no violence toward their settlements until the Scotch Irish arrived in the mid 1700's. They believed in social responsibility, and in Philadelphia created the most civilized, civic- centered city in the United States. It had libraries, fire departments, public water supply and sewage control, police, and street sweeping. It was orderly, quiet, friendly and prosperous. Although they professed self-effacing religious principles and no ostentation, they managed the most successful banks (Biddle) and merchant operations in the colonies and founded some of the best schools and colleges (Swarthmore, Haverford, Bryn Mahr for women) in the United States. Quakers led the abolitionist movement in England that ended the slave trade on the high seas, and Quakers in Pennsylvania did the same in the United States. They led the effort to ban slavery at the Constitutional Convention. They promoted fair treatment and equality for Indians and women, supported the "underground railway" during the pre-Civil War era, and sought an end to slavery, but were not aggressively confrontational toward the South as were the New Englanders.

Scotch-Irish

Notable Scotch-Irish: Andrew Jackson; John Calhoun; Admiral Halsey; George Patton

Scotch-Irish were late comers, arriving in two large migrations, one in the 1720's, and the second in the 1770's, with regular but less numerous arrivals before, between, and after. ***This group turned out to be the dominant influence on the public character, outlook, and even entertainment of the United States.*** They are so important and so little understood that they deserve special attention. The term Scotch-Irish derives from the conquest and appropriation of lands in Ireland by Scottish northern border clansmen sent by James I to finally extirpate the unruly Irish Catholics. His resettlement of these "Scots" in Ireland accounts for the description Scotch-Irish. Originally these clans herded cattle in the region from Northumberland to lowland Scotland. The clans were warlike, ruthless, and proud. They lived in sod houses, owned scant possessions, were burned or forced out of their meager homes frequently as a result of clan wars, and were tough, independent, irreverent, and often brutal. They wore wide brimmed hats, "western" shirts, long pants and high boots. They were tall, long boned, large, strong, hardy and generally handsome having a strong admixture of Scandinavian blood from the invasions of the 9th-10th Centuries. The women were shapely, dressed in short skirts and tight blouses, showed their sexual appeal to advantage and were generally attractive, pert, and worldly wise. The "Western" look erroneously attributed to some adaptation of Spanish and Indian dress and the conditions of the new continent, including terms and slang, boots, hats, dresses, music and the like, all existed among the cattle driving clans of Northumberland and southern Scotland ***before*** they left for Ireland and America.

English who visited their lands reported with astonished horror on the personal behavior and sordidness of their personal lives. They seemed entirely indifferent to bathing, cleanliness, or propriety, as respectable gentleman of the 1750's in England understood those terms. These people, descended from Celts and Scandinavians, respected no masters and invariably took a mile for every inch they were conceded. In Ireland they ruthlessly expropriated and virtually enslaved the native Irish. When overcrowding reduced the net advantage of settling on Irish lands, a large number of Scotch-Irish decided to move on to America. At first encouraged by the settlers already there, they began to arrive in Massachusetts. In America they continued their extraordinarily repellent habits, and added new horrors. They shocked Bostonians by their violent tempers, readiness to fight, indifference to and disrespect for authority, and their entire unsuitableness for routine work. They were soon ejected from the Puritan settlements and moved into Western Massachusetts.

As land seemed scarce and already mostly occupied they moved south into Western Pennsylvania, occupying any land available, including that of the Indian tribes so carefully cultivated by the Quakers of Philadelphia. The Scotch-Irish, having dispossessed the Irish in Ireland, saw no reason to defer to savages unable to appropriately cultivate the lands of the New World. They provoked hostilities in order to justify driving the Indians away, incited them to the warpath, and then called on the Pennsylvania Assembly to assist them in fighting the Indians. The refusal of the Assembly to assist their unjustified aggression against the Indians led them to march on Philadelphia, in protest or conquest remained to be seen.

The deep contempt of the Scotch-Irish for the Quaker establishment, and the repugnance of the Quaker establishment for the Scotch-Irish was insurmountable. This Scotch-Irish antagonism was extended to Puritan New England in the 1790's when Senator John Clay of the Scotch-Irish western settlements of Pennsylvania joined the new federal Senate and ceaselessly expressed his personal contempt for Vice President John Adams. The Scotch-Irish western settlements in Massachusetts and Pennsylvania led the Whisky rebellion against federal revenuers, which forced President Washington to call out the federal militia. The distaste inspired by the Scotch- Irish was shared by Cavalier gentlemen, as evidenced in William Byrd's diary where he describes the inconceivable squalor of a Scotch-Irish immigrant and his Indian consort living near a swamp in Virginia.

Political Evolution of the United States

Democracy 1789-1900: The United States formed at a time unique in Western history that favored democracy. 'Amateur' weapons, which were easy to use (long rifle/Colt revolver), made cheap by interchangeable parts and mass production, were the most effective arms available and made every man more or less equal to any other. Largely invented and manufactured in the Connecticut River valley, these weapons were cheap and abundant in the United States but rare and costly in Europe and elsewhere. However, it made the industrial northeast the most powerful region in the United States, a fact clearly proved by the Civil War. Mass citizen armies using these amateur weapons could be motivated and disciplined only in support of democratic objectives. Consequently, everyone was equal and coercion difficult.

Cheap abundant land made it possible for the oppressed to move on and it was difficult for authorities to enforce compliance over a large territory and dispersed population. Weak executive and strong legislature meant that tax power was in control of representatives of wealth who controlled government and starved executive branch ambitions by opposing a standing army or other permanent government establishments. Parties were largely regional not national. Various groups scattered over the States came together to form a national party every four years. Otherwise, political strength was mainly in States not in the national government...

1900-1975 Plutocracy A gradual change from democracy to plutocracy occurred in social, economic, and political conditions from 1900-1975, with more centralization and executive control. Expensive, specialist weapons (F-18 fighter jets, aircraft carriers, guided missiles) no citizen could afford or manage to use meant higher defense taxes and expenditures and deference to national security. The key date was the end of the Draft in 1976, which marked the end of the mass citizen army and the recognition of a small, professional military class. Bureaucratic administration replaced legislation as the Executive power extended and became dominant. The National Security State formed, subordinating domestic interests to foreign objectives. Corporate control of agencies of government that affect them (oil Industry at State, Interior and CIA; agribusiness and timber at Agriculture, etc.) meant weakening of the Congress. Politicians' dependence on lobbyists, lack of ability to supervise agencies, less control over taxation, and parochial interests that offset each other further weakened the Legislative Branch. Federal taxation drains States and local governments of revenue, making them more dependent on centralized federal programs. This is especially dangerous because there is no limit on federal spending and no requirement to balance the federal budget, whereas most state governments are required by state law to balance their budgets. One national party was formed with two versions (Republican and Democrat) in 1900 after the defeat of Bryan in 1896, and both were controlled by the Eastern financial establishment until 1933. Regional political influence weakened. The New Deal tipped the Democratic party somewhat to the left to include labor and farmers with urban voters. WWII consolidated the labor, industry, government triangle that persists today. Both parties are basically united by the influences and national interests that prevail regarding most issues.

1975-Present National Security State *Dans ce système, les citoyens sortent un moment de la dépendance pour indiquer leur maître, et y rentrent.* (*Toqueville, De la Démocratie en Amérique*, II-435.) This period intensifies trends apparent from 1900 to 1975. Democracy is subsumed into a managed election process wherein predetermined choices are made early in primaries, there is little competition, and foreign and domestic policies of the parties are much the same. The Executive is controlled and vetted by the established corporate power. Media no longer provide news, just 'infotainment', and some networks actually censor news unfavorable to their preferred candidate. The period is characterized by:

1. End of democracy except in a pro forma election process.
2. Vastly expanded Executive power and federal bureaucracy.
3. Vastly increased federal spending.
4. Increasing corporate feudalism in which people are subject to employment coercion.

Stages of American History

Many ways of outlining the course of American history are possible, but six main periods provide the clearest structure by which to interpret past and current events.

1618-1789 Religion to Deism

The most significant development in American history throughout the colonial period was a universal move from religious sectarianism to secularism in which freedom of belief was accepted and the established Church was gradually disestablished and removed from influence on government. The dominant role of the Congregational Church in early New England settlements led to a repressive theocracy. Gradually, the democratic town forums developed a more tolerant and compromising view of society that allowed for greater freedom and less orthodoxy. The movement to secularism was typified in the shift from Calvinist *Cotton Mather* to Deist *Unitarianism* in New England. The movement reacted against Calvinistic doctrines developed during the 1700's within the Congregational churches by Puritans like Cotton Mather (1663-1728), who some believed had fomented the hysteria that led to the Salem witch trials of 1692. The Calvinists emphasized human sinfulness, damnation for all but a chosen few, and extremely rigid standards of public and private morality. Unitarians argued that such doctrines were inconsistent with the Bible and contrary to reason. The dispute in the United States between the liberal Unitarians and the orthodox Congregationalists became so bitter after 1805 that Unitarians formed the American Unitarian Association in 1825 organized as a separate religious body. Ralph Waldo Emerson in his *"Divinity School Address"*

(1838) and Theodore Parker in his sermon "*The Transient and Permanent in Christianity*" (1841) expressed a new point of view in philosophy and religion called Transcendentalism that people have an experience of reality that transcends the experience of the senses. More relaxed Anglican Church standards prevailed among the Cavalier society of Virginia and South Carolina, and Presbyterian and populist Baptist sects had a strong following in the rural Southern backcountry. The mix of religious practice and belief made colony-wide religious orthodoxy impossible. The spread of Masonry, Deism, and liberal secular ideas from Europe to the educated elite, including Washington, Jefferson, and others, made religious tolerance politically expedient. Liberating political organization from religious orthodoxy was a significant step toward the shift from the King to revolution and a Republican system of government.

1783-1815 Confederation to Federalism

The American Colonies won their independence from the United Kingdom in the Revolutionary War in America (1775-1783). They founded the first national government of the United States in 1781 under a document called the Articles of Confederation. Under the Articles, however, the states kept much of their independence. The national government could not collect taxes, regulate trade, or force states to fulfill their obligations. Such leaders as George Washington, Benjamin Franklin, James Madison, and Alexander Hamilton feared that the weak national government would collapse. This concern about the Articles of Confederation led to the Constitutional Convention of 1787 in Philadelphia. The state delegates at the convention wanted a strong national government but feared that it would not respect the independence of the states and the liberties of the people. In framing the Constitution, they used ideas from the constitutions of New York, Massachusetts, and other states. The delegates created a new system of government--the *Constitution of the United States*. The document went into effect on June 21, 1788, when New Hampshire became the ninth state to ratify it. The first 10 amendments, called the Bill of Rights, were ratified in 1791. For the last time the four folkways, safely ensconced in their respective regions, joined more or less unanimously to establish the United States under a strong central government defined by the Constitution. Compromises were made to assuage folkway interests. Cavaliers wanted slaves included in the census used for districting Congress. Puritans and Quakers wanted a date set for the end of slave trade. Scotch-Irish wanted state authority strengthened and Congressional taxing power limited. All groups got something and conceded something. This never happened again in US history.

1820-1875 Rural/Agrarian to Urban/Industrial

The most important change during the period from 1820 to 1875 was the decisive shift from a rural agricultural society to an urban industrial society. Industrial enterprise and invention in the Connecticut River Valley, Lowell cotton mills, development of the railroads, and mass immigration revolutionized manufacturing and created a capitalist system that grew as settlement and markets grew in the western territories. The prerequisite for this growth was the Louisiana Purchase of 1803, which changed the United States from an eastern seaboard nation to a continental nation. This undermined the power of New England politically, but the industrial revolution centered in New England increased its economic power. The shift from agrarian to capitalist values and influences created major cultural shock throughout the period, obscured only by the largely tangential but extremely volatile issue of Slavery. While the battle over slavery raged and divided the two agricultural sectors irreconcilably, capitalist entrepreneurs gradually secured the dominant position in the nation's economy. The Constitution did not authorize the acquisition of land, but it did provide for the making of treaties, so that Jefferson felt the **Louisiana Purchase** from France and Napoleon of new territory was constitutional. He admitted that he had "stretched the constitution until it cracked." But he thought of himself as a guardian who made an investment of funds entrusted to his care. In a message to Congress on Oct. 17, 1803, Jefferson said:

> *Whilst the property and sovereignty of the Mississippi and its waters secure an independent outlet for the produce of the Western States and an uncontrolled navigation through their whole course,……the fertility of the country, its climate and extent, promise in due season important aids to our Treasury, an ample provision for our posterity, and a wide spread for the blessings of freedom and equal laws.*

The U.S. Senate ratified the treaty on October 20. The basic structure of politics from 1820 to 1865 was a three-part division into:

- **Capital and industrial interests in New England and New York**
- **Free soil farmers in the Ohio Valley extending across the Mississippi to Missouri, Nebraska and Kansas.**
- **Slave cotton States of the South.**

Whigs under Henry Clay and others linked **Eastern** capital and industrial interests with the **Western** agricultural producers by sponsoring public transportation systems via canals, roads, and railroads and tariffs to promote domestic manufacturing. Free soil farmers supported the program, tolerating tariffs that raised the prices of some goods they purchased in order to promote transportation systems to get their crops to urban markets in the East. Because cotton was shipped to mills in England, the South opposed tariffs and was reluctant to provide tax money to support transportation systems in the northern states. They bartered their votes for the Whig program in return for concessions on the extension of slavery to new territories. These compromises advanced the economic growth of the North and Midwest far beyond the growth enjoyed in the South. When compromise with Slavery became politically unacceptable in the late 1850's, Civil War became inevitable.

The ***Missouri Compromise of 1820*** allowed slavery in Missouri in return for which the South accepted a tariff that protected New England manufacturing. In 1818, the Territory of Missouri, which was part of the Louisiana Purchase, applied for admission to the Union. Slavery was legal in Missouri and most people expected Missouri to become a slave state. When the bill to admit Missouri to the Union was introduced, there were an equal number of free and slave states. Six of the original 13 states and five new states permitted slavery, while seven of the original states and four new states did not. This meant that the free states and the slave states each had 22 senators in the United States Senate. The admission of Missouri threatened to destroy this balance. This balance had been temporarily upset a number of times, but it had always been easy to decide whether states east of the Mississippi River should be slave or free, Mason and Dixon's Line and the Ohio River formed a natural and well-understood boundary between the two sections. No such line had been drawn west of the Mississippi River. In addition, some parts of Missouri Territory lay to the north of the mouth of the Ohio River, while other parts of it lay to the south.

The Missouri Compromise was a plan to settle the debate over slavery in the Louisiana Purchase area. Because the free states dominated the House of Representatives, the slave states felt they must keep the even balance in the Senate. Maine applied for admission to the Union so Missouri and Maine could be accepted without upsetting the Senate's balance between free and slave states. The compromise admitted Maine as a free state and authorized Missouri to form a state constitution. The compromise also banned slavery from the Louisiana Purchase north of the southern boundary of Missouri, the line 36 30' north latitude, except in the state of Missouri. The people of Missouri believed they had the right to decide about slavery in their state. They wrote a constitution that allowed slavery and restricted free blacks from entering the State. Henry Clay, the Speaker of the House, helped work out the final agreement. It required the Missouri legislature not to deny black citizens their constitutional rights. With this understanding, Missouri was admitted to the Union in 1821. In 1848, Congress passed the ***Oregon Territory Act***, which prohibited slavery in the area. President James K. Polk signed the bill because the Oregon Territory lay north of the Missouri Compromise line. Later proposals tried to extend the line by law across the continent to the Pacific Ocean. These efforts failed. The Missouri Compromise was repealed by the Kansas-Nebraska Act of 1854.

The ***Kansas Nebraska Act of 1854*** presented this three-way power struggle in stark, amoral clarity. It provided that two new territories, Kansas and Nebraska, were to be made from the Indian land that lay west of the bend of the Missouri River and north of 37 degrees north latitude. Senator Stephen A. Douglas of Illinois, a famous railroad lawyer, introduced the bill into Congress. It attempted to meet the needs of settlers and also clear the way for Southern support for a railroad from Chicago to the Pacific Coast. Douglas included in his bill a provision for "popular sovereignty" in Kansas and Nebraska. This provision stated that all questions of slavery in the new territories were to be decided by the settlers rather than by Congress. This provision was designed to win the support of the Southern congressmen and was directly contrary to the Missouri Compromise of 1820. The Missouri Compromise had declared that all land in the Louisiana Purchase north of 36 30', except for the state of Missouri, was to be free. Douglas was persuaded by the Southerners to declare the Missouri Compromise *"inoperative and void."* Antislavery people furiously attacked the Kansas-Nebraska Bill. The debate in Congress was long and bitter. But President Franklin Pierce supported the bill, and it became law. The Kansas-Nebraska Act made slavery legally possible in a vast new area. The act revived the bitter quarrel over the expansion of slavery, which had died down after the Compromise of 1820, and it hastened the start of the Civil War.

1875-1933 Capitalism to Income Redistribution The principal result of the Civil War was to permanently split the northern farm bloc from the southern farm bloc, the former resolutely Republican and the latter resolutely Democratic. The Grange and rural populist movements of the late 1880's failed to unite farmers on both sides of the Mason Dixon line against the railroads (high rates) and the gold standard (*'cross of gold'* and reduced credit). This division persisted and allowed the eastern capitalist establishment to dominate politics in the United States until the election of Franklin Delano Roosevelt in 1932. Throughout this period and after, the dominant issue in American politics and presidential elections has been explicitly or implicitly income distribution. The election of 1876 focused on the recession and the growing labor unrest. In the election of 1896, William Jennings Bryan (at 36 the youngest Presidential candidate in US history) led the Democratic Party for free silver and against eastern bankers' *'cross of gold'*. Republicans won. The civil War barrier still kept northern farmers in the Republican Party because they did not feel solidarity with the Democratic urban labor voters in the north and none at all with Southern Democrats.

Eventually eastern capital got control of both parties so fringe and third-party movements formed around income distribution issues. From 1906 to 1925, Senator Robert La Follette of Wisconsin advocated strict railroad regulation, lower tariffs, and conservation. Although nominally a Republican, when Calvin Coolidge was nominated for president in 1924, La Follette accepted the presidential nomination of a new Progressive Party, backed by independents and many labor groups. Similarly, the IWW and Socialist Parties emerged as fringe groups. By the time of the Depression, a great variety of right wing and left-wing parties and movements emerged, perhaps the best organized being the Communist Party. The issue of income redistribution overtook the prospect of prosperity in the minds of many who lost jobs and faced financial ruin in 1929. It became the major political issue of the 1932 campaign.

1933-1975 Income Redistribution to Post Industrial Society from the New Deal to 1975, income was redistributed through government spending on WWII and welfare and public works projects that created jobs and by the gradual accommodation between capital and labor to insure industrial peace in which wage increases were paid for by increased prices. Concurrent rising prosperity made this arrangement feasible, profitable, and affordable. Absence of competitors, cheap prices for oil and other natural resources, and strong demand for American products worldwide reduced inflationary pressure from other markets and insured increasing growth rates, jobs, and opportunity. This meant that consumers who paid the steadily increasing prices were enjoying steadily increasing wages, so the increased prices were acceptable.

The Labor capital arrangement broke down in the 1970's when competition from Japan in autos and electronics and rising domestic wages and lower price for foreign products put pressure on profit margins. Speeding up production and lower quality control undermined the competitiveness of domestic autos in particular and the market share gradually decreased. Public spending to achieve income redistribution peaked in the 1960's under the War on Poverty, but expenditures for the Vietnam War and a massive defense budget squeezed by increased foreign competition reduced the tax dollars available. Growing opposition to welfare programs made additional programs unlikely. But the major event of the 1970's was the definitive shift from rustbelt industries to high technology and service industries that were not unionized. These new sectors provided enormous growth rates in the following decades. Organized labor as a percentage of the nonagricultural workplace declined from 36 percent in 1945 to a low of 14 percent in 2000.

American Subcultures

A subculture often provides subconscious models, certain methods and styles of behavior that gradually are assimilated by the dominant population, usually by the youth in rebellion against the dominant culture. These influences are so pervasive, and the interactions between the dominant groups and with each of the subcultures are so important, that American history can largely be explained by these confrontations.

The main subcultures that influenced American culture and society were the Indian, Black, and Proletarian.

Indians: Early and often American Indians influenced every aspect of colonial life. However, the Indians never became part of colonial or later national society. To their credit the plains Indians remained warriors who opposed the advance of the White Man. They were defeated in war and were forced to sign peace treaties and accept assigned reservations for their settlement. They were isolated in rural ghettos and excluded partly by choice from the developing American society, except that they became the mythic vector of the natural nobility, freedom and the American spirit in western novels of the 19th Century and in the most pervasive public form of entertainment ever invented of the 20th Century: movies. The Indian influence on American culture began with James Fennimore Cooper who wrote his 'leatherstocking' novels (*Last of the Mohicans, etc.*) in Paris in the 1820's. He had complained about the poor quality of American novels and took a bet to see if he could write one. He is one of the greatest American writers. Practically every literary development in the United States originates with his novels (Henry James is prefigured in **Home as Found**; **Huckleberry Finn** is prefigured in Cooper's use of dialect colloquialism).

Ironically the Battle of Little Big Horn in 1876 became a symbol of national vulnerability. It came at the Centennial when severe economic depression and labor unrest in the economy and corruption in the second Grant administration had undermined national optimism. Crazy Horse and Sitting Bull became national hero/villains and Custer became the perennial symbol of fighting to the last. Mythic stuff. Eventually the Indians were brutally eradicated by Generals Sherman and Sheridan. But they returned in Wild West Shows of Wild Bill Hickock, Sitting Bull finding retirement income both here and in England and Europe where the Wild West was deliriously popular. The most popular German author, ***Karl May***, wrote Westerns though he had never been in the United States. His novels were read avidly and admiringly by young Adolf himself. In 1905, *The Virginian*, by Theodore Roosevelt's friend and neighbor at his ranch in Dakota Territory, **Owen Wister**, a Pennsylvania Quaker patrician, gave a literary and social cachet to the Western and a model for many movie scripts. About the same time, Sigmund Freud spent a year teaching at Clark College in Worcester Massachusetts. After dining in Back Bay homes in Boston, he observed that they all looked like Indians, stiff, stoic, and laconic. Of course, his English may not have invited fluent expression. The model of stoic, noble, laconic, stiff, long suffering, bravery was embodied in film by the ultimate '*White Indian*' Gary Cooper. The ultimate '*White Negro*', Marlon Brando, elaborately refused his Academy Award for The Godfather in 1972 in protest against the treatment of Indians in South Dakota and elsewhere, a remarkable confluence of cultural pluralism. We now have a very prosperous Indian community of tribes given 'national' status within the United States and enjoying oil revenues and profits from casino gambling, which have helped raised economic prospects and improve health services and education opportunity.

Blacks: From minstrel shows to hip-hop, Black subculture has emerged as the dominant American popular culture since 1950. What Sigmund Freud had postulated during his lecture tour to Clark College in Massachusetts in 1912 has come to pass. He had visited prominent Boston families during that tour and observed that the women looked and behaved like 'white Indians', with their expressionless faces and rather rigid posture. He opined that America would never be properly integrated psychologically until it became 'negrified'. Minstrel shows in which whites in black face imitated Blacks were common from the 1830's and the form continued in the Amos and Andy radio series, featuring two whites as the leads, which ran from 1926 to 1960, the longest running show in entertainment history. **Uncle Tom's Cabin** published in 1852 was the bestselling novel in American history until **Gone with the Wind** published in 1936, both focused on the south and slavery. **Huckleberry Finn** (1887) was the most important American novel to present the Black subculture in the form of Huck *hisself* and Nigger Jim his traveling companion. Finn legitimized the colloquial Scotch-Irish language that came to dominate popular culture. However, the effects of the Civil War produced a strong reaction in the Ku Klux Klan and racial segregation. Plessy vs. Ferguson in 1893 established separate but equal as a standard in public education and by 1913 **Birth of a Nation** crystallized national rejection of Black equality (even President Wilson requested a private showing at the White House). Prejudice prevailed until Brown vs. Topeka Board of Education (1954) reversed separate but equal and initiated the Civil Rights movement of the late 1950's. But the greatest influence on the eventual triumph of Black subculture was Rock and Roll and the various forms of black music that dominated popular culture after 1960. In addition, Marlon Brando dubbed the preeminent *'white nigger'*, introduced a Black physical style and manner of speech that gained wide acceptance. The War on Poverty, Civil Rights legislation, school busing, and other measures forced Black integration and white flight from urban areas, but the Black subculture steadily gained dominance in the white suburban living rooms and schools, such that it is nearly exclusively dominant today. Sports have lifted black players to the role of national heroes. Blacks have joined the mainstream culture, one of the best examples being Morgan Freeman, outstanding film actor and gentleman free of the BLM special pleading and the race crutch used by some manipulators of our Black community. When I see Morgan I never see him as 'black' or some 'category'. I see a great guy, a great actor, and a person I would be proud to have as a friend.

Proletariat. The urban proletariat subculture emerged after the Civil War when transportation and industrial labor unions first began to organize, and city political corruption and manipulation of newly arrived immigrant populations first became a national scandal. It was an urban subculture alien to most of American society which was small town and rural in outlook. Cities were hotbeds of crime and evil and the urban proletariat was largely immigrant and suspect. The proletarian subculture was confined by the national commitment to the middle class success story embodied in Horatio Alger stories and other booster literature. The ugly side of urban industrial society first became a subject of investigation in the muckraking era, with Upton Sinclair and his exposures of meatpacking (**The Jungle** 1906) and other industries. Prohibition introduced a further element, organized crime, gangsters, and mafia rule of city political machines largely based on Italian and Irish ethnic minorities. Detective literature emerged in the late 1920's and early 1930's, pitting private investigators usually of proletarian background against criminals of the upper income class. Movies depicting such situations, gang warfare and detectives fighting for justice, were standard in the 1930's but died out after WWII.

Another strain of proletarian subculture emerged in the socialist dramas and literature of the Depression Era, notably the plays of Clifford Odets. Torn T- shirts or naked torsos and proletarian speech continued into the 1940's and 1950's most notably in **On the Waterfront** (1953) which combined gangsters, corrupt labor unions, strikebreakers, and a proletarian hero who challenges the lot. The emergence of lower class diction and lack of grammar had spread in the 1930's through popular music and films but became standard in the 1950's the film **From Here to Eternity**, where nearly everyone spoke like a High School dropout from Jersey City, which Frank Sinatra happened to be. In the 1930's, the cliché that upper class people who spoke proper English and had manners were phony as compared with the honest and down-to-earth commoners was well established, although the **Philadelphia Story** drew swords with that point of view. Moss Hart's **You Can't Take it With You**, follows that theme, although the 'upper class' family in the play were actually parvenus from the same working class background as the prospective bride.

Proletarian subculture gained preeminence in American politics through the 1930's, but lost ground after WWII. Americans indoctrinated in upward mobility could not for long stop admiring the rich whom they hoped shortly to join at least at some level of affluence. However, with their success, proletarian values and habits of thought simply migrated to higher levels of society so that today the entire middle class to some degree is proletarianized and negrified in its tastes in music and entertainment and sexual and social behavior.

Social Development

From 1789 to the present, the United States has moved from a patrician society based on authority, through a middle class society based on wealth, to a proletarian society based on income. The transition introduced fundamental changes in values, from the high purposes of the revolution and Federal Constitutional period to the focus on elderly medical benefits, teenage drug use, sexually transmitted disease, and job growth of the consumer era.

1789-1860 Patrician Society. Patrician society consisted of prominent Southern landed and Northern merchant families who led the political and social life of the regions of the United States during 18th and part of the 19th Centuries. Many were comfortably off economically, but many like the Adams family of Massachusetts had quite modest land holdings and annual incomes. Such patrician families were present throughout the colonies but resided predominantly in the coastal areas and larger towns and cities. Virginia provided the model for the class, George Washington, the greatest patrician of them all. Without qualification Washington is the greatest American President and possibly the most distinguished political figure in history. He adhered to a code of service and honor and has a record of achievement no one has matched. His personal authority throughout the fledgling United States made success of the new government possible. Without him it simply would have failed. The United States owes its existence to George Washington.

Such patrician authority was based on character and on years of selfless public service in the interest of all the community. The patrician class generally observed a code of honor and service that tended to subdue insurrection and discourage corruption. With nothing to gain and everything they considered of worth to lose (honor, reputation), the patrician class gave stability and continuity to State and federal government and pursued reforms and innovations that benefited the entire society. It always does wherever it exists. John Quincy Adams following the patrician path of duty served as Ambassador to all major capitols of Europe, was Secretary of State under James Monroe, elected 6th President in 1824, then returned to the House of Representatives. Typical patricians include Teddy Roosevelt, Harvard Porcellan, author, politician, social reformer, and war hero who busted trusts and cleaned out the 'spoils system' helped along by hundreds of fellow patricians. The last great patrician was Franklin Delano Roosevelt whose balanced temperament, sense of duty and justice, and impeccable judgment of men and their abilities and weaknesses led the United States through Depression and War.

1860-1933 Middle Class Society: Much touted for its 'values' and morality, the middle class in history has demonstrated a level of criminality, corruption, venality, and larceny that equals more exalted Roman or Renaissance figures. The misdemeanors of Enron and other executives today are trifling examples of middle class character. The underlying amorality of the middle class has been obscured by its much-vaunted 'enterprise' as described by Max Weber in "*The Protestant Ethic and the Spirit of Capitalism*" (1904-1905). Weber argued that the Calvinist belief in working hard and avoiding luxury promoted capitalism and the expansion of business enterprise. According to Weber, the Calvinist doctrine of business success as a sign of spiritual salvation justified the desire for profits. The middle class rose in towns during the middle ages and was insecure from the start, having no recognized or essential status within the feudal society of church, lords, and peasants. ***The key to understanding the middle class is that it has property in wealth (intangible economic assets) not land***. Wealth is unstable, insecure, and constantly subject to increase or decrease beyond the protection of ownership. Corporations were invented in the 18th Century as legal 'persons' to allow for perpetual transfer of accumulated wealth, but that did not change its fundamentally fugitive nature. Insecurity bred conformity, a keeping up of appearances, an ostentatious sobriety (later followed by Veblan's ostentatious display), and a desperate fear of ruin. This neurotic combination of traits, under thick and usually black gabardine, concealed many demons (Victorian child prostitution) and outright criminal potentialities. If Calvin was the theologian of the middle class, Thomas Hobbes, whose brutal and uncompromising theories reduced human society to a carnivore feeding frenzy, was its philosopher. Their bleak and predatory views underlay the ostensible respectability of the bourgeoisie.

The United States developed a financial and industrial middle class of multimillionaires (Vanderbilt, Gould, Rockefeller, Morgan, and others) whose outlook was little mitigated by the inherent abundance of the nation's natural resources. Exploitation of labor was their most public expression, like the industrial slave mills of England itself. That the horrors of women and child labor, much less the degradation of male workers, should have occurred in a country as bountiful as the United States is simply appalling. It is the middle class outlook that made its peculiar savagery possible. The middle class also developed a colossal public relations campaign to sell the nation on its values and virtues. Because it controlled the press, pulpit and political parties, the rhetoric rolled in unison from every direction. Horatio Alger (1832-1899) wrote more than 130 books about boys who rose from poverty to wealth and fame through hard work, virtuous living, and luck. His books sold 40 million copies. Many of his boy heroes appeared in series, notably *Ragged Dick* (begun in 1867), *Luck and Pluck* (begun in 1869), and *Tattered Tom* (begun in 1871).

The middle class adopted the social Darwinism of Herbert Spencer (**First Principles** 1862 and **Principles of Ethics** 1879-1893) and William Graham Sumner, an American sociologist, who helped make social Darwinism popular in the United States. It was also reflected in the 'boosterism' of middle class small towns satirized by Sinclair Lewis (1995-1951) in his novels **Main Street** (1920) and **Babbitt** (1922).

The principal characteristic of the middle class is its self-interest, lack of solidarity and its belief that wealth, an essentially futile product, is the greatest value and measure of importance. The middle class rarely stands up publicly for principles. It is driven by conformity and personal advantage. Before expressing a view, it carefully assesses the opinion and views of its members and then resolutely adopts them, regardless of their intrinsic merit or moral quality. Hiding in their putatively 'secure' homes and gated communities, they actually believe that they are 'safe' and that their money will protect them. They are unwilling to 'get involved' when others are unjustly attacked, which is why middle class societies were the most favorable breeding ground for Nazism, and why Hitler hated and contemned the middle class more than any other, the very class that adored him most. As Hannah Arendt explained in her study of totalitarianism:

> *Nothing proved easier to destroy than the privacy and private morality of people who thought of nothing but safeguarding their private lives.*
> Hannah Arendt, Origins of Totalitarianism, 331.

1933-1950 Proletarian Society: In one of the brilliant coincidences of American history, an elegant and irrepressible patrician, Franklin Delano Roosevelt, was elected and presided over the age of the proletariat in the United States. Supported by the organized labor movement, Roosevelt gave labor access to government on a scale never before witnessed. Details of the New Deal programs are widely available. What is important is the different perspective of the proletariat and the organized labor movement that began to impinge on the dominant middle class ethos. Labor, like the middle class, presents inherent dangers to freedom in society. Labor does not require speech in its performance, although rhythmic music or chant is particularly helpful in carrying out labor and many such songs have been recorded in all cultures. Labor is therefore apolitical by nature. Labor consists of repetitive effort and has no product, unlike work. If applied to means of production organized for assembly line production, there is a product at the end of the laboring process aided by machines, but the laborer contributes only a small part to the outcome and the function he performs is usually monotonous, personally unrewarding, and machine-like. Labor in fields is equally metabolic. The lack of product identifies labor as a process, whereas work is distinguished by craft or skill applied to produce a product. Labor's highest value is life, and livelihood was the chief political subject of the labor movement and its political activities.

So long as the labor movement asserted principles of justice and dignity of laborers as human beings degraded by 12-hour days and 70-hour weeks, they spoke for social justice and benefited all parts of society and remained a positive political force. Once the benefits were obtained for the labor union members however, the movement withdrew into a lobbying group that pushed the interests of the union members, like any other lobbying group. This transition from leadership of a movement to improve the general welfare to a lobbying group happened gradually in the period 1933-1950. It climaxed in the early 1950's when capital and labor struck a bargain in which labor would get regular pay increases and capital would get industrial peace at the expense of higher costs to the consumer. Aggressive often violent unionizing actions in towns across the country in many cases led to substantial financial hardship callously inflicted by labor organizers at the expense of communities. Labor's reputation declined precipitously.

Labor continued powerful in traditional steel, auto, and heavy industry. The financial collapse of these industries, which were locked in to high-paying labor contracts and outmoded technology, occurred as they became subject to vigorous and more efficient foreign competition in the 1960's and 1970's. From 1970 to 1990, heavy industry restructured its organization, moved production offshore in some cases, and renegotiated benefits in labor contracts, while new high technology industries avoided unionization altogether. The role and influence of unions and the labor movement plummeted, as did the influence of the proletariat on American society.

1950-Present: Consumerism & Bureaucracy. In the 19th Century the American middle class industrialists analogized themselves to the European aristocracy, which was in decline and attracted to wealthy American debutantes. The United States did not have the social and political structure of a class society, but the influence of Europe from colonial times made monarchy and aristocracy a social model for the newly rich. Through schools (Philips Exeter, Groton and other prep schools modeled on Eton; Harvard, Princeton and Yale modeled on Oxford and Cambridge), social clubs, resorts, stately homes, and social events, the Eastern Establishment created a facsimile of European society as described by Henry James. As the more shabby genteel New England families receded in political importance they took refuge in the Ivy League Universities, which they ran until after WWII. An example is Henry Adams who taught American History at Harvard. The objective of the patrician class was formation of character, similar to the objectives of the English Public Schools. Academic achievement was secondary. Following WWII, a massive influx of GI bill students and academic careerists changed forever the class- dominated Ivy League prep schools and universities. The principal advantage went to Jewish students who had been subject to quotas, now removed. Although Walter Lippman and many other successful (and very Ivy League in form and manner) Jews had attended Harvard and done extremely well, following WWII the patrician class withdrew from academe altogether since the makeup and objectives of the student body were now so alien to their formation. The Ivy League schools following commission reports that recommended wider 'representation', both ethnic and geographic, changed admission policies. The hereditary family relationship no longer carried certainty of admission for sons and daughters of patrician families. Admissions were manipulated to achieve social goals, and sometimes rejected six and seven generation alumni for newcomers in rural Montana or a Chicago ghetto. Further, the patricians withdrew entirely into corporate boardrooms or to charitable work. In America today there are no patrician politicians and America is no longer a class society. It is a consumer society of jobholders divided only by income levels, but practically homogeneous in its cultural, social and economic outlook. How much one makes decides the relative importance or success of an individual.

Economic and social life has changed entirely since 1950 and the massive post WWII economic expansion. The fundamental change is that **_labor is no longer a major element in the economy_**. Formerly hard labor in mines, factories and farms was a fact of life and a political force. Now, machines, computerized robots, computers and specialized electric tools have eliminated physical labor and effort from nearly all forms of mass production and most other jobs. In fact, a nation of former laborers no longer labors. Jobholders now have enormous time and energy left over for other activities and interests. The staggering increase in popular entertainment and recreation is one consequence of the end of laboring. More time and money is spent on entertainment than any other sector of the economy. America is now a consumer society that is employed in largely effortless but neurologically wearing jobs consuming junk products and euphemistically 'working' in large process-driven bureaucracies. Most low level jobs are what the Russians call *sluzhba*, a form of time serving in which as they said in the Yeltsin era, '*You pretend to work and I'll pretend to pay you.*' At the high salary end are the professions, executives, scientists, doctors, lawyers and other occupations that still require exceptional skill, training, and intelligence. They constitute an elite group that basically runs the entire process. The middle group consists of sales, administration, and other white-collar jobs that carry out the routine processes of bureaucratic organizations. Trades, mechanics, construction, technical and other blue-collar jobs focus on production, building, maintenance, and other practical results. Blue collar workers often produce tangible goods, services, and products that pay as much or more than most mid-level administrative jobs. This led to a crisis among the petit bourgeois and an increase in religious fundamentalism, which derives its following mainly from the petit bourgeois threatened with being de-classed by cultural permissiveness, racial affirmative action, corporate restructuring and salary reductions. But the basic outlook of all jobholders is proletarian. Life and consumption are the primary 'values', and keeping the system functioning is the primary political duty of elected and appointed officials.

Mass Culture: For all its apparent variety, mass culture as it developed from the 1870's to the present had been characterized and made possible by two underlying innovations: amplification and duplication. These terms are used in the broadest sense. ***Amplification*** refers to all forms of increase in volume, size, and distribution. ***Duplication*** refers to repeating or copying in nearly infinite number. Without these innovations, modern mass popular culture would not be possible. Their significance is revolutionary. Until applied electronics in the mid-19th Century, no sound could be increased in volume or communicated more widely than the natural potential volume of the source would allow. Until mass printing and telecommunications, no image could be distributed more widely than engraving, lithography and letterpresses would allow. As a result of amplification and duplication, populations are now saturated with essentially identical sounds, images, and products produced in nearly infinite number and distributed to nearly every individual and location. These products have replaced the local and limited production of craft and performance cultural products. It has also shrunk the variety of information distributed as it vastly increased the audience. We have major benefits from the mass media of records, film, television and their derivatives (DVD, CD, video) which show us sights and sounds from all parts of society, foreign cultures, and individual lifestyles and character and provide 'role models' and even patterns of belief and behavior. They promote tolerance on one hand and a sense of alienation on another. Sexual behavior has been entirely liberated. This liberating influence may not be beneficial for the very young who are more easily misled, whereas it may help others overcome neurotic patterns of behavior. The double edge of advances in technology and knowledge is seen throughout the United States. Christian fundamentalists are frightened by the loss of family values and family control over their children's education. Liberated gays, lesbians and others feel threatened by this reaction. The culture wars center on such concerns.

SIDE BAR

Weapons Systems & Social Organization

Nature is founded on competition and violence between life forms for sunlight, water, nutrients, and shelter. The myth of the Garden of Eden is largely an expression of battle fatigue and wishful thinking. Mankind originally organized in groups of about 120 people of both sexes and three generations. Hunting and scavenging required agility, speed, coordination, and foresight, all elements that contributed to evolution of the species **homo sapiens**. By 10,000 BC, larger groups formed in hunter packs and organized warfare began to replace the episodic hostile confrontations of earlier periods. Stone-age weapons were blades, axes, and arrows. They were cheap, readily accessible and tended to equalize opponents. No group was much more effective than another. Two categories of weapons, contact weapons and missiles, survived unchanged to the present. Contact weapons and impact warfare usually involved sword, shields, spears, and eventually close order drill to protect the force as it advanced. The bow and arrow was the most accurate and deadly long range missile weapon (300 yards) until the invention of the long rifle and spiral barrel in the 18th Century. The advent of horses transformed warfare. In the grasslands of Central Asia fodder was abundant and horses cheap to feed and maintain. In the arid zones of Mesopotamia and Egypt, fodder was scare and horses were very expensive.

A further distinction is amateur and professional weapons and warfare. Citizens of Ancient Greek city states trained for armed conflict and sent citizen armies into the field. The Romans in the Early Republic did the same. This parity between soldiers and civilians favored democracy at least in the limited form practiced by those cultures. Warfare in Medieval Europe required horse, armor, constant training, and an authoritarian economic system, the manor, devoted to keeping an armed defender available. Kings of England required yeomen to train constantly with the long bow, the most effective weapon used at Agincourt and Crécy. The French nobility was 'gunned down' by English bowmen. Bowmen in England tended to be independent of authority and extensive forest throughout the island made refuge readily available. Robin Hood and his merry men were possible on the fringes of authority and kept alive the tradition of resistance that produced Nat Tyler and other renegades, to say nothing of the Puritans. The back and forth between amateur and cheap versus professional and expensive weapons and warfare is a central factor in any society. In the 18th and 19th Centuries, the United States enjoyed cheap weapons that made democracy possible, even necessary: long rifle, colt revolver, abundant forage for horses. Cheap amateur weapons made citizen armies feasible and democracy necessary from 1789 to 1945. Since 1945, technologically advanced weapons systems no citizen can learn to use in two or three years of military service have made the citizen army obsolete, created a professional military, and forced an end to the draft and citizen armies, with potentially adverse consequences for democratic government.

PART IX

Policy Making

As leader of Western Civilization, the United States faces challenges foreign and domestic. We enjoy an advantage and a burden in relation to all other nations. The advantage is that we have a fully developed and advanced infrastructure to support our power and the extension of that power worldwide. Not even Europe can match the advanced state of all levels of our society. Advances by other nations at one level, usually military, are unsupported by conditions overall in the countries. We have complete communication, transportation and power grids that serve all parts of the nation. Russia, China, and India, the only likely challengers to our supremacy, have limited systems that serve mainly urban areas while millions of their citizens live in pre-industrial conditions or worse.

We have the most advanced economic, corporate, educational and research institutions both capable and motivated to generate scientific and technological innovation and the capital and investment needed to produce it. The great burden we have is maintaining and improving our economic and military system to continue our current advantage. We bear the cost of protecting Japan and Europe, for example. Europe no longer faces the Soviet threat, so it has become independent and in the case of France and Germany competitive with United States policy and interests worldwide. Japan is threatened by North Korea and China, but we have the power to counter that threat. However, Japan can contribute more to offset our costs. India is vulnerable to attack from Pakistan.

Unfortunately, Islamic tribal states have no moral or ethical tradition that might restrain their irrational approach to conflict settlement.

The greatest threat to the United States is domestic, which has to do with the erosion of certain founding principles of our nation and civilization under influences from failed, mistaken, and corrupt notions derived from a corrupted 19th Century European intellectual tradition and their advocates that might undermine our society. Defending our tradition and Western Civilization against these influences is the major objective of both domestic and foreign policy.

Foreign Policy

In the 19th and 20th Centuries Western Civilization destroyed tribal societies and theocratic empires. Although the people in these areas have to varying degrees assimilated Western ***material*** culture, they retain most of the characteristics of their social and cultural heritage. Tribal society and theocratic empire underlie States that on the surface appear to be Westernized. In Moscow, Beijing, Damascus, Lagos, and elsewhere, high rises, BMW's, international airports, tailored suits, and Western academic degrees conceal rather than replace persistent cultural traditions. The following key points should be kept in mind when evaluating media and government information regarding foreign policy.

Democracy and freedom are not feasible objectives in tribal societies and societies derived from theocratic empires unless they are transformed into civil societies. This includes principally Russia, all of Africa and the Islamic world, and China. Only civil societies are capable of democratic government. Attempts to impose democratic procedures on tribal and theocratic societies simply entrench or rearrange existing power structures without changing fundamental conditions. A few tribal and theocratic states ***appear*** to be in transition toward secular civil society. ***Turkey***, under close control of their military, seems to be moving toward a secular democratic civil society despite strong Islamic influences and tribal divisions between Turks and Kurds. The success of this transition remains doubtful. Modern Turkey is westernized in Istanbul and a few other urban areas, but most of the rural population is strongly Islamist. Turkey's position in the Middle East is similar to that of Japan in Asia. They were once conquerors. Now Turkey is becoming more advanced economically, belongs to NATO, is under consideration for membership in the European Union, and provides a model for modernization for other Islamic nations as Japan does for China and the Far East. ***India*** is ostensibly democratic but is far from being a civil society in the Western sense despite all the rhetoric about being 'the world's largest democracy'. The privileged and educated ten percent of the population creates the impression that India is entirely secularized, democratic, and westernized, but this hardly applies to the hundreds of millions living in villages throughout India and not at all to millions of 'untouchables'. The ruling class is westernized sufficiently that change is biased toward westernization rather than revival of Hindu nationalism.

Japan is westernized in form and to some degree in spirit but remains a racial theocracy with an Emperor. The imperial family does not rule (just as it didn't rule under the Shoguns) but does provide the focus of authority and tradition for the Japanese. Japan can assimilate any form of culture, government, or economy without impairing the underlying racial theocratic outlook that unites all Japanese. Japan depends entirely on the United States for defense and will remain a loyal ally in the region.

In foreign policy, spreading democracy and freedom will be used to cover tangible resource and geopolitical objectives. Americans cannot be mobilized to sacrifice for oil or minerals but can be aroused by inspirational and benevolent claims to bring freedom to the world. Since Woodrow Wilson we have been led and misled by such projects with limited success. Whether you choose to believe or doubt such claims, the United States should never commit major ground forces to wars or upheavals in areas of tribal and theocratic societies.

In all cases, we should support local allies so they can carry out military objectives, as was done in Afghanistan. Given its imbedded Islamic tribal structure, **Afghanistan** will never achieve democratic civil society. **Iraq** was a disaster because Bush was pursuing Bush family economic and Israeli and Saudi political interests under the guise of avenging 9/11, interdicting a nonexistent nuclear threat, and (later) 'extending democracy and freedom to the Middle East'. Attempts to be a neutral broker among conflicting tribes in Iraq and elsewhere will fail.

United States power must be maintained and never used or withheld for reasons other than national security. World peace and security depend on the United States and to some extent on our European allies. Unfortunately, Europe is in decline demographically and economically and will be unable to substantially reinforce the United States worldwide. However, our allies can take the lead in political efforts to achieve peace and resolution in tribal and theocratic regions. With these basic principles in mind the following summarizes conditions and prospects for different regions worldwide to 2050.

Europe is in decline. The 2001 EURO currency union and end of national borders, customs and passports only releases funds formerly wasted on inefficient exchange, trade, travel, and market fragmentation but will provide only short-term improvements in economic conditions Europe-wide. The gains will temporarily help fund the unsustainable safety net of welfare, medical, and income support in Western Europe. Eventually those funds will run out and Europe's demographic contraction and socialist political systems will make impossible major economic growth much less military strength. Europe's population will decrease by 20-25 percent by 2050 (30 percent in Germany!). The number of elderly dependent will increase and combined with maturing workers who look forward to high retirement and health benefits will prevent political reform needed to deal with declining productivity. Immigration from low-income parts of Slavic Europe may offset some of the decline in young prospective workers. But all parts of Europe are in demographic decline, so this remedy will be short term. Immigration from Islamic nations is divisive and unpopular. A significant Euro-Islamic population is in place adding violence and welfare dependency to deplete domestic financial resources and, given high birth rates, a likely domination of European nations by 2070. Islam and the Western outlook are antipathetic and no accommodation to retrograde Islamic practices regarding women, education, science, and culture is feasible. Islamic immigrants have established extensive neighborhoods subject to sharia law in cities throughout Europe that project violence and chaos free of government control. Sweden a particular example of the devastating results of Islam. Their high birth rates are four times greater than the native population and will lead to political control and the overthrow of Western values by the end of the century.

United Kingdom is our most reliable ally, cultural patrimony, and (decreasingly) consanguineous friend, even though we fought two wars. UK has high achieving industrial, financial, scientific and technological institutions UK faces socialist and retrograde economic policies that may stultify growth and the university and secondary educational system needs competitive overhaul to sustain scientific progress. **France** is full of contradictions unresolved. Incredible native talent, scientific and engineering achievement, unsurpassed in agriculture, railroads, and aviation, all locked into a socialist mercantilist tradition that entrenches privilege and status and undermines initiative and change. Politically paralyzed, France may sink or swim depending on how successful it is in divesting this tradition. **Germany** has sunk from greatness to entitled inanition and now faces economic collapse having lost Russian gas supplies as a result of the Ukrainian war. Once it was the locus of leading research and universities, now its educational system is a mess. Industry is tied by labor privileges. The population is declining precipitously. Like France, it has to reverse every trend and undo every social contract to regain social and economic progress. **Italy** like France has enormous talent and ability undermined by chaotic political and social policies and systems. **Ireland and Spain**, oddly once the most retrograde nations in Europe, are now leaders in growth and economic innovation. **Scandinavia, Finland, and the Baltics** appear to be sustaining technological and economic advance based mainly on superior educational institutions, but Sweden faces a crisis of civil collapse as a result of their ruinous acceptance of Islamic 'refugees' who now are violent and disruptive and out of control. ***Eastern*** Slavic states, especially Poland and Hungary are thriving, having rejected the call to accept Muslim 'refugees' under European Union dictates.

Russia is in severe decline, its economy and population are deteriorating, and no improvement is foreseeable over the next fifty years. The population decline is particularly severe in the below thirty age group. Its nuclear missile system is obsolete. Putin's invasion of Ukraine exposed the parlous condition of its military, ineffective, poorly led, logistical failures and unable to maintain personnel, equipment, or develop advanced technology. Politically Russia is returning to traditional oligarchic authoritarian form with a privileged few controlling a passive mass population. However, the state cannot provide even the minimum standard of living Russians enjoyed under the Soviet regime. Unrest is possible and if widespread, the state is so weak that it cannot easily control it. Urban areas will be taken care of so most unrest will be rural and isolated. Russians want and respect strong man rule, whether Tsar, First Secretary, Vozhd, or President. Without strong state rule, Russians tend to anarchy and crime as the mafia and economic collapse of the 1990's show. They will elect a strong man but whether he can induce economic and social progress is entirely unlikely.

China is militarily weak, and its missile system systems do not pose a threat to the United States, although they could strike Japan. The prospect of unrest among the 400 million rural Chinese left out of the economic advances of the last 25 years forces the Communist Party to fund larger conventional forces to maintain order. The central government no longer controls many areas now run by party mafias. The Chinese economy is vulnerable to disruption in trade with the United

States and Europe and cannot maintain the prosperity of even the urban masses without United States trade. Chinese investment in African and Central Asian mineral and oil resources is good for worldwide energy development and strategically unimportant for the United States which can interdict supplies to mainland China from anywhere in the world. China is a remnant of the theocratic empire system, focuses on internal autonomy rather than territorial expansion, and poses no threat to the United States. It wants capitalism and international trade, but it is very unused to foreign investment and control of domestic companies. The United States wants inexpensive labor, which can be had anywhere in India and Southeast Asia. China has nothing we can't find elsewhere if necessary, whereas China needs United States trade in order to grow and prosper. This advantage will not change and will contribute to peace in the region.

Africa is a shambles and will continue its decline into tribal savagery and genocide, economic and political corruption, rampant starvation and disease, and most important demographic decay. HIV AIDS will thin the population drastically in Central Africa. Attempts to reverse these trends are largely futile because the tribal tradition is so endemic that no native sources of reform are present. Because of the domestic influence of Blacks in key electoral states, much of our African policy is designed to gain votes here rather than improve conditions there. The propaganda surrounding our African policies make it sound effective and responsive and long overdue. Yet all the money expended will benefit mostly *kleptocrats* there and political boondoggles here. International conferences and study groups, political rhetoric and photo opportunities create an impression of effective intervention to benefit African people, which is not the case. The United States should monitor the situation in Africa, attempt to reduce the conflict and maintain economic resource recovery and exploration there, establish pockets of political and economic stability, improve distribution of medical and economic aid to local people, but definitely not commit its military to ground operations of any kind.

Islam poses no threat to the United States despite the hand wringing about terrorism, 9/11, and the need to 'win over the minds of the Islamic peoples'. We do however need to insure access to oil reserves in the Middle East, restrain the irrational tendencies within nuclear Pakistan, prevent spread of nuclear weapons to other Islamic States, and offer economic incentives to moderates in the region to develop peacefully. This is the only region where strategic air strikes may be needed to disable rogue regimes from acquiring nuclear weapons. Iran will probably be the first to be attacked by Israel with US support. Otherwise, buying off the endemically corrupt regimes in the Islamic world should be the most efficient and economical method for maintaining order in the region. There is no prospect or need to promote democracy in the Islamic world. The tribal tradition and the Arabic outlook of Islam make this incompatible with their society and religious beliefs.

Israel, Saudi Arabia, and Iran: Iran is Shia and Saudi Arabia is Sunni. The Shia threaten the 'Kingdom' because the population in the Saudi oil region is Shia. Iran supports Shia Iraq which borders Sunni Saudi Arabia. Iran threatens both Israel and Saudi Arabia. In effect, Saudi Arabia is a *patent* enemy and a *latent* ally of Israel. Both oppose Iran and its prospective nuclear ambitions. Israel and Saudi Arabia welcome United States military commitment in Iraq to forestall a Shia takeover of that state. Saudi Arabia will be a covert supporter in the likely event of an Israeli attack on Iran. Typical of Islamic tribal society, much posturing will take place, but the power interests will be served.

North Korea is a second-rate dysfunctional state that poses no direct or immediate threat to the United States. Any threat their limited missile. capability poses is to Japan, South Korea, and China. The latter is the principal trading partner with NK and is not necessarily immune from blackmail similar to what NK has managed successfully with South Korea.

We should of course plan for a strategic strike against North Korea in case it becomes necessary, but for the short term it is best to await the departure of Kim Jong Il, from natural or other causes. Russia and China and Japan are the principal constraints on NK and they should lead any measures to bring that country to reason. The United States, however, should remain in the background with a very big stick pointed directly at Pyongyang.

India poses no threat to the United States and could become the next source of offshore labor and trade as did China over the past twenty years. In fact, India's greatest short term advantage for the United States is as a means of restraining China. India, however, may experience severe internal disorder over the next 50 years. Its population will increase by 200 million by 2050! Very few Indians have or are likely to benefit from the high-tech revolution that is taking place in Bangalore. If only 150 million Indians out of total population of 1.7 billion reap the benefits of this development, major unrest can be expected. Rising Hindu nationalism is confronting increased Islamic nationalism. The United States can promote more trade and investment but should not intervene in these internal issues except to urge restraint *vis a vis* **Pakistan**. But the nuclear imbalance that will follow any agreement to supply India more nuclear capability will aggravate this conflict. There is a distinct possibility that foolish policies by our government will lead to nuclear war in the subcontinent, perhaps the most dangerous international threat to peace we will face.

Communicable Disease: All other nations and parts of the world pose no threat to the United States in the next 50 years, except in the area of public health. Spread of communicable diseases from tropical areas is increasing, and so-called governments in most tropical areas are totally incapable of controlling spread of these diseases.

Domestic Policy

The United States is divided into interest groups that seek to control federal policies to their advantage. As mentioned already, industries control the committees of Congress and the Executive Departments and regulatory agencies that affect their interests. For example, energy industries (some 60 oil executives took positions in the federal government under G.W. Bush) control the CIA, State and Interior and chemical and agriculture industries control Agriculture and both when possible influence EPA. This is normal in a democracy where we all seek to advance our own interests, and such economic, social and regional divisions are common in our history. It is only when a limited group gets to decide issues of general importance that such predominance adversely affects the nation as a whole. Corporate interests influence both political parties, so their interests are invariably well served.

Certain public interest groups can publicize the worst consequences of this influence but that is about all that can be done. But these industries also support our economy and provide jobs and wealth to sustain our economy.

Minority groups within our society also pursue and gain objectives that are not necessarily in the long-term interests of all citizens. This is particularly evident in the areas of foreign, education and welfare, and health policy. The following examples will suffice to illustrate the pattern. Of the population of the United States, Jews make up 8 million and Blacks and Seniors (65 years and older) make up about 35 million each. Each minority determines expenditures and policies of the Nation in three crucial areas: the Jewish lobby dominates Middle East policy; the Black lobby dominates welfare and education policy; and the Seniors lobby dominates health and social security policy. As a consequence, the long-term interest of all citizens is not the priority in these areas.

Middle East Policy

In 1948 the Zionist militia Haganah seized control of Palestine after an underground terrorist campaign directed against the British-led Palestine Authority, which was trying to work out under United Nations mandate a joint Israeli-Palestinian State. International sympathy for Jews following the Holocaust combined with the ongoing Presidential election in the United States worked to gain immediate recognition of the new State of Israel by President Truman. Overlooked was the expropriation and displacement of 5 million Palestinian refugees. Initially Israel received funds from Jewish organizations in Europe and the United States. But these were inadequate to sustain Israel against Arab hostility throughout the Middle East. Jewish lobbies in the United States used political leverage gained from prominent corporate, academic, media, entertainment, and scientific influence to obtain taxpayer funds to support of the survival of Israel. Fundamentalist Christians also supported the policy despite decades of virulent anti-Semitism. Fortunately for Israel, it is a Western Civil society surrounded by Islamic tribal societies. In fact, Israel is a test case for the superior power of civil societies over tribal societies. That a nation of 6.5 million could fight, win, survive and even dominate surrounding Islamic nations amounting to tens of millions of people shows the power of western solidarity over the endemically divided and self-destructive characteristics of tribal societies.

The United States has armed and financed Israel in its hostilities with Arab States, leading to chronic disruption in the Middle East. Complaints of Palestinians are disregarded and their violent resistance to Israeli 'occupation' is dismissed as terrorism. United States interests would best be served by creating a Palestinian State, but without restoration of expropriated lands, Palestinians are unlikely to find this solution acceptable. Even better would be a joint Jewish and Palestinian State, but this is unacceptable to Israel. The Palestinian birthrate is so much greater than that of Israel that the Arab community would soon dominate the democratically elected parliament and gain control of the State.

Instead of resolving the conflict in its own interests, the United States has held itself hostage to Israel and its policies. This is partly because we side with Western civil societies when given a choice, even though the predicament of Israel is insoluble. There is no basis for agreement among civil and tribal societies, and the injustices done to the Palestinians are irreconcilable given the revenge-based culture endemic to Islamic tribal societies. The advent of terrorism and prospect of disruption of oil production is already familiar. The hostility of Muslims worldwide additionally places at risk American interests.

It is a measure of the strength and determination of the Jewish lobby that neither the Democrat nor Republican Party has dared to challenge this policy. Given the financial support and substantial leverage of the Jewish community in the United States, such a challenge is unlikely, and the dead end in the Middle East will continue indefinitely.

Education and Welfare Policy

Blacks were once the only minority in the United States. From colonial times, Indians were not part of the union so only blacks were a significant minority within the population. The Constitution counted them for purposes of allocating representatives to the Congress, but only after the Civil War did they become citizens and acquire the vote and other civil rights. State laws and Federal Supreme Court rulings (including the 1893 'separate but equal' ruling in Plessy vs. Ferguson) made segregation legal until the Brown vs. Board of Education ruling by the Warren Court in 1954. The requirement of 'integrated' therefore 'equal' education was extended to voting, hotel accommodations, transportation, and other equal access by Civil Rights Acts of the 1960's.

Since 1970, Hispanic and Asian immigration has shifted the balance of minority populations in the United States. Blacks once made up the most numerous minority group in major Eastern States. Now Hispanics nearly equal Blacks in New York, New Jersey, and Connecticut, outnumber Blacks in Massachusetts and Florida, and are close to the Black population in Illinois. In the West and Southwest Hispanics far outnumber Blacks, whereas in the Deep South, Michigan, Missouri, Ohio, and Pennsylvania Blacks substantially outnumber Hispanics. Because these latter states are strongly contested in Presidential elections, Blacks are still politically courted as a swing vote. Asians are a small percentage of the population in all states but California, but like Jews, their representation in professions, business, and academe give them disproportionate potential influence.

Hispanics have replaced Blacks as the dominant minority population. This change is noticeable in the steadily declining number of Blacks elected as mayors of large metropolitan areas and the declining political influence of Blacks in elections, except in key mid-Western states. Asians in California are running for local office and State legislatures along with Hispanics and both groups are likely to provide much of the urban political leadership over the coming decades. In Los Angeles, Blacks are now 10 percent of the population compared to 35 percent Hispanic. Blacks seek to conflate 'minority' interests, but the other minorities show little interest. Asians are the only minority that hasn't sought special legislation for subsidies and welfare. They are in fact discriminated against in schools and universities because they, like Jews, are disproportionately successful academically. Hispanics do not enjoy similar status but they are succeeding in jobs and education at a level beginning to approach the average for Whites and are integrated into the economy and society through their family orientation, religious commitment, and work ethic.

Percentage Hispanic, Black, and Asian Population			
State	Hispanic	Black	Asian
Arizona	**25.3***	3.1	1.8
California	**32.4***	6.7	10.9
Colorado	**17.1***	3.8	2.2
Connecticut	**9.4***	9.1	2.4
Florida	**16.8***	14.6	1.7
Illinois	**15.1***	12.3	3.4
Iowa	**2.8***	2.1	1.3
Kansas	**7.0***	5.7	1.7
Massachusetts	**6.8***	5.4	3.8
Michigan	3.3	**14.2***	1.8
Minnesota	2.9	**3.5***	2.9
Missouri	2.1	**11.2***	1.1
Nebraska	**5.5***	4.0	1.3
New Jersey	13.3	**13.6***	5.7
New York	15.1	**15.9***	5.5
Ohio	1.9	**11.5***	1.2
Pennsylvania	3.2	**10.0***	1.8
Texas	**32.0***	11.5	2.7
Washington	**7.5***	3.2	5.5
Wisconsin	3.6	**5.7***	1.7

* Predominant minority

Regardless of this shift in minority population, Blacks continue to set the agenda for education and welfare legislation nationwide because they are the primary minority recipients of public assistance. Since the 'Great Society' and 'War on Poverty' legislation of the 1960's, billions of dollars have been spent on overcoming the Black 'disadvantage'. The 'disadvantage' persists and the 'need' for funding continues. However, at some point the situation of 13 percent of the population will cease to interest the remaining 87 percent, particularly as Asian and Hispanic minorities assume political leadership in city, county, and state governments. Whites accede in Black-oriented social policies for reasons of guilt, political advantage, or social stability. Hispanics and Asians do not share this feeling and for the most part feel indifferent to Black concerns. Blacks have lowered the educational standards of public schools that most immigrant Hispanics and many Asians attend. and depend on public housing and welfare that working Asians and Hispanics feel no obligation to support.

Blacks occupy a unique position in American society that is not articulated because political correctness subsumed commitment to truth in the United States. This is especially unfair to Blacks. The role they play in a middle class society and in a proletarian society should be explained so they can cope with authentic conditions, not false ones. Blacks have always represented the bottom of middle class White society. In the South this was early understood and used by the dominant land-owning class to control the poor white, redneck, and white trash in their society. Whatever your place was in Southern white society, blacks were always below you. Somewhat the same role was played by urban blacks in the North following the great exodus from the South after the Civil War and especially after WWI and WWII. As the underclass, they had no way but up. This was oddly an advantage.

The middle class from its origins in the medieval towns has always lived with personal insecurity and the dread of poverty and of falling into a lower class. It is willing to commit or preferably condone any crime committed by others to prevent this outcome. It also attempts to appear as the upholder of order, morality, and principle. The middle class is a very conflicted group with constant internal contradictions and conflicts, personal, familial and social. Often children of the middle class understand the emotional hypocrisy underlying the outward pretence and rebel by adopting the characteristics of a subculture. Usually this is dress, music, and slang. Just as students at Eton speak cockney, American middle class youth began to adopt black music and slang in the 1920's. They also affected proletarian class values, but blacks were the most radical form of rebellion.

After WWII conflicts within the nuclear family, which isolated and confined intelligent middle class women, led to more rebellion, daughters especially seeking out and exposing the 'hypocrisy' of their inherited values. They turned to minorities for authenticity: Greeks (*Never on Sunday*), Jews (*Exodus*), blacks (*Guess Who's Coming to Dinner*). Blacks were in a position to appear real, authentic, not phony, and so on. Their music was sexual, personal, and uninhibited. Their needs were basic, their enjoyment open and wholehearted, their expression vigorous and soulful. The problem is that black subculture is no more authentic than any other, but for the period 1960-1990 it appeared to be, the real thing. Blacks were locked into a stereotype that denied them more demanding, varied, and rewarding paths of development. Churches were the refuge for responsible Blacks who wanted to get out of this cultural ghetto. The Civil Rights movement began in the Churches where principles were taught and upheld so far as possible.

Health Policy and the American "Health Crisis"

Senior citizens in the United States make up 15 percent of the population. They have enormous political clout because they consistently vote and own a substantial share of the nation's wealth. Consequently, they entirely dominate State and Federal health policy. This socially dysfunctional investment in the ailments and complaints of the elderly at the expense of the very young is entirely against the long-term interests of the United States. Given the stark comparisons between **diseases** that threaten survival in the underdeveloped world and **ailments** that result largely from self-indulgence in the major industrial economies, it is hard to take seriously the health crisis many people and all politicians in the United States claim is occurring. Constant complaints are provoked by the high rates of inflation in prices for medical services, drugs, and health insurance.

The health care issues of the younger population relate to obtaining affordable insurance for prenatal, natal, and infant care and for emergency health services. These requirements plus treatment of adult and child genetic and unavoidable health problems beyond the control of individuals, regardless of age, could be solved at reasonable cost and would not create a health crisis. All are legitimate and non-preventable health requirements. But the greatest drain on health care providers and the driving force in rising demand and rising costs for health services are ***preventable behavior-caused*** diseases and ailments, such as diabetes, heart disease, knee surgeries, and the like.

This "health crisis" is caused mainly by people over fifty years of age, a group that consumes a disproportionate share of health services directed at treating diseases and ailments that are preventable by responsible diet and exercise. The fact is many of our elderly are Medicare parasites, too fat, lazy, and self-indulgent to maintain their physical fitness, preferring medical interventions to self-discipline. Behavior-related diseases in their terminal stages entail numerous surgeries and hospital visits during the last eighteen months of life, incurring enormous cost with no prospect for recovery because the lifestyle that caused the ailment is unchanged and the deterioration is too far advanced to be corrected. Pharmaceuticals are the scapegoat for this preventable problem. If the ailing seniors changed to a healthy diet and moderate exercise, they would not need the dozens of medications that fill their medicine cabinets throughout the United States. Obesity and poor physical condition symptomatic of more than fifty percent of the population in the United States are preventable. The so-called health crisis would be measurably reduced if steps, especially in insurance, were taken to address behavior.

Politically the elderly are coddled and courted because they vote and have strong lobbies, so sending the message that personal responsibility for maintaining health is an obligation is not politically acceptable. Nevertheless, the growing cost and declining affordability of health care will force some recognition of this underlying cause of the so-called health crisis in the United States.

These are just a few of the areas in which special interest groups and lobbies representing business, special interest groups and organizations influence policy. In a democracy such influence is expected and so long as it is transparent and understood, can be dealt with. As mentioned before, each department of the federal government is funded through a committee of Congress which is in turn subject to the business or other interests affected by that department. Departments are staffed, from the Secretary on down, by representatives of the dominant interest group. Because the federal government is largely bureaucratic, with each department issuing regulations that determine the outcome of many issues, it provides unique opportunity for special influence. There are areas in which special interest and national interest coincide and for the most part anything egregiously contrary to national interest is likely to be thwarted by competing interests through Congress, the media, or the White House. Certain policies are essential for maintaining the national interest and the position of strength of the United States.

Military Supremacy

Maintaining United States military supremacy is the most important national policy. Since 1942, the best investment of tax funds has been the United States military. Despite constant and often legitimate complaints about defense spending waste and overruns, the military industrial complex, and the need for social welfare spending, our military have provided the greatest return on investment of any part of the federal government. Winning WWII was the least of the benefits. From 1942 to 1975, the draft military provided vocational training for millions of young men and women. They found lifetime employment as a result of training received in military radio and electronics schools, cooking schools, diesel engine and aircraft maintenance, military police, supply and inventory, truck driving and mechanics, and countless other MOS (Method of Service), the kind of training not available readily in civilian life. They learned discipline, self-respect, and work ethic. *The end of the draft in 1976 marked the end of the greatest educational adventure the United States had ever experienced* and introduced a period of deficient training for many who otherwise would have learned a trade in the services. The military also provided the GI Bill which offered civilian education to millions of veterans.

Our military, scientific and technological supremacy defeated *without conflict* the Soviet regime, which was unable to develop corresponding resources. The investment in military spending has also insured United States military supremacy. Contrary to propaganda and misinformation, Russia and China have little prospect of challenging American supremacy.

Education

Developing the talent, we need to continue our highest levels of science, engineering, and other fields is the primary national interest. Education policy must be based on freeing primary and secondary education from union and lobby control to develop the talent of the *best students* for science, engineering, and other disciplines essential to our economy and society. We must focus on intensive and successful teaching in mathematics and science and other formal disciplines. An indulgent social engineering that equalizes downward is undermining our students and the society they expect to work in and succeed. Health policy must be based primarily on newborn and child development rather than the 'needs' of irresponsible individuals.

CONCLUSION

Equality vs. Freedom

Western Civilization is the greatest civilization and the United States, as current leader of that civilization, is the greatest political society that ever existed. The greatness of our civilization has been discussed at length. The United States is *inclusive* and *representative* of all parts of the world's population. It is open, dynamic, and driven by endless contradictions. Every possible combination of people, resources, conflict, and challenge is present in the United States. No other nation contains such variety or attracts so much interest and emulation, hatred and fear. We represent the ongoing challenge of freedom and progress to the fragmented tribal and theocratic empire societies with which we must deal worldwide.

The greatness of the United States is founded on the Constitution, the most important political document in history. It was written in 1787 by landed and merchant patricians who had long political experience in representative and democratic institutions: town meetings, assemblies, courts. They represented people who owned land, worked and succeeded by their own effort, believed in solidarity, and opposed oppression at any price.

This was our heroic age. Nothing said in subsequent years begins to explain the greatness of these men and women. Thanks to them we inherited a form of government and society that could defend freedom *and* equality, justice *and* fair play, and that could survive mediocre and corrupt politicians, representatives, judges and Presidents; regional conflict; disparate goals and interests; economic greed; racial conflict and oppression; crime and war.

We owe everything to the patricians who established this amazingly resilient political society: above all George Washington, who presided over the Constitutional Convention and later served as the first and greatest of our Presidents; Hamilton, Madison and Jay who explained in *The Federalist* the intent of the founders; Franklin, who at a point of deadlock during the Convention gave the speech that overcame all objections in a spontaneous act of unity and solidarity; and countless others who rose to the challenge of public spirit and selfless commitment to the nation's interest and future. We have never seen their like again.

Part of the genius of the founders was that they included within and based the political formation of the United States upon the most contradictory elements imaginable. Contradiction is dynamic and provides creative tension to political, economic, and social life. It works well when no single point of view dominates entirely. It leads to stalemate and failure when no balance between contradictory factors can be agreed upon. The Constitution balances these elements and is our primary protection against the mediocrities who influence and govern and the self-interests that hover around our political institutions. This section reviews some of the conflicts, contrasts and anomalies within our society that give us such variety and dynamism. They are perhaps the most important thing to keep in mind when evaluating facts and policies, opinions and explanations presented by the media, politicians, and others.

Constitution vs. Declaration of Independence

The Constitution of 1787 is a ***legal*** document; the Declaration of Independence. of 1776 is a ***moral*** document. Both provide the foundation of the United States. One is the ***law*** of the land; the other is the stated ***aspiration*** of the people. The Declaration cannot be enforced in court; the Constitution can. They served different purposes and, in many respects, reflect different points of view. They came at different times and dealt with different circumstances.

The Declaration provided the inspiration required to carry out the Revolution. It was what citizens fought for, had in mind, and believed at Valley Forge and elsewhere. The Constitution combines both freedom and, in the Bill of Rights (first10 Amendments), equality as goals. The Declaration emphasizes equality and proclaims freedom. Both documents reflect the primary underlying contradiction in the United States, equality and freedom, which has driven us toward great progress and achievement when kept in balance, but always threatens to reverse that progress whenever that balance is not maintained.

Contrary to the Declaration of Independence (and Rousseau), men are not born equal or free, have no inalienable rights, and the pursuit of happiness is a fools errand if understood as a goal rather than the by-product of work and effort. Oddly enough, such rights are only possible under a political organization committed and able to bestow and defend them. They are not 'natural' however desirable. Equality is a legal, social, and moral convention, and freedom exists only to the extent that a society or state has the power to confer and defend it. Liberty is a condition of being independent from economic or physical constraint but is not Freedom, which presupposes Liberty but exists only in association with peers.

A provocative and oddly productive sense of entitlement began with the declared natural right to equality and happiness in the Declaration of Independence. This prescriptive document has confused domestic, social, political, and even personal life in the United States ever since.

Equality is a legal fiction appropriate to specific and defined application. Equality before the law is legitimate as an assumption of innocence and right to fair trial. Equality as in 'first come first served' is expedient and fair. Equality of opportunity is much more vague and impossible to insure but expresses the desire to be fair to everyone in our society. Its corollary, privilege, is unacceptable in a democracy as a means of advancement, but in fact economic advantage confers privilege and governs much of society. Confusing the goal of fairness with the desire for equality is a common misunderstanding. Correspondingly, unbridled freedom when used to serve privilege rather than merit leads to tyranny and stagnation.

Men are born equal so far as basic needs are concerned, somewhat equal to the extent that human physiology is common to the species, but unequal in individual physical and intellectual endowment and potential. This is basically because each human is unique while partaking of the undefined common potential of the species. Only talent and work can lead to success, freedom, happiness, or whatever term is used to describe self-improvement, achievement and the good life. Equality of outcome or condition is always downward to the lowest common denominator. Men cannot be equalized upward. They differ too widely in talent and ability. The communist doctrine 'from each according to his ability to each according to his need' replaces freedom with equality and destroys human plurality. The only practical equivalent for 'equality' is 'equity'.

Men are not born free, but rather are entirely dependent from birth on the parents, family, and the society that receives them and nurtures them. Long dependence and slow development especially of the brain and neural system lead to individuation and distinction. This becomes most evident after puberty when growth, talent, and opportunity distinguish each individual from others. There are common interests, skills, aptitudes and achievements, but they do not apply to everyone, only to classes within the society. Concert pianists, particle physicists, neurosurgeons, postmen, chefs, and countless other categories of endeavor are exclusive despite the common humanity of their practitioners.

Personal freedom is achieved by increasing one's command of financial and social power. In that sense the slogan *Arbeit macht frei* is true. The least gifted usually remain subject to financial and social constraint. Only a small percentage of the population enjoys freedom from economic constraints and no one is entirely free of the "*heartache and thousand natural shocks that flesh is heir to.*" All this is obvious but ignored in certain policy debates, notably education, health care, and broad claims for 'social justice'.

A 'natural' right to happiness is the oddest political claim ever made. 'Happiness' is a personal matter that is apolitical and yet Jefferson and the makers of revolution in 1776 place it at the forefront of American political objectives in the Declaration of Independence. The pursuit of happiness became a political right, defended and presumably abetted by the State. The absence of happiness, equality, and liberty, all social conditions, became a political issue. Victims who suffer from lack of liberty, equality, and happiness became a constituency for political and other opportunists looking for an issue to ride into office. What would normally be a personal matter became an issue for political and social discontent and when developed into a class action, attracted political attention. The sense of entitlement expressed in the Declaration of Independence has been broadly, almost unconsciously, and certainly mistakenly accepted. For example, men are not 'entitled' to health care by birth. This is a service provided by trained physicians whose services require reimbursement. The market place, as with most things, is the best arena for sorting out how much and to whom health care is provided. Forms of health insurance sort out the distribution of health services. Unfortunately, the sense of entitlement has eroded and in many cases eliminated any sense of responsibility. The fat, lazy, unexercised, badly fed, self-indulged, parasitic appear to expect health care and even sympathy for their heart disease, diabetes, and other medical conditions often self-inflicted. When poor health is self-inflicted and the patient refuses to adopt corrective diet and healthful exercise, no sympathy is merited.

The issue of public education is more complicated. Education is a public interest and should be provided to all children. The wealthy always have educational opportunity. Public education was intended to offer children of poorer families an opportunity to develop their talent and learn skills for personal growth and future employment. In this case public education is an extension and enrichment of the family or should be. When education is taken over by teacher unions and unqualified or minimally qualified teachers are carried along in the system then public education must be reformed. Similarly, state universities and colleges were established to provide higher education to talented students and are a social benefit that must be supported. These institutions must teach and serve the goals of the society that pays for them. The breakdown in rigor and even common sense within the non-scientific disciplines due mainly to fragmentation of subjects and faculties into interest groups and other politically correct so-called programs has led to a high degree of mediocrity and irrelevance in so-called higher education.

An odd but prevalent social problem is the child whose entitlement to happiness unconnected to work, effort, discipline, or achievement is the obsession of parents. There is no natural happiness, although some people have physiological and neurological systems, so called temperament, that are more disposed to a sense of well-being than others. But there is no happiness without effort and the problem of 'teenage' rebellion and malaise is largely the result of incredible idleness and absence of demands on their ability and time. Such drifting mediocrity doesn't serve the child or society.

Semitic mythology explained the human condition as a result of the 'fall' from innocence caused by the ***sin of knowledge of good and evil.*** The issue centers on notions of guilt versus innocence, nature versus artificiality. Knowledge and guilt having to do with man's awareness of the evolution of higher brain function as compared to stronger but encoded animal behavior.

Innocence seems to have to do with either unconsciousness or nonviolence, as the lion lying down with the lamb. The fall of Adam (man in Hebrew) caused by the serpent working through Eve appears to have affected all creation, whose predatory instincts were then aroused. That Cain slew Abel was an extension of the Fall's broader release of violence throughout creation. Violence, the only means animals have to claim control and insure survival in the natural world, was the underlying manifestation of guilt and the Fall. Innocence was and continued to be a sort of fatuous belief in innate goodness (nonviolence) to which men and creatures could be recalled, a kind of return to the garden. Alternatively, consciousness and conscience appear to be associated with the Fall.

Rousseau reversed the Semitic Garden of Eden myth. He claimed that individuals are born innocent (sinless). Evil is in Society and corrupts individuals. The Semitic accusation of knowledge as the cause of evil and the Fall brings a desire to return to unconscious innocence and nonviolence, a desire that has tormented Indo-Europeans for millennia. Rousseau and the tradition of anti-intellectualism derive from this Old Testament dilemma. We have been bewitched with this conundrum ever since, the United Nations a sort of institutional attempt to reverse Genesis. Dostoevsky's **Idiot** and Melville's **Billy Budd** are literary critiques of this wish to return to Paradise.

The question of natural versus artificial is confused and convoluted. Natural is everywhere approved; the artificial (read insincere) is universally despised. And yet there is nothing 'natural' about humans as compared with other animals, and nearly everything about men is 'artificial', if understood as conventional rather than determined, because we have the power of thought and speech. Rousseau really meant to say that man was born natural but is made artificial by society, whereas in fact man is born artificial and is everywhere tormented by not being natural.

Rousseau discovered in the 'natural' a theory that has tyrannized everyone since the 1700's. The English garden, breastfeeding, domestic tranquility, Marie Antoinette's Hameau at Versailles, and the other Rousseauist innovations in decoration, art, manners, dress, and sentiment show the 'artifice' of naturalism. Cultural Romanticism overcame art, literature, and social ethics and misled millions into believing they were unnatural, vicious, and depraved if they didn't share the experience. Of course, they may have been, but not because there was a particularly authentic or universal version of natural and innocence. The 18th Century assumed the natural goodness and innocence of the Indians because they wore feathers and deerskin, conveniently overlooking the scalps on their belts. It took Levi-Bruel to uncover the neurotic lethal fables and obsessions that dominate 'primitive' man.

Secular State vs. Religious Society

Article I of the Bill of Rights Amendment to the Constitution states: *'Congress shall make no law respecting an establishment of religion, or prohibiting the free exercise thereof.'* This was a statesmanlike, expedient and rational solution to the insoluble contradictions in religious belief and practice among the regions of the new United States. The tension, not to say conflict, between our dominantly religious society and our secular state has been the most dramatic in our history. It all began with the original settlements of the four principal regions of Anglo America. Colonial America had four distinct views of religion, almost entirely incompatible.

Puritan New England emphasized the Old Testament, sin, conscience, community intervention in individual conduct and belief, and God's final Judgment. Established as a Theocracy, the Massachusetts colony was intolerant of dissenters, such as Quaker ladies who were burned at the stake for daring to preach. Preachers were college educated and formally ordained.

Quaker Pennsylvania emphasized the Gospel, humility, brotherly love (Philadelphia) and God's Love and Mercy. Perhaps the most humanist and ethical view of the Christian message in history. Quakers had no ministers or hierarchy; each member of the congregation was welcome to 'witness' to God's love.

Patrician Virginia emphasized Deism, the established Anglican Church, and social order, outward conformity rather than conscience, all externals. Internals were left alone, e.g., Washington, Jefferson and most others were Free Masons. Churches and ordained Ministers were supported by land (glebe) and taxes. Aristocrats were pragmatic as Elizabeth I, who tried to create an Anglican catechism that would stretch sufficiently to satisfy Popish Catholics with High Church paraphernalia and Low Church dissenting Calvinists with Protestant locutions.

Backcountry Scotch-Irish emphasized Fundamentalism, 'Born Again' Salvation, and community autonomy (clan systems and conflicts typical of Scotch-Irish settlements, like the Hatfield and McCoy feud, were left to the participants to settle). Religion was a matter of overcoming sin (mainly whisky) and turning to Jesus. It was personal, and no established church was needed or acceptable. Anglican and Presbyterian ministers sent to their communities were often tarred and feathered.

With such an incompatible combination, the genius of the founders led to complete disestablishment of religion in the Constitution. However, the religious outlook of each region persisted. During the Constitutional Convention Quaker representatives tried to outlaw slavery, a practice particularly repugnant to them on religious grounds. Quakers had taken the lead in the Abolitionist movement in England which abolished slavery and used its Navy to interdict slave trading. Quakers managed to set a date for an end to import of slaves (1807) in the Constitution, but in return slaves were counted (2/3 of a person each) in the population census used for districting members to the House of Representatives.

The South found this an attractive compromise because slavery in the Piedmont tobacco region was becoming less productive as soils were depleted and it was assumed that slavery would simply be phased out of the economy. The slave population was not that numerous in any case. Interestingly, the Brown family of Rhode Island (founders of Brown University) and a number of Massachusetts shipping magnates engaged in the trade of Slaves from Africa to the Caribbean and Brazil, and Sugar/Rum to the States. Only much later did Abolition become a major theme in Puritan New England.

The United States was to some extent founded on Slavery and Genocide, in the broadest sense of the latter term: chattel slavery on Southern Plantations and wage slavery in Northern mines and factories; genocide of Indian tribes, and metaphorically of fish and wildlife (extermination of buffalo, grizzly bear, wolf, salmon, etc.), forests through strip cutting, lakes, rivers and streams through industrial pollution.

Invention of the cotton gin by Eli Whitney in 1797 revolutionized textiles. Until then cotton was a comparatively expensive and difficult fabric to make. Cotton boles included many seeds that had to be picked from the cotton fiber before carding and making useable thread. That took much time and made mass production impractical. The gin provided a mechanical way to remove seeds rapidly. Cotton became an abundantly available and desirable fabric for the first time. Only wool and flax and linen had been practical for wide general use.

The cotton gin entrenched plantation slavery in the South after 1800 to produce cotton, and industrial slavery and child and women's labor in the North to produce cotton cloth. Owners of the first cotton mills in Lowell Massachusetts attempted to provide civilized work conditions and reasonably well-paying jobs for young white respectable females of good but rather poorer families. The experiment proved uneconomical and such altruistic programs were abandoned for exploitative employment of men, women and children. But the religious sanctimony of New

England and the arrogance of Gentry South clashed over the common guilt and interest in cotton. The North began to favor immigration to obtain cheap labor for mills and factories. First Irish then Germans then South Europeans then East Europeans were brought over to feed the Northern industrial expansion with cheap factory labor. Railroads later recruited settlers to purchase land grants the companies received for building the rail lines westward. The South wanted to acquire more slaves to work their cotton plantations. Slaves were sold from the Piedmont tobacco region of Virginia as land gave out. Other slaves were smuggled into the South after the Constitutional ban on imports came into effect in 1807. Slavers from New England profited from this trade. Yet the regions clashed and provoked a Civil War rather than acknowledge their complicity.

The cotton gin also gave impetus to the industrial revolution in the United States. It led to progress, introduction of machines to replace manual labor, use of steam, electricity and petroleum as energy rather than human or animal power, and eventually liberated the average man and woman from the onerous need for heavy manual labor. Yet Blacks remained more or less in slave status, especially in the South, from 1789 to 1965, when the first Civil Rights Acts were passed. Wage enslavement of industrial workers, especially of women and children, lasted to 1935 when the National Labor Relations Act was passed. Child labor laws were bitterly resisted in the first decade of the 20th Century on grounds of free enterprise and rights of free labor' to negotiate contracts.

Genocide of Indians was completed throughout the 19th Century. The story is familiar. However, the attitude that slaughter of helpless Indian women and children and of the animals they depended on for survival was acceptable and even patriotic provided a dark and violent heritage in the culture of the United States. The Environment didn't get federal protection until the Environmental Policy Act of 1969 and subsequent laws protecting water, air and natural resources.

Each struggle aroused the religious 'instincts' of each region in our heritage, both for ***and*** against the particular issue. Particular hatred arose in New England during the pre-Civil War era. Much of this was a nearly psychotic transference on the part some leaders, particularly Charles Sumner, Senator from Massachusetts, who 'discovered' the abolitionist message late and rode it, attacking Southern Senators with hysterical venom and provoking the caning that made him a hero in the North. The source of this fanaticism was later revealed when he married a very attractive Boston widow. She divorced him soon on grounds of nonperformance of husbandly duties, which she, being attractive, fairly young and physically very vigorous, fully expected. Similar psychotic hatred of the North was common in the South. So we had a brutal Civil War over an issue that most Whites did not want to pursue. Northern States (Illinois, Ohio, Indiana, etc.) had passed prohibitions of Black inmigration. No Northern State wanted to increase its black population much less send sons to die to liberate them.

Fights against political corruption and for Prohibition were invariably led by Churches and their members. But the culmination of Church influence was symbolized in the 'Monkey Trial' of 1924, that posed Darwin and Evolution against Genesis (William J. Bryan). Science and Religion confronted each other in court. Biological Evolution is established in the record, which shows many forms of the genus homo derived from the ape/chimpanzee line. Homo sapiens, the culmination of this evolution, presumably shares about 97 percent of his genetic makeup with chimps. The difficulty with all scientific findings is that they may be true as fact but contribute to false implications. A reductionist view might conclude that man is an animal much like other primates and derive false social and ethical conclusions. Given the constant flow of discovery and revision in scientific theory, nothing should be taken as 'conclusive'.

Social Values vs. Individual Rights

Article I of the Bill of Rights Amendments to the Constitution also states that Congress shall make no law 'abridging the freedom of speech'. This succinct statement liberates and protects personal expression under the law, thereby setting up a controversy between social values and individual rights.

Ironically, no part of the United States practiced or approved of individual freedom of speech when it contradicted prevailing community values, least of all the New England theocracy where religious orthodoxy, rigid ethical standards, public morals, and punishment of private derelictions were constant preoccupations. Burning witches and Quaker female preachers, exiling nonconformists, and liberal use (the only liberal aspect of Puritan New England) of the stocks were characteristics of the region.

The Scotch-Irish clans in the hill country of the South were equally intolerant of government, revenuers, outside ideas, and strangers. The Clans were led by a prominent member who through bravery and personal conduct most represented clan values of manhood gained authority. The most famous clan leader was Andrew Jackson. Clan law was enforced by 'Regulators', bands of clansmen who executed 'justice' quite literally. The Ku Klux Klan was derivation of the Regulator system.

Patrician Virginia was not so much intolerant as repelled by crude and uncivilized Scotch-Irish and pious hypocritical Puritans. Quakers were too simple, kind, and Christian to be objectionable, but the other regions found something to dislike, especially the Scotch Irish who hated them nearly as much as New Englanders for their pacifism.

Freedom of expression was, however, freely exercised in matters that affected all regions. Political campaigns were vicious, slanderous, and sustained. It began with the election of 1796 pitting Jefferson and Adams in a regional free for all. Jefferson was accused in the Federalist press of bedding his father-in-law's mulatto daughter. Adams was accused in the Republican press of neglect of office (he spent most of the year in New England). It never let up from that election to the latest.

Political expression was always loud and forceful. But society had established laws and unspoken rules in townships, counties, and states regarding individual conduct and expression. The different regions were vastly different in these respects. New England strictly regulated sexual caprice (of which there was quite a bit anyway). Quakers, invariably subdued and kind, appeared to be in less turmoil over this matter. Patrician Virginia shared the attitude of the English Aristocracy, *'do what you like, just don't create a scandal'*. The Scotch-Irish were randy, open and frequent in regard to sexual conduct. Many of their place names are virtually unpronounceable in mixed company: Cunt Hollow, Pussy Creek, etc., in case these terms seem to be more modern allusions. Pornography and prostitution existed in cities throughout the United States and whisky, the distilled and transportable product of rye and other grain alcohol, was a 'currency' of trade, in fact equivalent to dollars and cents especially in the Southern States.

Propriety and family values were always at odds with each generation's propensity for the currently available form of sex, drugs, and rock and roll. Opiates (laudanum), cocaine and even heroin advertised, sold, and widely available in 'drug stores' during the 19th Century, and were available and unregulated until 1951 when the Durham Humphrey Amendment to the Food and Drug Act which designated drugs whose sale and use (opiates especially) were restricted to medical prescription. Throughout the 19th Century laudanum and other mild and not so mild opiates were readily available to cope with female 'moods', 'vapors', and worse male conditions. During the Civil War, morphine was widely used and some 200,000 addicts left the trenches in 1865. The 14th Amendment of 1918 prohibited sale of wine, beer and liquor of more than three percent alcohol content. Of course drinking and prostitution (locally regulated) continued and heroin use was introduced widely after WWII but use of drugs had been continuous.

Until television, movies, and recordings, propriety could isolate and quarantine parts of the town, county, or state where 'vice' was available. With the advent of Victorianism and the nuclear family, home became a refuge for wife, children and the provider. He might enjoy a child prostitute at a certain location, but appearances were maintained in the business district, neighborhood, and home. Home was a citadel protected by middle class propriety and the church.

Radio, recordings, television and the automobile changed that protected status. Movies were perhaps the first subject of concern, but at least one had to go out of the home to see them and they could be regulated to maintain moral standards. This happened early, in 1934, when the review board was established to ensure propriety in films.

The major threat to 'family values' was not what could be seen but what could be heard. Rock and roll introduced a revolution in popular music and thereby in society. The energy and relatively free sexual implications of R&R were first released by Elvis and never subsequently entirely eclipsed. But this was an energetic and ultimately romantic impulse, not down and dirty. He might be 'all shook up' but that was because he 'can't help falling in love with you'. Television and movies were still regulated, but in the 1960's, drugs and 'acid rock' with increasingly sexual and explicit lyrics and throbbing rhythms overturned the middle class hold on public morals.

Hearing is the most suggestive and compelling faculty. Most languages use verbs of hearing to express command, obedience, and the like: 'Listen to me', 'Do as I say', 'Listen up'. Serge Gainesbourg, the French popular singer and BB lover, issued a record in the 1960's of a woman having sex and reaching orgasm. Listening to her moans and heavy breathing is more compelling, suggestive and exciting than any film could be. It sold well as might be expected but aroused as it were some concerns. Use of formerly prohibited words (fuck, motherfucker) in recordings, movies and to some extent in regulated television is now common. Foreplay and simulated fucking in films is commonplace, even though pornographic DVD's are readily available showing close up every possible combination. Rap music is a machismo degradation of women in no uncertain terms. The fact that all this is now introduced into the home and available to children has overturned the protected status of the family and home. Values outside have far more influence than parents and churches. The Culture Wars are clearly being lost by the once all-powerful middle class family. And the middle class family hardly cares. At least half end in divorce and infidelity, and the children are more inconvenient than matters of concern.

The decline in tone, style, manners and content from the heroic Federal age to the clearly mixed 'Atomic' age is striking. George Washington, Thomas Jefferson, and Alexander Hamilton when compared with Mick Jagger, Jimmy Hoffa, and Howard Stern clearly belong on different planets. The Federalist Papers and Deep Throat belong to different solar systems. It is an irony that the Supreme Court has ruled that prayer in schools is illegal and that pornography is a 'right of free expression' under the Constitution. Nothing could more symbolize the confusion and decay of American social values since 1789.

But the cultural landscape is more interesting than the contest of ultimately boring pornography versus family values. While so-called popular culture was becoming more 'realistic', an antique cultural form associated mainly with lorgnettes, long gowns, and diamond tiaras became the greatest cultural growth industry in the United States.

Since 1980 the United States has established more opera houses and opera seasons that any other nation, even though less than 1 percent of Americans has ever seen an opera. Whether in Biloxi, Grand Forks, or Rapid City, one can see at least the chestnuts, *Tosca, Madama Butterfly,*

Carmen, Traviata, Barbiere, performed by locally assembled or itinerant opera companies in albeit brief but invariably sold-out annual seasons. Every major city has a substantial opera season, and several have world class permanent companies. To judge from TV, radio, CD sales and IPOD records, black music (performed by blacks or others no matter) is all we listen to. Yet we are the major purchasers of and principal market for opera and classical music recordings. A small percentage admittedly, but being in the majority is the issue. The United States has the most live theater of any nation. Although symphony orchestras are facing major financial difficulties (concertgoers usually have high end stereo systems and enjoy music better at home) they still constitute the principal musical institution in every major city.

The issue is freedom, not conformity. Any attempt to suppress others' freedom in order to restore family values will fail. The best is always preferred by those who recognize it, which has always been a small but leading percentage of the population. And that includes the best popular music. American songs since 1920 have transformed our emotional and as it were lyrical understanding of love and relationships between men and women, the only authentic subject of great art. The titles are numerous, and everyone has particular favorites that somehow give words and music to the joy and sorrow that love brings. Likewise, the glories of Handel, Bach, Mozart, Beethoven, Verdi, Bellini, Wagner, Puccini and others are now becoming familiar to more and more people who find a narrowly 'sexploitative' popular music and film far from fulfilling. The debasement of women that underlies much of the worst of this popular culture may die off as it begins to bore and offend people who seek meaning not diversion in their lives.

Obsolescence and the End of History

Mythology was the organizing principle for prehistoric societies. Mythology included a foundation myth for the people and a series of stories involving divine creatures often mingling with and directing mortals. Most familiar is the Jewish mythology of the Creation, Garden of Eden, Fall (caused by a woman of course), and the subsequent wandering from the grace of Yahweh. Greek and Germanic mythologies were variants of an original Indo-European system of belief. All these mythologies held nomadic peoples together in the face of birth, death, disease, catastrophe, and constant movement through the overwhelming forces of time and space.

The Historic period, which began in the West with the Ancient Greeks and Romans, relied on tradition embodied in religion and history sustained and carried indefinitely into the future by political societies established in States. Greeks had the founding stories of heroes of the Trojan Wars celebrated by Homer. Romans had the founding of Rome by Romulus and Remus (characteristically Romulus killed Remus as Cain killed Abel, making all political life a kind of crime) as the beginning of their political community and tradition. The historic period continued to about 1945. We are now in a post historic society still in transition to a new and largely uncertain foundation.

The balance of generations has always been skewed to elders. Life expectancy was half or less what it is today. Seniority, revered in the Roman Senate, had tradition and wisdom gained by age and experience to compel authority. Rome fell because the system of authority was corrupted, decayed, and lost support. The Greeks collapsed because they had no way of restraining personal glory in favor of community survival. Western Civilization inherited this Classical historical system of religion and secular tradition. The United States was the highest expression of that tradition. The Founding Fathers studied ancient authors to discover the source of political stability and authority. We live on that achievement, without which our society would long ago have collapsed under the pressure of social greed, personal avarice, and organized violence.

Tradition, history and religion no longer have a hold on society, and the teenager and Generation Gap, unique creations of post WWII

American society, began the revolution in time that we have yet to come to terms with. That is why we have 'culture wars' opposing born-again Christians and gay and lesbian pornographic permissive liberals. No agreed final source of authority exists. Science has made the future, read youth, the most likely source of innovation and progress. Obsolescence in every aspect of society means that each generation not only becomes physically older and less able but also intellectually obsolete. Professional degrees become obsolete within ten years as discovery overturns current doctrine.

The net effect is that the past no longer is of primary significance to the future. It no longer serves as a guide or model for what is to come. No generation is interested in what has gone before, so parents, teachers, politicians, judges and like sources of authority simply are no longer relevant, except as nuisances who have money and advantages youth needs to advance. No one under twenty is the least bit interested in anyone over twenty. And they, too, soon will be irrelevant.

Interestingly this affects education more than any other aspect of our society. Education is the means by which tradition was conveyed to the next generation. It assumed that there were certain principles and knowledge essential to becoming part of the society. Today there is no agreement, except that language skill and mathematics and science are essential to success.

History, formerly the guiding element in socializing members of the community, is irrelevant to a mix of populations whose ancestors had nothing to do with Caucasian Europeans. Blacks and to some extent women rewrite his-story from their own unflattering perspective. Asians and Latin Americans have no idea and care less about Washington, Lincoln, or the Roosevelts. Teachers are not particularly well educated themselves and certainly have no 'orthodox' or traditional views to pass on.

The fact is that schools no longer know what to teach, other than praxis diversions and social mixing activities. Even fundamentals like language, math, and science are unavailable because few teachers are qualified or able to teach them. The few who try and occasionally do are too few to make a difference. Ignorance has become a conceit, where knowledge was once an ideal. Fortunately, Asians and some Caucasians are determined students of math and science and can provide the professional leadership we require.

The past is no longer a guide to the future, which requires freedom for the young to explore and discover new ways of doing things. Change and innovation are essential to our heritage. But the past is a guide in the matter of principles, which were present at the founding of Western Civilization and continue undiminished. However different our future social and historical circumstances may be, honor, respect (for women particularly), a willingness to forgive each other's mistakes and press on toward a creative and fulfilling future, solidarity, and the amazing Christian gift of faith, hope and love as the foundation of character can never be replaced because they are the basis for the success and achievement of our nation and civilization. Nothing compares with or can compete with or replace this magnificent heritage.

www.ingramcontent.com/pod-product-compliance
Lightning Source LLC
Chambersburg PA
CBHW052028030426
42337CB00027B/4904